Windows PowerShell for .NET Developers

Second Edition

Efficiently administer and maintain your development environment with Windows PowerShell

Chendrayan Venkatesan

Sherif Talaat

BIRMINGHAM - MUMBAI

Windows PowerShell for .NET Developers
Second Edition

First published: January 2014

Second published: October 2015

Production reference: 1161015

Published by Packt Publishing Ltd.
Livery Place
35 Livery Street
Birmingham B3 2PB, UK.

ISBN 978-1-78528-743-5

www.packtpub.com

Credits

Foreword

There is no doubt that Windows PowerShell is a great tool that you must have in your toolbox, whether you are a developer or an IT Pro. Windows PowerShell is not just another scripting language, but a complete management and automation platform with endless possibilities.

For a very long time, there has been a myth about scripting languages and who should use them. This myth states that automation tools, such as scripting tools and automation languages, are meant to be used by IT Pros. I think the reason for this misconception about scripting and automation is the limited functionalities and capabilities of those tools back then. However, this is no longer the case with PowerShell. For instance, Windows PowerShell is the first object-based scripting language because it is built on top of the .NET framework, which makes it easy to access all the powerful libraries underneath. Also, out of the box, it easily works with XML, ADSI, WMI, COM, and so on.

Today, for developers, Windows PowerShell is a core component of development tools such as Visual Studio and Team Foundation Server. You can use PowerShell to build your own automated test cases, provision and deploy applications, extend your software by building a PowerShell automation and management interface, and more interesting stuff that will be discussed in this book.

As the author of the first edition of this title, I was asked to write the second edition too. However, due to the fact the I was busy with another writing project I had to nominate someone to write it. Honestly, I couldn't think of anyone but Chendrayan Venkatesan (also known as Chen V), not only because he is a fellow MVP but also because of his enthusiasm and passion for PowerShell that allow him to always come up with great ideas and unique ways to do impressive things (you will find some of it in this book) with PowerShell.

Windows PowerShell for .NET developers is the jump-start reference for any developer looking for a consolidated resource to learn about Windows PowerShell. It is a fast-paced guide with short, crisp, and to the point real-world examples. This book takes you through a learning journey that starts with an overview of Windows PowerShell capabilities, components, and architecture. Then it walks you through the PowerShell syntax (which is pretty close to C#), working with objects, how to write scripts, functions, workflows, and so on.

Then you will learn how to use your .NET development experience to benefit from PowerShell. The book will show you how to work and manipulate .NET objects, COM, XML, WMI, CMI, and so on. After that, you will be introduced to PowerShell **Desired State Configuration (DSC)** and how to use it. DSC is a very useful component when it comes to standardizing your environments, which is important when you are deploying an application or even building a development and test environment that has to be identical to the production one.

Next the journey gets more interesting with cool stuff about using Windows PowerShell with the web technologies such as RESTful Web services, OData, and so many more. And finally, you will explore PowerShell API and SDK.

I am sure that you will enjoy the time you spend reading this book and learning these cool things brought to you by the one-and-only Chen V.

Ladies and gentlemen, get ready. The fun is about to start.

Sherif Talaat
PowerShell MVP

About the Authors

Chendrayan Venkatesan (Chen V) is a SharePoint IT Professional who has worked for the Information, Computer and Technology industry since 2005. Chen V started his career as Windows XP technical support engineer and became a SharePoint IT Pro in the year 2007. He mainly focuses on automating Microsoft Technologies such as SharePoint, LYNC, and Exchange. He was awarded the Microsoft **Most Valuable Professional (MVP)** in 2014. He speaks on Windows PowerShell, SharePoint Servers, Content Management, and IT Process Automations. He blogs in `http://chen.about-powershell.com` and is mentoring three IT professionals in PowerShell. He is a TechNet Wiki addict and has introduced Windows PowerShell as a category in the TechNet Wiki Guru award competition. To connect with Chen V you can visit his web site `http://about-powershell.com` or choose your favourite social media twitter `@ChendrayanV` or LinkedIn `nl.linkedin.com/in/chendrayanv`.

Sherif Talaat is a young computer science addict. He holds many technology certificates. Sherif has been working in the ICT industry since 2005. He has worked on the Microsoft's core infrastructure platforms and solutions with more focus on the cloud and data center management, IT Process Automation (ITPA), and scripting techniques.

Sherif is one of the early adopters of Windows PowerShell in Middle East and Africa. He speaks about Windows PowerShell at technical events and user groups' gatherings; he is also the founder of Egypt PowerShell User Group and the author of the first and only Arabic PowerShell blog. He has been awarded the Egyptian MCIT Shield and has won the Microsoft Most Valuable Professional (MVP) award for PowerShell seven times in a row since 2009. He is also the author of three different Windows PowerShell titles for IT professionals and developers. Last but not least, he is also a TED conference speaker.

You can learn more about him at `http://sheriftalaat.com` and follow him on Twitter `@SherifTalaat`.

About the Reviewers

Richard Gibson lives in London and has worked as a .NET developer for eight years. His work has taken him into the world of DevOps and Powershell, which has become a necessary skill for the automation of everyday tasks.

He currently works for `http://www.asos.com/` as a senior developer, spending most of his Powershell time providing continuous deployment for the business through TeamCity.

Richard blogs on various issues related to .NET and PowerShell at `http://richiban.uk/`.

Mayur Makwana is a software professional holding a Computer Engineering degree with more than six years experience in the information technology field covering Microsoft, Citrix, and VMware technologies. Presently he leads the infrastructure operations on Citrix (XenApp/Xendesktop) and Windows (WSUS/SCCM) projects in one of the leading Fortune 500 companies.
He is a huge believer in certifications and holds the following titles:

- **Citrix Certified Administrator (CCA)** for Citrix XenApp 6.5
- **Microsoft Certified Professional (MCP)**
- Microsoft Specialist (Microsoft Server Virtualization with Windows Server Hyper-V and System Center)
- **VMware Certified Associate-Data Center Virtualization (VCA-DCV)**
- **Information Technology Infrastructure Library (ITIL)** V3 Foundation
- ChangeBASE AOK (application compatibility testing and remediation)
- **Oracle Certified Associate (OCA)**

He reviews technical books and writes technical blogs (`www.all-about-software-applications-repackaging.com`).

He has attended several courses and conducted training in the following fields:

- Licensing Windows Server
- Advanced Tools and Scripting with PowerShell 3.0 Jump Start
- Deploying Windows 8
- Licensing Windows 8
- Migrating from Windows XP to Windows 7
- Networking Fundamentals
- Introduction to Hyper-V Jump Start

I would like to thank my mother Beena Makwana who has always encouraged me to utilize my potential and help people by sharing my expertise and knowledge. Thanks to the Packt Publishing team for giving me this opportunity.

Laxmikant Patil is a Senior Technical Architect on various Microsoft Technologies. He has 13 years of experience in building complex software systems from devices running Linux and BerklyDB to Cloud-based highly scalable systems and SharePoint-based Portal and Content systems. He has written many papers on Cloud adoption, technology migrations, ERP integrations, knowledge management, and cost-effective designing areas. His passion is to apply technology to business problems to supply solutions that will fit into customers' budgets. His dream project is to develop a platform for children that will help them develop analytical and logical thinking abilities. During his spare time, he enjoys watching cartoon movies. He writes on his blog site `http://laxmikantpatil.com/`.

I would like to thank my family, especially my lovely wife Vasudha for her understanding and sacrifices during this period. Love you!

My thanks to the PacktPub team for believing in me. It was a great experience working with you. Thank you, team!

www.PacktPub.com

Support files, eBooks, discount offers, and more

For support files and downloads related to your book, please visit www.PacktPub.com.

Did you know that Packt offers eBook versions of every book published, with PDF and ePub files available? You can upgrade to the eBook version at www.PacktPub.com and as a print book customer, you are entitled to a discount on the eBook copy. Get in touch with us at service@packtpub.com for more details.

At www.PacktPub.com, you can also read a collection of free technical articles, sign up for a range of free newsletters and receive exclusive discounts and offers on Packt books and eBooks.

https://www2.packtpub.com/books/subscription/packtlib

Do you need instant solutions to your IT questions? PacktLib is Packt's online digital book library. Here, you can search, access, and read Packt's entire library of books.

Why subscribe?

- Fully searchable across every book published by Packt
- Copy and paste, print, and bookmark content
- On demand and accessible via a web browser

Free access for Packt account holders

If you have an account with Packt at www.PacktPub.com, you can use this to access PacktLib today and view 9 entirely free books. Simply use your login credentials for immediate access.

Instant updates on new Packt books

Get notified! Find out when new books are published by following @PacktEnterprise on Twitter or the *Packt Enterprise* Facebook page.

Table of Contents

Preface

Windows PowerShell is no longer a secret in the world of IT. Starting in 2006, it's been growing and has now turned out to be a massive automation platform especially for Microsoft products and technologies.

Windows PowerShell 5.0 for .NET Developers is your self-start guide to performing automation using Windows PowerShell. This book will help you to understand the PowerShell syntax and grammar and will also teach you techniques to remove the rough edges of manual deployments. Packed with PowerShell scripts and sample C# codes to automate tasks, it also includes real-world scenarios, such as administrating office servers to help you save time and perform deployments swiftly and efficiently.

What this book covers

Chapter 1, *Getting Started with Windows PowerShell*, covers the basics of Windows PowerShell, the importance of object-based shells, and how ISE helps us in building scripts.

Chapter 2, *Unleashing Development Skills Using Windows PowerShell 5.0*, explores XML and COM automation and NET objects for Admin and Development tasks. You will also get acquainted with the PowerShell modules and how script debugging works.

Chapter 3, *Exploring Desired State Configuration*, gets you started with **Desired State Configuration** (**DSC**) concepts such as installing WMF 5.0 April 2015 Preview, Imperative versus declarative programming and their significant features. It also explores Windows Remote Management and CIM, and teaches you to create configurations scripts.

Chapter 4, *PowerShell and Web Technologies*, starts with the installation and configuration of Web Access, and explores Web requests, services, and REST API.

Chapter 5, Exploring Application Programming Interface, covers the key benefits of the API and using it in Windows PowerShell, Exchange Web Services, LYNC Client-side API, and SharePoint Client Side Object Model; you'll walk through a demo to create a PowerShell module in C# for office servers.

What you need for this book

The following is a list of software required and supported operating systems for this book:

- Windows Management Framework 3.0 and advanced (Windows 7)
- Windows Management Framework 5.0 (Windows 7, Windows Server 2008 R2 SP1 and advanced)
- Windows Management Framework 5.0 (Windows 7, Windows Server 2008 R2 SP1 and advanced)

Who this book is for

If you are an IT professional or developer who has worked on the .NET platform and you want to learn about automation using Windows PowerShell, then this book is for you. This self-start guide takes you from the basics and gradually moves to an intermediate level to show you how to perform professional scripting.

Conventions

In this book, you will find a number of text styles that distinguishe between different kinds of information. Here are some examples of these styles and an explanation of their meaning.

Code words in text, database table names, folder names, filenames, file extensions, pathnames, dummy URLs, user input, and Twitter handles are shown as follows: "`$MaximumHistoryCount` is a built-in variable that returns the actual value of the command's history."

Any command-line input or output is written as follows:

```
(Get-Host).UI.RawUI
(Get-Host).UI.RawUI | GM
```

New terms and **important words** are shown in bold. Words that you see on the screen, for example, in menus or dialog boxes, appear in the text like this: " Using the **Options** tab, we can see **Cursor Size**, **Command History**, and **Edit Options**, and adjust them as we require."

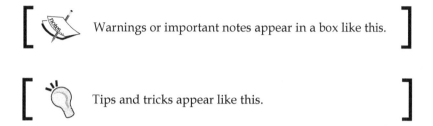

Warnings or important notes appear in a box like this.

Tips and tricks appear like this.

Reader feedback

Feedback from our readers is always welcome. Let us know what you think about this book—what you liked or disliked. Reader feedback is important for us as it helps us develop titles that you will really get the most out of.

To send us general feedback, simply e-mail feedback@packtpub.com, and mention the book's title in the subject of your message.

If there is a topic that you have expertise in and you are interested in either writing or contributing to a book, see our author guide at www.packtpub.com/authors.

Customer support

Now that you are the proud owner of a Packt book, we have a number of things to help you to get the most from your purchase.

Downloading the example code

You can download the example code files from your account at http://www.packtpub.com for all the Packt Publishing books you have purchased. If you purchased this book elsewhere, you can visit http://www.packtpub.com/support and register to have the files e-mailed directly to you.

Downloading the color images of this book

We also provide you with a PDF file that has color images of the screenshots/diagrams used in this book. The color images will help you better understand the changes in the output. You can download this file from `https://www.packtpub.com/sites/default/files/downloads/7435EN_ColouredImages.pdf`.

Errata

Although we have taken every care to ensure the accuracy of our content, mistakes do happen. If you find a mistake in one of our books—maybe a mistake in the text or the code—we would be grateful if you could report this to us. By doing so, you can save other readers from frustration and help us improve subsequent versions of this book. If you find any errata, please report them by visiting `http://www.packtpub.com/submit-errata`, selecting your book, clicking on the **Errata Submission Form** link, and entering the details of your errata. Once your errata are verified, your submission will be accepted and the errata will be uploaded to our website or added to any list of existing errata under the Errata section of that title.

To view the previously submitted errata, go to `https://www.packtpub.com/books/content/support` and enter the name of the book in the search field. The required information will appear under the **Errata** section.

Piracy

Piracy of copyrighted material on the Internet is an ongoing problem across all media. At Packt, we take the protection of our copyright and licenses very seriously. If you come across any illegal copies of our works in any form on the Internet, please provide us with the location address or website name immediately so that we can pursue a remedy.

Please contact us at `copyright@packtpub.com` with a link to the suspected pirated material.

We appreciate your help in protecting our authors and our ability to bring you valuable content.

Questions

If you have a problem with any aspect of this book, you can contact us at `questions@packtpub.com`, and we will do our best to address the problem.

1
Getting Started with Windows PowerShell

In this chapter, we will cover the following topics:

- What is **Windows PowerShell**?
- Installing **Windows Management Framework 5.0** on **Windows Server 2012**
- The **Windows PowerShell console**
- Setting up the console using GUI and PowerShell
- Benefits of the **Windows PowerShell ISE**
- Creating snippets in the PowerShell ISE

Scripting the cmdlet style

This is a self-paced guide for you to learn Windows PowerShell in order to perform IT automation. The management goals of IT are to simplify the creation and operation of computing environments. IT professionals and developers need to complete their daily tasks swiftly in order to avoid chaos.

Windows PowerShell is an object-based and distributed automation platform that enables IT professionals and developers to speed up their development tasks and deployments. The Windows PowerShell scripting language makes daily tasks more productive.

The goal of this book is to share the features of Windows PowerShell 5.0 and how developers can utilize its benefits. Let's dive into Windows PowerShell 5.0 so that we can design our infrastructure, automate our daily tasks, manage drifts in our environment, quicken the deployment tasks, and so on.

The IT industry is growing rapidly; to adapt and minimize the impact, we need to plan and design our infrastructure so as to meet the growing needs with minimum chaos. It's challenging and really difficult to automate the tasks without PowerShell. Windows PowerShell plays a major role by not only enabling task automation, but also allowing us to design our infrastructure with the help of IT professionals and developers.

Developers from the .NET background can quickly understand PowerShell. Developers can easily create their own **cmdlets** (cmdlets, pronounced as command lets, are nothing but the lightweight commands used in Windows PowerShell) and leverage it in the infrastructure as needed. Thus, the deployment tasks become easier and the productivity increases by automation.

Come, let's dive into Windows PowerShell 5.0 and its features.

 Before we begin, let's note that Windows PowerShell 5.0 is not a stable release. So, if you identify any bugs in the command, you can file a case at `http://connect.microsoft.com`.

This self-paced guide will discuss the following:

- Working with PowerShell cmdlets
- PowerShell scripting
- Exploring PowerShell modules
- Exploring the XML, COM, and .NET objects
- Exploring JSON, REST API, and Web Services
- Features of Windows PowerShell 5.0
- Exploring DSC to configure servers
- Exploring web technologies using PowerShell
- Consuming API in C# and PowerShell
- Using PowerShell codes in C#

 If you are interested in knowing the origin of Windows PowerShell 5.0, you should read Monad Manifesto at:

`http://blogs.msdn.com/cfs-file.`
`ashx/__key/communityserver-components-`
`postattachments/00-01-91-05-67/Monad-Manifesto-`
`_2D00_-Public.doc`

Introducing Windows PowerShell

Windows PowerShell is an object-based command-line interface with a very powerful scripting language built on .NET. Windows PowerShell is designed with access to several cmdlets, functions, filters, scripts, aliases, and executables.

From Windows Management Framework 4.0 onward, a new configuration management platform has been introduced in PowerShell 4.0, which is Windows PowerShell **Desired State Configuration (DSC)**.

Windows PowerShell is very enhanced in the version 5.0 April 2015 Preview release. This is not a stable release, but we will explore the new features introduced in Windows PowerShell 5.0. The current stable version is Windows PowerShell 4.0.

IT professionals and developers use their own statements or definitions based on the way they use PowerShell. Mostly, they define PowerShell as a scripting language. Yeah! This is true but not completely because Windows PowerShell does much more. However, the official page of Windows PowerShell defines PowerShell as an automation platform and scripting language for Windows and Windows Server that allows you to simplify the management of your systems. Unlike the other text-based shells, PowerShell harnesses the power of the .NET Framework, providing us with rich objects and a massive set of built-in functionality to help you take control of your Windows environments. Refer to the following URL:

```
https://msdn.microsoft.com/en-us/powershell
```

You may wonder, why Windows PowerShell? Why not VBScript? This is a very common question that most administrators think. It's good to know both, but VBScript is fading, and compared to PowerShell, it is very limited. Windows PowerShell can access all .NET libraries, which helps us explore DLLs easily; on the other hand, VBScript has limitations. If you are a beginner Windows PowerShell will be a better choice because it is easier to understand and very powerful. The Windows PowerShell cmdlets are rich and very easy to understand. Using Windows PowerShell, we can avoid repeated steps, automate administration tasks, avoid GUI clicks, and do much more. This is not limited to IT Professionals; developers can also do much more by exploring Windows PowerShell, such as performing development tasks faster than before.

From Windows PowerShell 5.0 onward, we can develop classes, parse structured objects using the new cmdlets, and do the package management easily using the `PackageManagement` module. This module is introduced in version 5.0 but was formerly known as the `OneGet` module; many such modules are enhanced in the new version.

But wait, this is not all; you can refer to the following link to get a list of the new features in Windows PowerShell 5.0:

```
https://technet.microsoft.com/en-us/library/hh857339.
aspx#BKMK_new50
```

Installing Windows Management Framework 5.0

Before we explore the PowerShell console host and the PowerShell ISE, let's install Windows Management Framework 5.0 April 2015 Preview (Latest Build). Windows Management Framework 5.0 is now supported on Windows 7 and Windows Server 2008 R2 SP1 – this will be covered in *Chapter 3, Exploring Desired State Configuration* in detail. Windows Management Framework is shipped out of the box in the Windows 10 operating system and Windows Server Technical Preview. So, there is no need for manual installation.

To start the demo, we need to perform the following functions in our machine environment:

- Set up Windows 2012 R2 Data Center
- Download .NET Framework 4.5 (Included in Windows Server 2012)
- Download Windows Management Framework 4.0
- Download Windows Management Framework 5.0

 Windows 2008 R2 has PowerShell 2.0 by default. To install Windows Management Framework 5.0, we need to upgrade from Windows Management Framework 4.0.

To open Windows PowerShell, perform the following functions:

1. Click on the start icon.
2. Type `Windows PowerShell` in **Search programs and files**.
3. It lists **Windows PowerShell ISE** and **Windows PowerShell**.

Here, ISE is short for Integrated Scripting Environment.

 Ignore x86 – it's a 32-bit Windows PowerShell application (we will not use it in any of our examples in this book).

It's best practice to know your PowerShell version before you start doing an exercise or start using scripts from the Internet.

To check the current version of PowerShell, you can simply run the following code:

```
$PSVersionTable
```

The following screenshot illustrates the output:

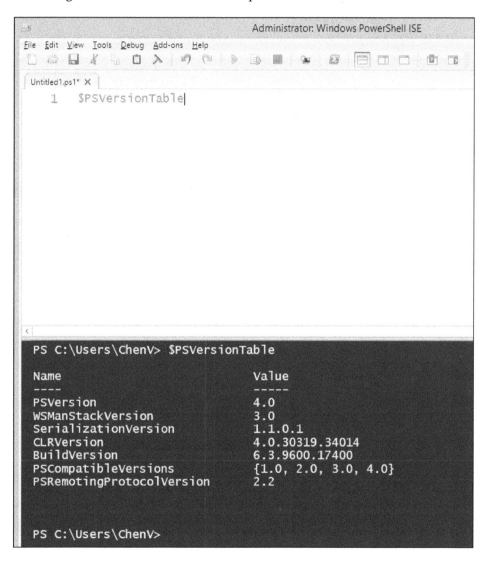

Windows Server 2012 R2 has WMF Version 4.0 by default. Let's upgrade it to WMF 5.0. If you are performing this task on Windows 7 or Windows 2008 R2 with SP1, install WMF 4.0 prior to WMF 5.0.

Following are the links where you can download the .NET framework and WMF from:

- .NET Framework 4.5 — `http://www.microsoft.com/en-us/download/details.aspx?id=30653`

- WMF 5.0 — `http://www.microsoft.com/en-us/download/details.aspx?id=46889`

 Do read the system requirements before proceeding into the production environment. The installation of WMF 5.0 requires a reboot.

Once the .NET framework 4.0 is in place, update it to the .NET framework 4.5.

As per the Microsoft Document, the .NET framework 4.5 is included in Windows 8 and Windows Server 2012. We can skip the .NET framework 4.5 installation.

We need to identify and install the correct package of WMF 5.0. For Windows Server 2012, we need to download the 64-bit version of it, which is `WindowsBlue-KB3055381-x64.msu`.

Open the MSU package and you will see the prompt, as shown in the following screenshot:

1. Click on **Yes**.

2. Read and accept the license agreement, as shown in the following screenshot:

3. After this, the installation begins, as shown in the following screenshot:

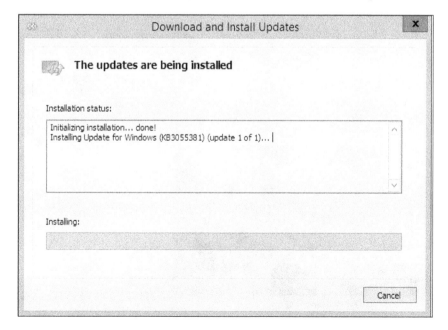

4. Click on **Restart Now** when you see the following window on your screen:

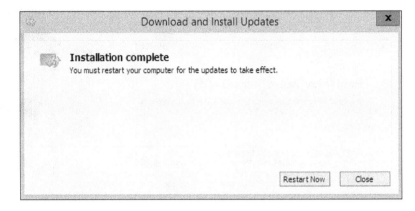

We have successfully installed WMF 5.0. As an outcome of this upgrade, now we also have the updated versions of Windows PowerShell, Windows PowerShell **Desired State Configuration (DSC)**, and the Windows PowerShell ISE. Package manager and network switches cmdlets are included with this version.

The following image illustrates the Windows PowerShell 5.0 ISE:

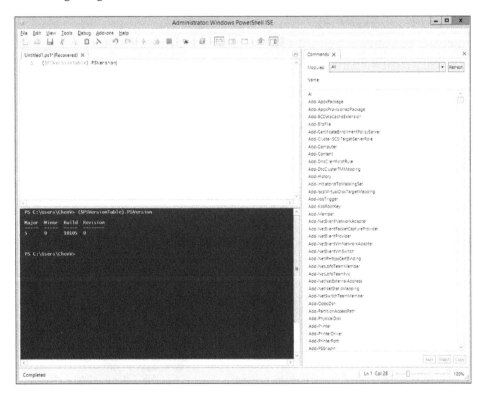

The Windows PowerShell consoles

Windows PowerShell has two different consoles: the console host and the Windows PowerShell ISE host, which is GUI. To verify this, click on the start icon and search for `PowerShell` on Windows Server 2012.

The following image illustrates the results of PowerShell:

 Ignore x86 in the Windows PowerShell ISE (x86) for now. This is a 32-bit ISE, and throughout this book, we will focus only on the 64–bit ISE.

The location of the Windows PowerShell console host and ISE is:

`C:\Windows\System32\WindowsPowerShell\v1.0`

The file name `powershell.exe` is the console host and `powershell_ise.exe` is the Integrated Scripting Environment.

The Windows PowerShell console host

This is where we begin with the PowerShell cmdlets. It's easy for on-the-fly cmdlet executions. The following image illustrates the PowerShell 5.0 console host:

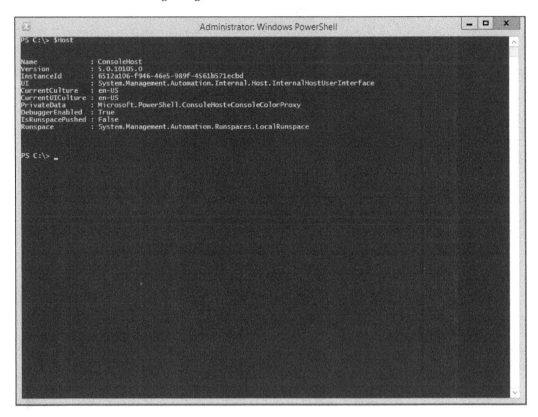

By default, the background color is blue, and in the foreground, the color of the text is white.

There is no need to type out the complete command; the PowerShell console allows Tab Completion. For example, Get-Se + *Tab* completes the Get-Service command. Tab completion is not only for the commands and parameters; we can also select the properties using tab key.

To execute the following PowerShell code:

```
Get-Service -Name BITS | Select -Property Name , Status
```

Windows PowerShell allows tab completion like this:

```
Get-Ser + Tab -N + Tab BITS | sel + Tab -Pro + Tab N + Tab, s + Tab
```

There are multiple ways to start a PowerShell console: we could either use the **Run** dialog box, or type `PowerShell` in an open command-line window. These techniques allow you to pass arguments to Windows PowerShell, including the switches that control how Windows PowerShell works and the parameters that execute additional commands. For example, you can start Windows PowerShell in the no-logo mode (which means that the logo banner is turned off) using the startup command, `PowerShell -nologo`. By default, when you start Windows PowerShell via the command shell, Windows PowerShell runs and then exits. If you want Windows PowerShell to execute a command and not terminate, type `PowerShell /noexit`, followed by the command text.

We can use this to schedule our script in task schedulers. To see all the switches, run the following command:

```
PowerShell.exe /?
```

Downloading the example code

You can download the example code files from your account at `http://www.packtpub.com` for all the Packt Publishing books you have purchased. If you purchased this book elsewhere, you can visit `http://www.packtpub.com/support` and register to have the files e-mailed directly to you.

Setting up the console host using GUI

We can change the look and feel of the console host using GUI. To do this, we need to perform the following steps:

Click on the Windows PowerShell icon, which appears in the upper-left corner and select **Properties**. This has four tabs—**Options**, **Font**, **Layout**, and **Colors**. Let's explore each tab.

- **Options**: Using the **Options** tab, we can see **Cursor Size**, **Command History**, and **Edit Options**, and adjust them as we require.

  While setting the cursor size, we have three options: **Small**, **Medium**, and **Large.** Here, small is 25 pixels, medium is 50 pixels, and large is 100 pixels.

The following image illustrates the **Options** tab:

By default, the command history retains the last 50 commands in a buffer. We can customize this by increasing or decreasing the **Buffer Size** value.

 $MaximumHistoryCount is a built-in variable that returns the actual value of the command's history. This takes precedence over GUI.

- **Font**: Using the **Font** tab, we can change the size, style, and type. Before applying changes, we can preview the console host using the preview window.

  The following image illustrates the **Font** tab:

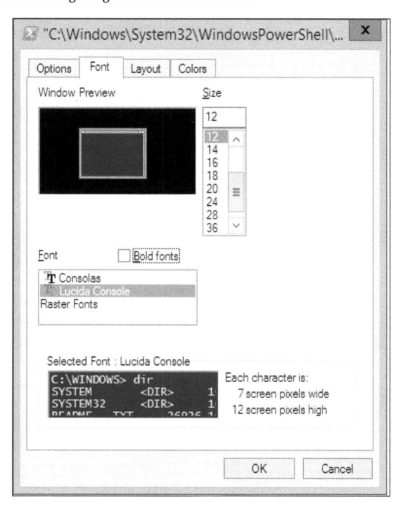

- **Layout**: Using the **Layout** tab, we can set the screen buffer size, window size, and window position. Similarly to the **Font** tab, this also has preview window.

  The following image illustrates the **Layout** tab:

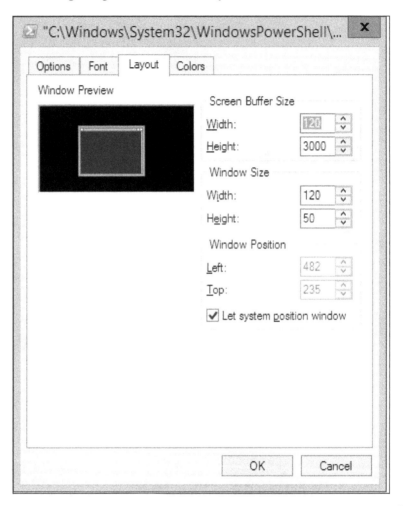

- **Colors**: Using the **Colors** tab, we can set the screen text, screen background, pop up text, and popup background values. The current RGB values are shown in the **Selected Color Values** section. The modifications can be previewed before applying.

The following image illustrates the **Colors** tab:

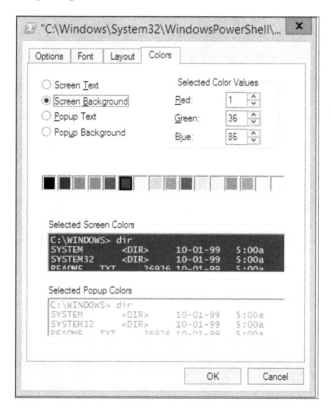

Press *F7* to see the history; this pops up a tiny window as shown in the following image:

Setting up the console host using PowerShell

The steps we explored under **Graphical User Interface (GUI)** are limited; we can actually do more using PowerShell. Here comes the importance of objects. In this exercise, we will adjust our console settings. To do all this, we need to know is Get-Host command-let.

The Get-Host cmdlet is used to do more of the Windows PowerShell console setup. In this exercise let's change the title of the PowerShell console host.

The default console host title is shown in the following image:

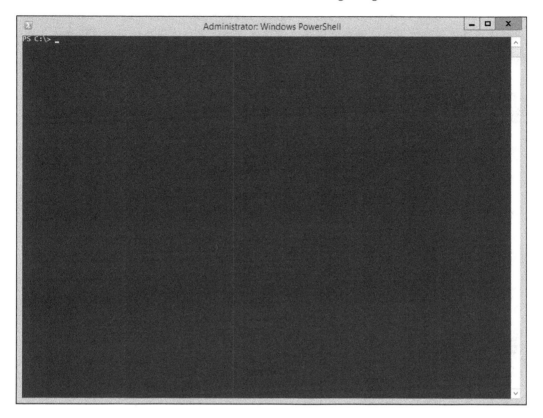

Administrator: Windows PowerShell is the default title. Now let's change this to
`Windows PowerShell 5.0 April 2015 Preview`. Run the following commands:

```
(Get-Host).UI.RawUI
```

```
(Get-Host).UI.RawUI | GM
```

The preceding code returns the current settings and its members.

The output is illustrated in the following image:

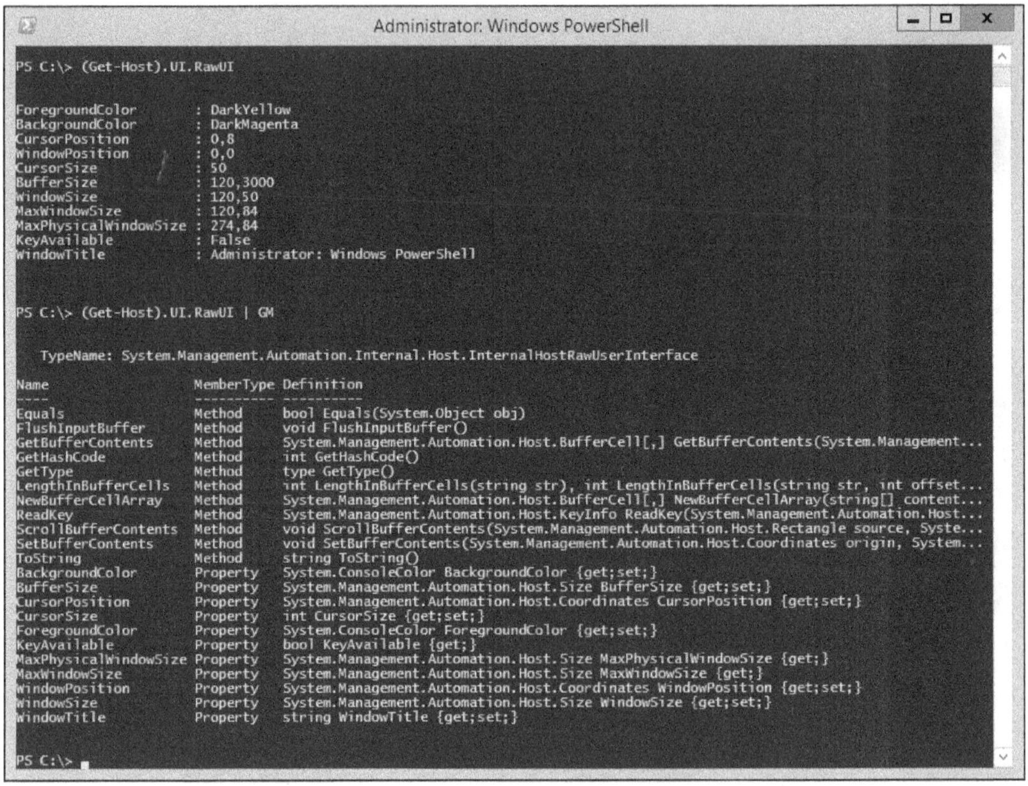

`WindowTitle` is a property for which we can get and set a value and whose datatype is `String`. We will discuss this in detail in the *Understanding Objects* section. Now, let's execute the following code to change the title of the console host:

```
(Get-Host).UI.RawUI.WindowTitle = "Windows PowerShell 5.0 April 2015
  Preview"
```

The change appears as illustrated in the following image:

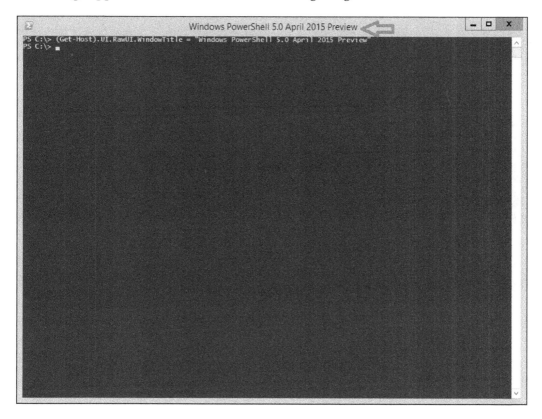

Using GUI, we can set the cursor size to small, medium, or large, which allows only 25, 50, or 100 respectively. But, PowerShell allows us to customize more by executing the following command:

```
(Get-Host).UI.RawUI.CursorSize
```

The previous command returns the current cursor size. Run the following command:

```
(Get-Host).UI.RawUI.CursorSize.GetType()
```

This command returns the type as shown in the following image:

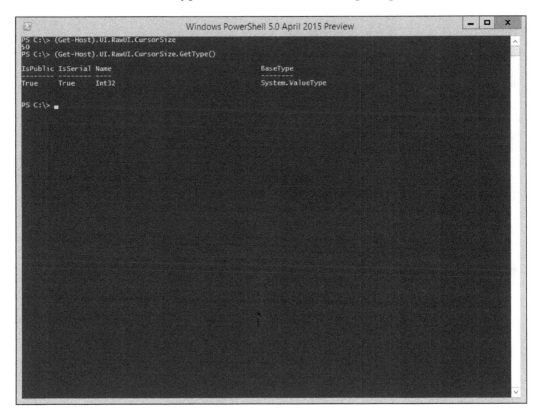

Now, let's change the cursor size to 72 by executing the following command:

```
(Get-Host).UI.RawUI.CursorSize = 72
```

The output is illustrated in the following image:

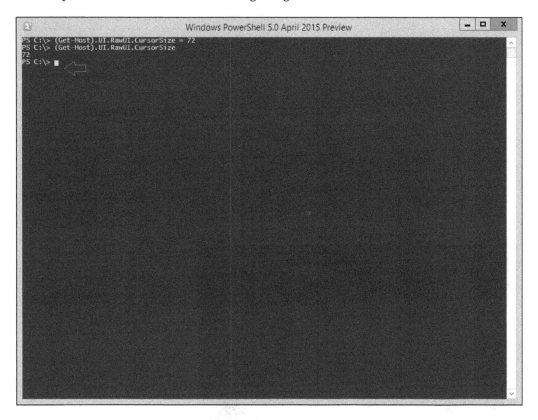

Exploring the Windows PowerShell ISE host using GUI

The Windows PowerShell ISE host is enhanced and exciting in version 5.0. This version has lots of new features and is user friendly. The ISE helps us to write scripts faster than a console. We will explore the features of ISEs in *Chapter 3, Exploring Desired State Configuration*.

Opening the PowerShell ISE is similar to opening the console host. Click on the start icon, search for PowerShell, and open **PowerShell ISE**. The executable file for the PowerShell ISE resides in the same location as console host:

```
%windir%\system32\WindowsPowerShell\v1.0\PowerShell_ISE.exe
```

The following image illustrates the PowerShell ISE:

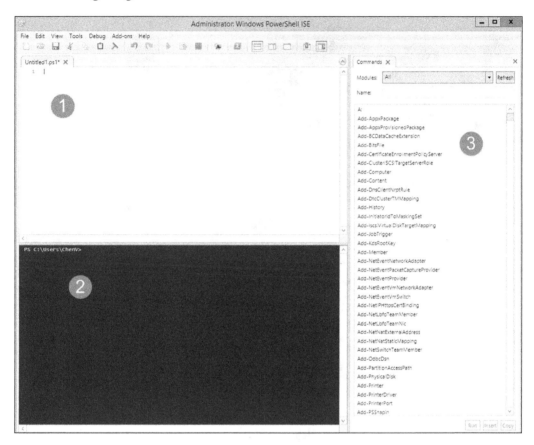

The PowerShell ISE host is divided into the following sections:

- **1**: Script pane
- **2**: Command pane
- **3**: Commands add-on

The script pane's visibility can be adjusted using the keyboard shortcuts, *Ctrl + 1*, *Ctrl + 2*, *Ctrl + 3*, which sets the script pane to top, right, and maximized, respectively. This makes it easy for us to view the command and result that we need.

The command pane will be hidden if we maximize the script pane.

Let us learn more about commands add-on pane:

1. By default, all the available modules will be shown. Click on the drop-down list to view the modules.

2. Click on **Refresh** if any new modules are loaded.

3. Type the command name, and it will show the output as illustrated in the following image:

4. Enter the command.

5. Select the command.

6. Click on the help icon, and this opens up the help in GUI.

7. Enter the parameters as required. The * sign denotes mandatory.

8. The common parameters are not always required, but we will use them in the next chapters.

9. We can run the code, copy it, or click on **Insert**, which appears in the command pane. Ensure that you haven't maximized the Script Pane.

An ISE allows us to cut, copy, paste, start IntelliSense, and start the snippets. Similarly to other windows operations, *Ctrl + X*, *Ctrl + C*, and *Ctrl + Y* will cut, copy, and paste, respectively.

IntelliSense gives us a better discoverability of cmdlets. A bunch of related commands will be shown in the drop-down menu, so we can easily choose the cmdlet we need. The Syntax tooltip lists the parameters to be used with the command, as shown in the following image:

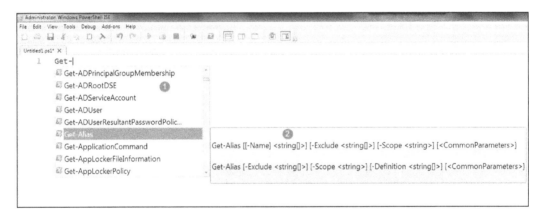

1. As soon as we start typing, IntelliSense shows us the list of commands that begin with the text that is typed. We can scroll down and choose the command we need to execute.

2. The syntax tooltip shows the syntax of the command that we choose.

To get help about the command, simply type the command, select it, and press *F1*.

The output is illustrated in the following image:

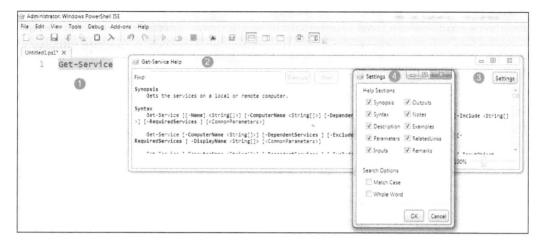

The points marked in the figure are explained in the following list:

- **1**: Select the command.
- **2**: Press *F1*, which brings up the help window.
- **3**: Click on **Settings**.
- **4**: Select the sections you need to know. For example, unselect **Examples** to hide the example section in the help window.

Benefits of an ISE

In comparison with the PowerShell console host, an ISE has a lot of benefits, and I will list a few of them here:

- It's easy to use
- It's very user friendly
- There are shortcut keys to manage the script
- Writing the DSC configuration code is easy
- The snippets make our job much easier
- There is a script browser
- We have the Command add-on
- It shows a squiggly line in case of errors

The PowerShell ISE script browser

PowerShell ISE has a script browser feature that allows us to search for the script in TechNet's script gallery. This is optional but worth using! This is because using **Script Browser,** we can download and use the scripts available in TechNet's script gallery.

The following image illustrates Script Browser:

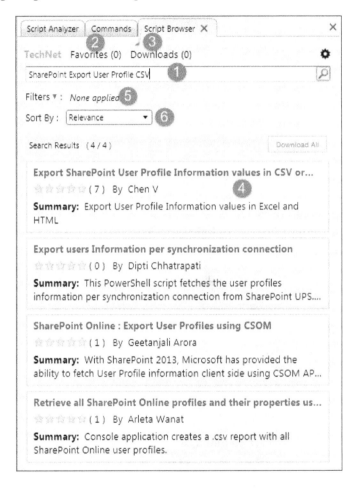

Following are a few options in **Script Browser**:

- You can search for the script you need. Type the script's name in the textbox provided, right-click on the script, and select either **Add to favorites** or the **Download** option.
- Your favorite scripts appears in the **Favorites** tab.

- The scripts that you download will appear in the **Downloads** tab.

- You can set the language, download locations and network settings by clicking on the settings icon in the upper-right corner.

The following image shows the **Settings** window of **Script Browser**:

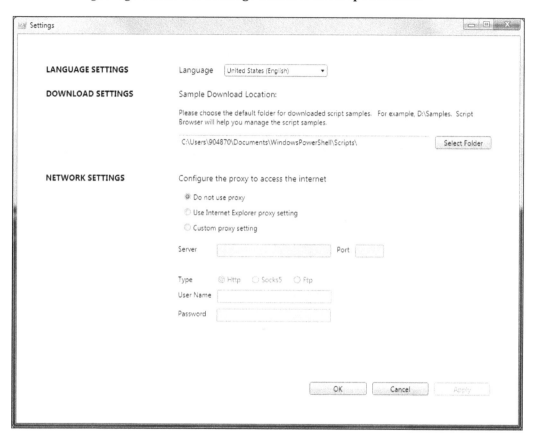

Some benefits of Script Browser are as follows:

- Script Browser allows us to filter the search based on technologies

- Script Browser allows us to sort the script by popularity, ratings, and so on

 The link to download Script Browser is http://www.microsoft.com/en-us/download/details.aspx?id=42525.

Using an interactive shell

Windows PowerShell can be used either interactively or as a script automation. Before we take a look at script automations, let's explore the use of an interactive shell.

We can do arithmetic operations in Windows PowerShell as follows:

```
2 + 2
```

This will return 4. Consider the following operation:

```
2 + 2 * 3
```

This will return 8.

Windows PowerShell does left-to-right arithmetic operations according to the precedence rules. In the preceding expressions, PowerShell performed the operation as 2 * 3 + 2. We need to use parenthesis, as with (2 + 2) * 3, which return the result as 12. Here, (2 + 2) is known as grouping.

Using Windows PowerShell, we can do much more, such as system unit calculations, hexadecimal conversions, and so on, and few examples are as follows:

```
4GB / 1MB
```

This returns 4096.

```
(0xc85).ToChar($_)
```

This returns the following character:

```
'⌷'
```

In Windows PowerShell, we can use .NET classes. Here's an example:

```
[System.Math]::PI
```

This returns the value of pi, which is 3.14159265358979.

Windows PowerShell allows us to use class directly, without using the namespace, shown as follows:

```
[Math]::PI
```

Refer to the following MSDN link for the `System.Math` class: `https://msdn.microsoft.com/en-us/library/system.math%28v=vs.110%29.aspx`

The command shown before was just an example. With reference to this, we can build code as per our needs using .NET classes.

Windows PowerShell cmdlets

In this topic, we will cover the following:

- Exploring Windows PowerShell commands
- Exploring Windows PowerShell modules
- Getting help
- Understanding aliases, expressions, objects, pipelines, filtering, and formatting
- Scripting with Windows PowerShell

Windows PowerShell is designed to execute four kinds of named commands:

- Cmdlets: These are .NET programs designed to interact with PowerShell
- Scripts: These are files with the `FileName.PS1` extension
- Functions: These are a block of code that are very helpful for script organization
- Native window commands: These are internal commands such as MKDIR, CHDIR, and so on

The internal commands of Windows PowerShell are called cmdlets. Cmdlets are always named in the verb-and-noun combination. This appears as *Verb-Noun*, for example `Get-Service` and `Stop-Service,` where `Get` and `Stop` are verbs, and `Service` is a noun.

(Verb) — Action

(Noun) — Something to be acted on

For example, `Get-Service`

Let's execute the following command:

```
Get-Command
```

The output of this command is illustrated in the following image:

```
Administrator: Windows PowerShell
PS C:\> Get-Command

CommandType     Name                                              Version      Source
-----------     ----                                              -------      ------
Alias           Add-WAPackEnvironment                             0.8.7        Azure
Alias           Begin-WebCommitDelay                              1.0.0.0      WebAdministration
Alias           Disable-WAPackWebsiteApplicationDiagnostic        0.8.7        Azure
Alias           Enable-WAPackWebsiteApplicationDiagnositc         0.8.7        Azure
Alias           End-WebCommitDelay                                1.0.0.0      WebAdministration
Alias           Fix-It                                            1.2.0.132    pspx
Alias           Get-AzureStorageContainerAcl                      0.8.7        Azure
Alias           Get-WAPackEnvironment                             0.8.7        Azure
Alias           Get-WAPackPublishSettingsFile                     0.8.7        Azure
Alias           Get-WAPackSBLocation                              0.8.7        Azure
Alias           Get-WAPackSBNamespace                             0.8.7        Azure
Alias           Get-WAPackSubscription                            0.8.7        Azure
Alias           Get-WAPackWebsite                                 0.8.7        Azure
Alias           Get-WAPackWebsiteDeployment                       0.8.7        Azure
Alias           Get-WAPackWebsiteLocation                         0.8.7        Azure
Alias           Get-WAPackWebsiteLog                              0.8.7        Azure
Alias           Import-WAPackPublishSettingsFile                  0.8.7        Azure
Alias           Invoke-Hive                                       0.8.7        Azure
Alias           New-WAPackSBNamespace                             0.8.7        Azure
Alias           New-WAPackWebsite                                 0.8.7        Azure
Alias           Remove-WAPackEnvironment                          0.8.7        Azure
Alias           Remove-WAPackSBNamespace                          0.8.7        Azure
Alias           Remove-WAPackSubscription                         0.8.7        Azure
Alias           Remove-WAPackWebsite                              0.8.7        Azure
Alias           Restart-WAPackWebsite                             0.8.7        Azure
Alias           Restore-WAPackWebsiteDeployment                   0.8.7        Azure
Alias           Save-WAPackWebsiteLog                             0.8.7        Azure
Alias           Select-WAPackSubscription                         0.8.7        Azure
Alias           Set-WAPackEnvironment                             0.8.7        Azure
Alias           Set-WAPackSubscription                            0.8.7        Azure
Alias           Set-WAPackWebsite                                 0.8.7        Azure
Alias           Show-WAPackPortal                                 0.8.7        Azure
Alias           Show-WAPackWebsite                                0.8.7        Azure
Alias           Start-CopyAzureStorageBlob                        0.8.7        Azure
```

The previous command will list all the installed commands from the computer and retrieve only the cmdlets, functions, and aliases.

To retrieve only cmdlets, we can use the `CommandType` parameter, as shown in the following command:

```
Get-Command -CommandType Cmdlet
```

> Windows PowerShell supports tab completion. For example, let's run the following command:
>
> Get-Comm + *Tab* +   -Co + *Tab* + C + *Tab*
>
> When we type out this command, it will result as follows:
>
> ```
> Get-Command -CommandType Cmdlet
> ```

Now, let's explore the commands. In the following example, we will take a look at the cmdlet `Get-Service`. Since we know the cmdlet up front, let's collect more information such as the cmdlet version and source, as follows:

```
Get-Command Get-Service
```

The output of the preceding command is illustrated in the following image:

The points marked in the figure are explained in the following list:

- **1**: This is the type of the command
- **2**: This is the name of the command
- **3**: This indicates the version (From Windows PowerShell 5.0 onward)
- **4**: This indicates the module's name

To retrieve the commands for a specific module, we need to use the `Module` parameter, which accepts the module name (**Source**) as we saw in bullet 4. The following is an example of the command:

```
Get-Command -Module Microsoft.PowerShell.Management
```

This outputs all the commands available in the `Microsoft.PowerShell.Management` module.

The `Get-Service` command will retrieve all the services running on your local computer.

Refer to the following link to get more information on the `ServiceController` class:

`https://msdn.microsoft.com/en-us/library/system.serviceprocess.servicecontroller%28v=vs.110%29.aspx`

Let's see the alternate of the `Get-Service` cmdlet using the .NET class. To do this, let's find the TypeName of the `Get-Service` cmdlet by executing `Get-Service | Get-Member` and this gives the `TypeName` as `System.ServiceProcess.ServiceController`. Windows PowerShell allows us to use this directly as follows:

```
[System.ServiceProcess.ServiceController]::GetServices()
```

Now, let's take a look at how the command that we just discussed works.

Here, we will consume the .NET `ServiceController` class in PowerShell and invoke the `GetServices()` method.

The `GetServices` method has an overload with a `machineName` parameter. To find this, we will execute the following command:

```
[System.ServiceProcess.ServiceController]::GetServices
```

The difference is that here, we did not use parentheses. The output of `OverloadDefinitions` is as follows:

```
OverloadDefinitions
-------------------
static System.ServiceProcess.ServiceController[] GetServices()

static System.ServiceProcess.ServiceController[] GetServices(string
machineName)
```

We can query the service information of a remote computer by passing the host name of the remote computer as the `machineName` parameter, as follows:

```
[System.ServiceProcess.ServiceController]::GetServices('RemoteServer')
```

Getting help

This is the most important and interesting topic. No matter what technology we consume, all we need to know is the way to get help for it. Most IT professionals and developers say that they use Google to find this.

For PowerShell, help is much more focused. It's very difficult to remember all the commands. So, we can search for a command and find help for the same. Let's take a look at how to seek help for Windows PowerShell cmdlets.

```
Get-Help Get-Service
```

The output is illustrated in the following image:

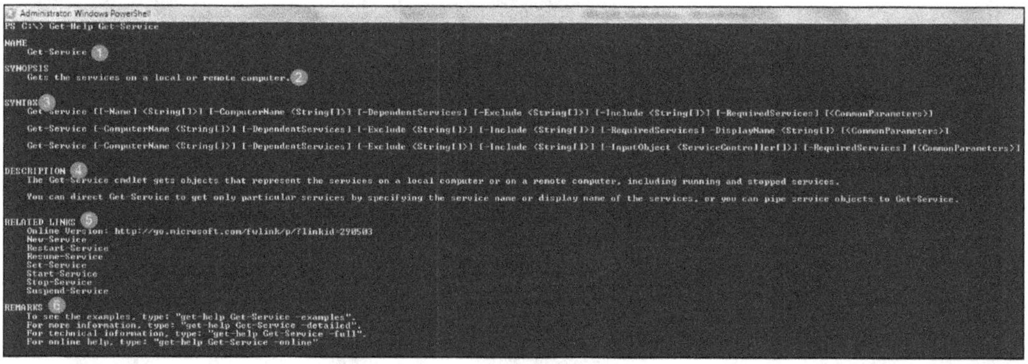

The sections in the image are explained as follows:

- **NAME**: This is the name of the command (`Get-Service`)
- **SYNOPSIS**: This is the abstract of the command
- **SYNTAX**: This gives us the syntax of the commands, which includes all its parameters and its type
- **DESCRIPTION**: This is the description of the command whose help we are looking for
- **RELATED LINKS**: This contains the URL of online versions of the command, and other commands related to the one we are looking for help regarding
- **REMARKS**: This will guide us to explore examples, detailed information, full help, and online help

If more information than that fitting the page view is to be displayed, the console is paginated. For example, if we execute the `Get-Help Get-Service -Detailed |` `more` command, the details will output as shown in the following image:

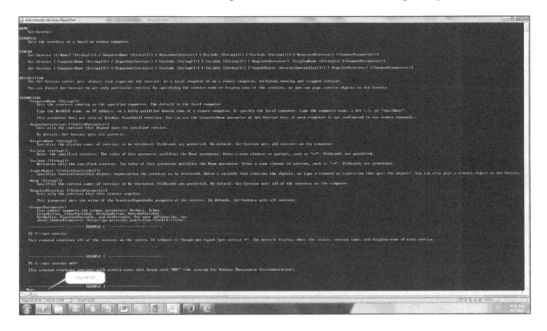

If we press *Enter*, we can view one line after another, whereas pressing the space key will give a page view.

Keep your files updated using the `Update-Help` cmdlet as shown in the following command. Ensure that your machine has internet connectivity and execute the following command:

Update-Help -Verbose

This cmdlet is designed to download and install help files on our computer. The output is illustrated in the following image:

Ensure that you have an Internet connection while updating your help. The reason for updating help is to keep the help document up-to-date. Let us learn more about the Get-Help cmdlet:

- The Help cmdlet is an alias for Get-Help (Aliases will be covered in the next section).

- The Get-Help cmdlet allows us to view the online help using the Online parameter. The following command will open the online URL in the default web browser:

```
Get-Help Get-Service -Online
```

- The Get-Help cmdlet allows us to view the help content in a separate user interface. The following is the command that needs to be executed:

```
Get-Help Get-Service -ShowWindow
```

The output of the preceding code is illustrated in the following image:

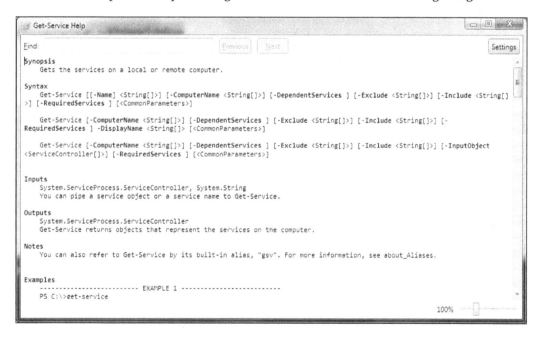

- To view only syntax, we can execute the following code:

```
(Get-Help Get-Service).Syntax
```

Understanding aliases

Using aliases in Windows PowerShell is not advised by many. The reason for this is readability and understandability. Developers are comfortable using an alias because it's easier, but the difficulty is in remembering the alias for each cmdlet.

The bottom line is that aliases are shortcuts for Windows PowerShell cmdlets.

Windows PowerShell has two types of aliases:

- The built-in alias: This is an alias that represents PowerShell's native cmdlets
- The user-defined alias: This is an alias created by us for specific needs.

The following command retrieves all the commands available in the `Microsoft.PowerShell.Management` module:

```
Get-Command -Module Microsoft.PowerShell.Management
```

The following image shows the output of the previous command:

Using the following alias, we can achieve the same output as with `-like`:

```
gcm -Module Microsoft.PowerShell.Management
```

Here, `gcm` is an alias or shortcut for the `Get-Command` cmdlet.

Let's explore all the commands related to an alias. The module name for aliases' commands is `Microsoft.PowerShell.Utility`:

```
Get-Command -Name '*Alias*'
```

The output of this command is illustrated in the following image:

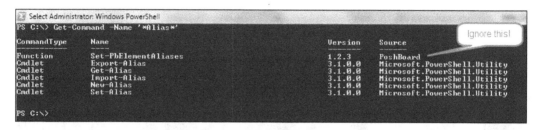

For now, ignore the `PoshBoard` module; we will discuss modules in *Chapter 2, Unleashing Development Skills Using Windows PowerShell 5.0*.

To find an alias of any given command, we can simply execute the following code:

```
Get-Alias -Definition Get-Alias
```

The output of this command is as follows:

```
PS C:\> Get-Alias -Definition Get-Alias


CommandType     Name
  Version       Source

-----------     ----
-------         ------

Alias           gal -> Get-Alias
```

Here, `gal` is an alias of the `Get-Alias` cmdlet. The `Get-Alias` cmdlet will retrieve all the available aliases in your local computer.

PowerShell allows us to create aliases for any given valid cmdlet. To create a new alias, we execute the following command:

```
New-Alias -Name W -Value Get-WmiObject -Description "Learning
  PowerShell" -Verbose
```

The output of the command we just discussed is as follows:

```
VERBOSE: Performing the operation "New Alias" on target "Name: W Value:
  Get-WmiObject"
```

Now, let's take a look at how the command we just discussed works.

The New-Alias command is used to create an alias.

The W part is a friendly name. You can choose any name you need, but you can't create a new alias with the existing, used names.

The Value command is used here. We also used the Get-WmiObject command, and that's our definition.

The Description parameter is for our reference.

The Verbose parameter just shows the action performed by the message.

The output of the preceding command is illustrated in the following image:

```
PS C:\windows\system32> Get-Alias -Name W | Select *

HelpUri               : http://go.microsoft.com/fwlink/p/?linkid=290505
ResolvedCommandName   : Get-WmiObject
DisplayName           : W -> Get-WmiObject
ReferencedCommand     : Get-WmiObject
ResolvedCommand       : Get-WmiObject
Definition            : Get-WmiObject②
Options               : None
Description           : Learning PowerShell③
OutputType            : {}
Name                  : W ①
CommandType           : Alias ④
Source                :
Version               :
Visibility            : Public⑤
ModuleName            :
Module                :
RemotingCapability    : OwnedByCommand
Parameters            : {[Class, System.Management.Automation.ParameterMetadata], [Recurse,
                        System.Management.Automation.ParameterMetadata], [Property,
                        System.Management.Automation.ParameterMetadata], [Filter,
                        System.Management.Automation.ParameterMetadata]...}
ParameterSets         :
```

The sections in the image are explained as follows:

- **Name**: This is the name of the alias.
- **Definition**: Here, this is the Get-WmiObject command. It may be any command.
- **Description**: This is the description of the alias.
- **CommandType**: Here, this is Alias.
- **Visibility**: Here, this is Public.

Using the `Set-Alias` command, we can do the same, but it allows us to change the association later. In the preceding example, we created an alias named W for the `Get-WmiObject` command. If we try to create an alias with the same name for another command, the following error appears:

```
PS C:\> New-Alias -Name W -Value Get-Service -Description Learning
New-Alias : The alias is not allowed, because an alias with the name 'W' already exists.
At line:1 char:1
+ New-Alias -Name W -Value Get-Service -Description Learning
+ ~~~~~~~~~~~~~~~~~~~~~~~~~~~~~~~~~~~~~~~~~~~~~~~~~~~~~~~~~~~~~
    + CategoryInfo          : ResourceExists: (W:String) [New-Alias], SessionStateException
    + FullyQualifiedErrorId : AliasAlreadyExists,Microsoft.PowerShell.Commands.NewAliasCommand
```

In this scenario, we can use the `Set-Alias` command to change the alias' association. Run the following code:

```
PS C:\> Set-Alias -Name W -Value Get-Service -Description 'Change
  Association' -Verbose

VERBOSE: Performing the operation "Set Alias" on target "Name: W Value:
  Get-Service"
```

> Best practice to use an alias is when you are controlling the environment entirely.
>
> Ensure that you have made a note about alias in your script. This helps others to understand and troubleshoot in case of any failures.

If you create more aliases in your machine, you can move them to other machines using the following two cmdlets:

- The `Export-Alias` cmdlet
- The `Import-Alias` cmdlet

In this exercise, we will create an alias for the `Test-Connection` cmdlet and use it in other machines. The `Test` part will be the alias of `Test-Connection`. Following is the command to set the alias' name:

```
New-Alias -Name Test -Value Test-Connection -Description "Testing"
  -Verbose
```

Let's test the functionality using the following command:

```
test localhost
```

This command returns the following output:

```
Destination    IPV4Address    IPV6Address                        Bytes    Time(ms)
-----------    -----------    -----------                        -----    --------
localhost      127.0.0.1      ::1                                32       0
localhost      127.0.0.1      ::1                                32       0
localhost      127.0.0.1      ::1                                32       0
localhost      127.0.0.1      ::1                                32       0
```

Let's use the `Export-Alias` cmdlet and export only this alias using the following command:

```
Export-Alias -Name test C:\Temp\CustomAlias.txt –Verbose
```

We will get the following output:

```
# Alias File
```

```
# Exported by : ChenV
```

```
# Date/Time : Tuesday, August 25, 2015 1:57:28 PM
```

```
# Computer : CHENV
```

```
"Test","Test-Connection","Testing","None"
```

Move this text file to another computer and use the `Import-Alias` cmdlet to do this.

Look at the following image:

```
PS C:\> Import-Alias C:\Temp\test.txt –Verbose  ①
VERBOSE: Performing the operation "Import Alias" on target "Name: test Value: Test-Connection".

PS C:\> Get-Alias -Name Test ②

CommandType     Name                                    Version    Source
-----------     ----                                    -------    ------
Alias           test -> Test-Connection  ③


PS C:\> test localhost  ④

Source          Destination     IPV4Address     IPV6Address                        Bytes    Time(ms)
------          -----------     -----------     -----------                        -----    --------
CHENWIN8        localhost       127.0.0.1       ::1                                32       0
CHENWIN8        localhost       127.0.0.1       ::1                                32       0
CHENWIN8        localhost       127.0.0.1       ::1                                32       0
CHENWIN8        localhost       127.0.0.1       ::1                                32       0
```

The steps marked in the image we just discussed are explained as follows:

- **1**: Here, I used the `Import-Alias` cmdlet and have given the path where I copied the text file
- **2**: Here, I used the `Get-Alias` cmdlet to verify the existence of the alias
- **3**: This indicates the result—**test -> Test-Connection**
- **4**: This verifies the functionality of the alias

There is no direct cmdlet to remove an alias, such as *Remove-Alias*. So, how do we do this?

Alias is one of the items in the PowerShell drive. Yes! We can use the `Remove-Item` cmdlet to remove the alias. Execute the following command:

```
Get-Item Alias:\test
```

The command that we just discussed returns the following output:

```
PS C:\> Get-Item Alias:\test

CommandType        Name                                        Version    Source
-----------        ----                                        -------    ------
Alias              test -> Test-Connection
```

So, you can simply use `Remove-Item` to delete the alias. Execute the command as shown in the following image:

```
PS C:\> Remove-Item Alias:\test -Verbose
VERBOSE: Performing the operation "Remove Item" on target "Item: test".

PS C:\> |
                                                                    Alias
```

Understanding expressions

Windows PowerShell supports regular expressions. We know that PowerShell is built using the .NET framework. So, it strongly supports the regular expressions in .NET.

Developers prefer to use regular expressions to solve complex tasks such as formatting display names, manipulating files, and so on.

Regex can either be used by comparing operators or implementing the .NET class.

The MSDN reference link for the regex class is `https://msdn.microsoft.com/en-us/library/system.text.regularexpressions.regex%28v=vs.110%29.aspx`.

In this topic, we will cover the following:

- Operators and comparison operators
- Implementing regex using the .NET class
- Where do we use regular expressions?

Before we proceed with regular expressions, let's explore a few things about operators.

To know about operators, we can run the following code:

```
help about_Operators -ShowWindow
```

The output is illustrated in the following image:

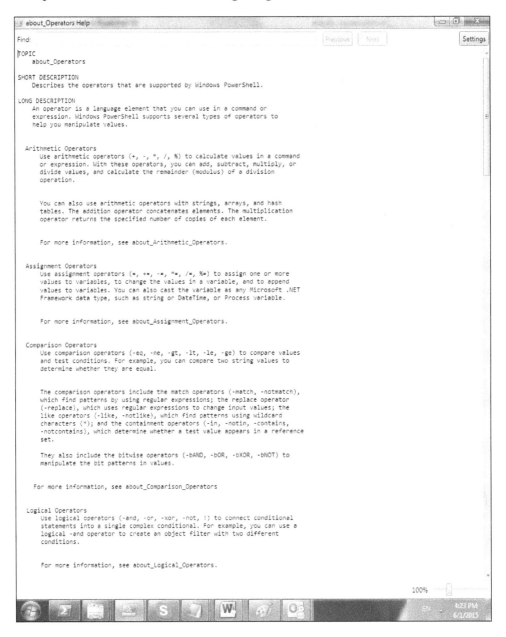

To retrieve help for all the operators in Windows PowerShell, you can run each of the following lines of code and explore their usage:

```
help about_Arithmetic_Operators
help about_Assignment_Operators
help about_Comparison_Operators
help about_Logical_Operators
help about_Type_Operators
help about_Split
help about_Join
help about_Redirection
```

Windows PowerShell has operators such as arithmetic operators, assignment operators, comparison operators, logical operators, redirection operators, split and join operators, type operators, format operators, static member operators, and so on.

As we are exploring regular expressions, we will focus only on the comparison operators.

Comparison operators are used to compare values and to find the matching pattern. By default, comparison operators are not case sensitive.

We can also perform case-sensitive pattern matching using c before the operators.

Let's consider both these in the following example:

```
#Case In-Sensitive
"PowerShell" -match "PowerShell"
```

This command returns the output as true.

```
#Case Sensitive
"PowerShell" -cmatch "powershell"
```

This command returns the output as false.

Now, it's time for us to use the .NET regular expressions in Windows PowerShell with the comparison operators

> The MSDN link for a quick reference guide to regular expressions is https://msdn.microsoft.com/en-us/library/az24scfc%28v=vs.110%29.aspx

Here is a command that uses a regular expression to check whether the first three characters are digits in a given string.

For example, the given string is `123-456-ABC`. Then, the command would be as follows:

```
"123-245-ABC" -match '^\d{3}'
```

This command returns the output as true.

```
"EFG-245-ABC" -match '^\d{3}'
```

This command returns the output as false.

Now, let's take a look at how the command that we just discussed works, in the following list:

- `^`: This is the beginning of the string.
- `\d`: This is to check the digits.
- `{3}`: This matches the previous elements *n* times. In our case, it's three times.

Use the following regular expression to remove the white space characters from any given string:

```
"Power Shell" -replace '\s' , ''
```

This returns `PowerShell`.

> In case of replacing a string with null with the help of the `replace operator`, we can execute the following command:
> ```
> "Power Shell" -replace '\s'
> ```
> There is no need to explicitly mention replacing a string with a non-white space character.

The given input string is `Power Shell`. The expression removes the white space between `Power` and `Shell` in the string and outputs the `Powershell` word. The white space is removed as explained in the following steps:

- In the preceding code, we used the comparison operator, `-replace`
- The `\s` character is the white space character in regex
- This is replaced with a non-white space character

We can swap strings using regular expressions.

Consider the given string as `FirstName LastName`:

```
#Given Name: FirstName LastName
#Required Output: LastName, FirstName
"FirstName LastName" -replace "([a-z]+)\s([a-z]+)" ,'$2, $1'
```

The commands that we just discussed return the output as `LastName, FirstName`.

Consider the given string as `FirstName12345 LastName`:

```
#Given Name: FirstName12345 LastName
#Required Output: LastName, FirstName
'FirstName12345 LastName' -replace "\d+" -replace "([a-z]+)\s([a-z]+)"
  ,'$2, $1'
```

The commands that we just discussed return the output as `LastName, FirstName`.

The output of the previous two expressions is illustrated in the following image:

```
Administrator: Windows PowerShell ISE
File  Edit  View  Tools  Debug  Add-ons  Help

PS C:\> #Given Name : FirstName LastName
#Required Output: LastName, FirstName
"FirstName LastName" -replace "([a-z]+)\s([a-z]+)" ,'$2, $1'

#Given Name : FirstName12345 LastName
#Required Output: LastName, FirstName
'FirstName12345 LastName' -replace "\d+" -replace "([a-z]+)\s([a-z]+)" ,'$2, $1'
LastName, FirstName
LastName, FirstName

PS C:\> |                          Output
```

Similarly, PowerShell allows us to use the `regex` class to perform the same tasks. Execute the following code:

```
[Regex]::IsMatch('PowerShell' , 'PowerShell')
```

 The MSDN TechNet article for the regex class is at the following link:
https://msdn.microsoft.com/en-us/library/system.
text.regularexpressions.regex%28VS.80%29.aspx

The `IsMatch` method is a member of the `regex` class. This method is overloaded, which indicates whether the regular expression finds a match in the input string. This is a simple example to check whether a string contains another string.

 The MSDN TechNet article for the regex class members is at the following link:
https://msdn.microsoft.com/en-US/library/system.text.regularexpressions.regex_members%28v=vs.80%29.aspx

Developers can easily understand and implement regex. However, IT professionals or system administrators may have difficulties in understanding the arguments to be passed.

What arguments should we pass for members? It's not always necessary to refer to the MSDN article. Instead, we can use PowerShell to find the overloaded definitions.

In the following example, we will use the `Replace` method (the public method of the regex class):

```
[Regex]::Replace
```

The output of the code that we just discussed is illustrated in the following image:

```
PS C:\> [Regex]::Replace          Overloaded Definitions          Arguments Type

OverloadDefinitions
-------------------
static string Replace(string input, string pattern, string replacement)
static string Replace(string input, string pattern, string replacement, System.Text.RegularExpressions.RegexOptions options)
static string Replace(string input, string pattern, string replacement, System.Text.RegularExpressions.RegexOptions options, timespan
matchTimeout)
static string Replace(string input, string pattern, System.Text.RegularExpressions.MatchEvaluator evaluator)
static string Replace(string input, string pattern, System.Text.RegularExpressions.MatchEvaluator evaluator,
System.Text.RegularExpressions.RegexOptions options)
static string Replace(string input, string pattern, System.Text.RegularExpressions.MatchEvaluator evaluator,
System.Text.RegularExpressions.RegexOptions options, timespan matchTimeout)
```

To remove the numbers from the given string using regex, we execute the following command:

```
[Regex]::Replace('12String' , '\d{2}' , '')
```

The command that we just considered returns the output as `String`. We get this output as explained in the following steps:

- Using the Regex class, we invoked the public method, `Replace`.
- As per the overloaded definitions, we have an option to pass three arguments—string, pattern, and replacement string.
- The `'\d'` shorthand character represents the digits and `{n}` checks *n* times. In our case, it's two times.
- This was replaced with empty values.

Understanding objects

In general, a term object is something that we can touch and feel, and the same is applicable for PowerShell as well. An object in PowerShell is a combination of methods and properties:

Objects = Properties + Methods

A property is something that we can get or set. In short, properties store information about the object.

A method is an action to be invoked on a particular object.

Objects are constructed using their types, properties, and methods.

In this section, we will cover the following topics:

- Getting help about objects, properties, and methods
- Exploring objects, properties, methods, and types

Before we explore objects, let's have a look at the help documentation using the following commands:

```
help about_Objects
help about_Properties
help about_Methods
```

The objects that we see in PowerShell are a part of the .NET framework, and PowerShell will allow us to create custom objects as well.

> From Windows PowerShell 5.0 onward, we can create objects using a class. This will be covered in the *Chapter 2, Unleashing Development Skills Using Windows PowerShell 5.0*.

Now, let's explore objects in detail. In the following example, we will use the Get-Date command:

```
$Date = Get-Date
```

Here, $Date is a variable in Windows PowerShell and Get-Date is a cmdlet to get the current date and time.

Once we run the preceding code, $date will be a DateTime object. Let's take a look at the type of the $Date variable:

```
$Date.GetType()
```

The output of this command is as follows:

The Get-Member cmdlet is our friend, and helps us to explore the members and properties. To take a look at the available properties and methods, we can run the following code:

```
Get-Date | Get-Member -MemberType All -Force
```

The preceding command retrieves all the properties and methods.

The list will be huge; so, to view the properties and methods, we can change the MemberType value to either Property or Method. Let's execute the following code:

```
Get-Date | Get-Member -MemberType Property -Force
```

The output of this code is illustrated as follows:

```
PS C:\> Get-Date | Get-Member -MemberType Property -Force


   TypeName: System.DateTime

Name          MemberType Definition
----          ---------- ----------
Date          Property   datetime Date {get;}
Day           Property   int Day {get;}
DayOfWeek     Property   System.DayOfWeek DayOfWeek {get;}
DayOfYear     Property   int DayOfYear {get;}
Hour          Property   int Hour {get;}
Kind          Property   System.DateTimeKind Kind {get;}
Millisecond   Property   int Millisecond {get;}
Minute        Property   int Minute {get;}
Month         Property   int Month {get;}
Second        Property   int Second {get;}
Ticks         Property   long Ticks {get;}
TimeOfDay     Property   timespan TimeOfDay {get;}
Year          Property   int Year {get;}
```

The definitions of the property is shown as {get;}. Let's explore the property now, as follows:

```
(Get-Date).DateTime
```

The command that we just considered displays the current date and time of the local machine.

Now, let's take a look at how the command that we just discussed works, in the following list:

- Get-Date: This is the Windows PowerShell cmdlet.
- .: This is the property deference operator.
- The DateTime property shows the current system's date and time.

Alternatively, we can use the DateTime object, as follows:

```
[DateTime]::Now
```

We will get current date and time as output. For example, Tuesday, June 02, 2015 12:15:51 PM.

The operator used here is the static member operator, ::.

To invoke the methods of an object, we will follow the same procedure. But, if the method needs arguments, we need to pass it accordingly, as shown in the following command:

```
Get-Date | Get-Member -MemberType Method -Force
```

 We used the -Force parameter to retrieve all the methods, including the hidden ones.

Execute the following code:

```
(Get-Date).AddDays(1)
```

Here, we added one day to the current day and the output is as follows:

```
Wednesday, June 03, 2015 12:55:35 PM
```

Alternatively, we can write ([DateTime]::Now).AddDays(1).

The $psISE object is the root object of the Integrated Scripting Environment. Using this we can toggle settings of the ISE, as follows:

```
$psISE | GM -Force
```

The output of the command we just discussed retrieves all the members of $PSISE. One of the property options that hold all the options of the ISE is as follows:

```
$psISE.Options
```

To modify the zoom, use the following code:

```
$psISE.Options.Zoom = 150
```

To modify the Intellisense timeout seconds, we execute the following code:

```
$psISE.Options.IntellisenseTimeoutInSeconds = 5
```

To change the script pane's background color, we execute the following code:

```
$psISE.Options.ScriptPaneBackgroundColor = 'Green'
```

Understanding pipelines

A Windows PowerShell pipeline is used to join two or more statements with a pipeline operator. The Pipeline operator is '|'.

We have used pipelines in previous examples; let's know about pipeline use case scenario.

In this section, we will cover the following:

- Using a pipeline operator
- Where to use a pipeline operator

Windows PowerShell is designed to use pipeline. Here's an example of pipelines:

```
Command1 | Command2 | Command3
```

Here, Command1 sends the object to Command2; the processed object will then be sent to Command3, which will output the results. Take a look at the following command:

```
help about_Pipelines -ShowWindow
```

A pipeline works in the following way:

- The parameter must accept input from a pipeline (however, not all do so)
- The parameter must accept the type of object being sent or a type that the object that can be converted to
- The parameter must not already be used in the command

Now, let's take a look at the following example:

```
PS C:\> Get-Service -Name BITS

Status     Name               DisplayName
------     ----               -----------
Running    BITS               Background Intelligent Transfer Ser...
```

The Get-Service cmdlet gets the object representing the BITS service.

Using the Stop-Service cmdlet, we can stop the service. The -Verbose parameter is to show the operation handled, as shown in the following code:

```
Get-Service -Name BITS | Stop-Service -Verbose
```

The output of the command we just discussed is illustrated in the following image:

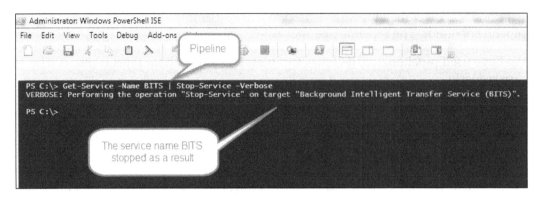

Using pipeline, we can do many more tasks, such as sorting, grouping, looping, and so on.

How do we find the parameter that accepts pipeline? Using help and pipeline, we can do this as shown in the following code:

```
help Get-Service -Parameter * | Select name , PipelineInput
```

The output of the command we just discussed is illustrated in the following image:

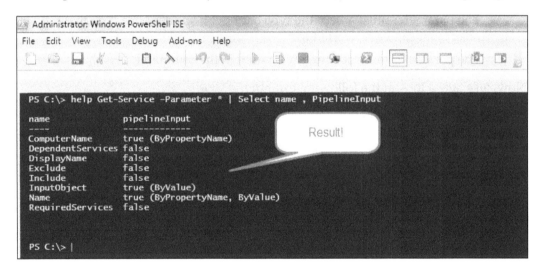

To retrieve the Windows services of the remote machine, SharePoint001, we can write the command as follows:

```
'SharePoint001' | %{Get-Service -ComputerName $_}
```

In short, the pipeline passes the output to another command so that the next command has something to work with or simply connects the output to other commands. This helps IT professionals automate tasks such as inventorying, reporting, and so on.

Exporting a running process to a CSV file

Let's take a look at the following command:

```
Get-Process | Export-csv C:\Temp\Process.csv `
-NoTypeInformation -Encoding UTF8
```

Refer to the following image:

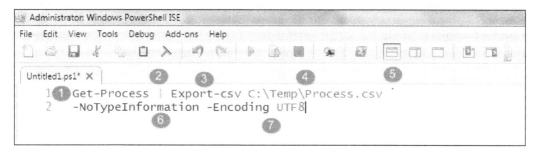

The points marked in the image are explained as follows:

- **1**: The Get-Process cmdlet is used to retrieve a running process in your local machine. Alternatively, the gps alias can be used
- **2**: This is the pipeline operator used to pass the output to the next command
- **3**: The Export-csv cmdlet is used to save the output in the CSV format
- **4**: This is the complete path of the output file
- **5**: This is the PowerShell line continuation character
- **6**: The NotypeInformation switch parameter is used to avoid #TypeInformation in the CSV header
- **7**: The Export-CSV cmdlet has an encoding parameter, which can be ASCII, UTF7, UTF8, BigEndianUnicode, OEM, or so on

The CSV output is shown in following image:

I prefer to export data in the XML format using the Export-Clixml cmdlet because it holds a lot more information. Take a look at the following command:

```
Get-Process | Export-Clixml C:\Temp\Process.xml
```

The output is shown in the following image:

Using `Import-Clixml` and `Import-Csv`, we can view the output we exported:

`Import-Clixml C:\Temp\Process.xml`

The output of the command we just discussed is shown in the following image:

Using pipelines, we can connect multiple commands and get effective solutions, as explained in the following list:

- We can start, stop, or set a service
- We can export the output to report, for inventories, and so on.
- They connect commands and display the output as required
- They help in sorting, filtering, and formatting objects

Understanding filtering and formatting

In Windows PowerShell, filtering and formatting are used in most places to get the output in the desired format. Select-Object is very useful cmdlet to filter.

In this section, we will cover the following topics:

- Basics of filtering
- Basics of formatting

Consider the following command:

```
Get-Command -Noun Object
```

The output is as shown in the following image:

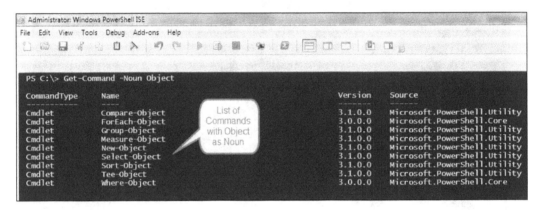

Use the following Help commands:

```
Help Select-Object -Examples
Help Where-Object -Examples
```

Using the Select-Object cmdlet, we can select the first and last *n* items from the collection of objects. The Select-Object cmdlet can be used to retrieve only unique values (ignoring duplicates).

Now, let's explore `Select-Object` for filtering. Let's consider that we have a set of objects from 65 to 90; to select the first 10, we need to pipe and use `Select-Object`, as shown in the following command:

```
65..90 | Select -First 10
```

We will get the output as 65 to 74.

Consider the following command:

```
1,2,2,3 | Select -Unique
```

Here, we will get the output as 1, 2, and 3.

Take a look at the following command:

```
1,2,2,3 | Select -Last 1
```

Here, we will get the output as 3.

Consider the following command:

```
1,2,2,3 | Select -SkipLast 1
```

We will get the output as 1, 2, and 2.

Take a look at the following command:

```
1,2,2,3 | Select -Skip 2
```

Here, we will get the output as 2 and 3.

To get help for all the parameters in `Select-Object`, use the following code:

```
help Select-Object -Parameter *
```

The `Where-Object` cmdlet is used to filter data returned by the other cmdlet. This cmdlet accepts comparison operators.

Let's explore the syntax of the `Where-Object` cmdlet, as follows:

```
(help Where-Object).Syntax
```

The output of the command we just considered is illustrated in the following image:

```
PS C:\> (help Where-Object).Syntax

Where-Object [-Property] <String> [[-Value] <Object>] [-EQ] [-InputObject <PSObject>] [<CommonParameters>]
Where-Object [-Property] <String> [[-Value] <Object>] [-InputObject <PSObject>] -Contains [<CommonParameters>]
Where-Object [-FilterScript] <ScriptBlock> [-InputObject <PSObject>] [<CommonParameters>]
Where-Object [-Property] <String> [[-Value] <Object>] [-InputObject <PSObject>] -GE [<CommonParameters>]
Where-Object [-Property] <String> [[-Value] <Object>] [-InputObject <PSObject>] -GT [<CommonParameters>]
Where-Object [-Property] <String> [[-Value] <Object>] [-InputObject <PSObject>] -In [<CommonParameters>]
Where-Object [-Property] <String> [[-Value] <Object>] [-InputObject <PSObject>] -CContains [<CommonParameters>]
Where-Object [-Property] <String> [[-Value] <Object>] [-InputObject <PSObject>] -CEQ [<CommonParameters>]
Where-Object [-Property] <String> [[-Value] <Object>] [-InputObject <PSObject>] -CGE [<CommonParameters>]
Where-Object [-Property] <String> [[-Value] <Object>] [-InputObject <PSObject>] -CGT [<CommonParameters>]
Where-Object [-Property] <String> [[-Value] <Object>] [-InputObject <PSObject>] -CIn [<CommonParameters>]
Where-Object [-Property] <String> [[-Value] <Object>] [-InputObject <PSObject>] -CLE [<CommonParameters>]
Where-Object [-Property] <String> [[-Value] <Object>] [-InputObject <PSObject>] -CLike [<CommonParameters>]
Where-Object [-Property] <String> [[-Value] <Object>] [-InputObject <PSObject>] -CLT [<CommonParameters>]
Where-Object [-Property] <String> [[-Value] <Object>] [-InputObject <PSObject>] -CMatch [<CommonParameters>]
Where-Object [-Property] <String> [[-Value] <Object>] [-InputObject <PSObject>] -CNE [<CommonParameters>]
Where-Object [-Property] <String> [[-Value] <Object>] [-InputObject <PSObject>] -CNotContains [<CommonParameters>]
Where-Object [-Property] <String> [[-Value] <Object>] [-InputObject <PSObject>] -CNotIn [<CommonParameters>]
Where-Object [-Property] <String> [[-Value] <Object>] [-InputObject <PSObject>] -CNotLike [<CommonParameters>]
Where-Object [-Property] <String> [[-Value] <Object>] [-InputObject <PSObject>] -CNotMatch [<CommonParameters>]
Where-Object [-Property] <String> [[-Value] <Object>] [-InputObject <PSObject>] -Is [<CommonParameters>]
Where-Object [-Property] <String> [[-Value] <Object>] [-InputObject <PSObject>] -IsNot [<CommonParameters>]
Where-Object [-Property] <String> [[-Value] <Object>] [-InputObject <PSObject>] -LE [<CommonParameters>]
Where-Object [-Property] <String> [[-Value] <Object>] [-InputObject <PSObject>] -Like [<CommonParameters>]
Where-Object [-Property] <String> [[-Value] <Object>] [-InputObject <PSObject>] -LT [<CommonParameters>]
Where-Object [-Property] <String> [[-Value] <Object>] [-InputObject <PSObject>] -Match [<CommonParameters>]
Where-Object [-Property] <String> [[-Value] <Object>] [-InputObject <PSObject>] -NE [<CommonParameters>]
Where-Object [-Property] <String> [[-Value] <Object>] [-InputObject <PSObject>] -NotContains [<CommonParameters>]
Where-Object [-Property] <String> [[-Value] <Object>] [-InputObject <PSObject>] -NotIn [<CommonParameters>]
Where-Object [-Property] <String> [[-Value] <Object>] [-InputObject <PSObject>] -NotLike [<CommonParameters>]
Where-Object [-Property] <String> [[-Value] <Object>] [-InputObject <PSObject>] -NotMatch [<CommonParameters>]
```

Consider an array from 1 to 5. To select values greater than 3, we use the Where-Object alias, ?, next to the pipeline operator, as shown in the following command:

```
1..5 | ? {$_ -gt 3}
```

From Windows PowerShell 4.0 onward, we can avoid pipelines for the ForEach and Where objects, as follows:

```
(65..90).ForEach({ [char][int]$_ })
```

The output of the code we just discussed is shown in the following image:

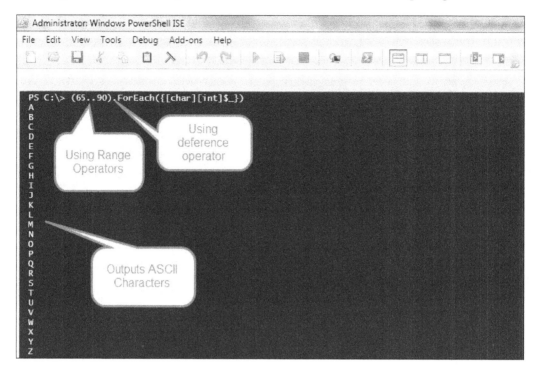

Now, let's take a look at how this works in the following list:

- The `(65..90)` range uses the range operator, `..`; these are the ASCII values of A-Z
- We used the dereference operator, `.`, to invoke the `Foreach` method
- The `Foreach` method accepts expressions and arguments, as shown in the code we just considered.

Now, let's take a look at the following code:

```
(1..10).Where({$_ -ge 5})
```

The output of this code is shown in the following image:

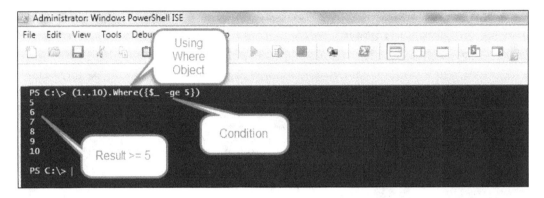

Now, let's take a look at how this works in the following list:

- The (1..10) range uses the range operator, ..; this is the 1 to 10 array of the object
- We used the dereference operator, ., to invoke the Where method
- The Where method accepts the expression, mode, and number to return

We can use the Where statement with different modes. In the following example, we will select the first three values, where the number is greater than or equal to 5. Now, let's consider the following code:

```
(1..10).Where({$_ -ge 5}, 'First' , 3)
```

The output of this code is illustrated in the following image:

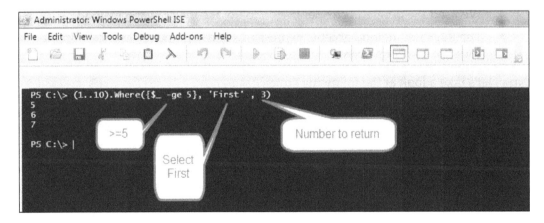

Now, let's take a look at how this works in the following list:

- The (1..10) uses the range operator, .., and this is the 1 to 10 array of the objects

- We used the dereference operator to invoke the Where method

- In this expression, {$_ -ge 5} is an object greater than 5, First is the mode, and 3 is the value for the number to be returned.

Similarly, we can use the Split mode as well. Using this, we can split the given collection of objects, as shown in the following code:

```
$section1 , $section2 = (1..100).Where({$_ -le 50} , 'Split' , 0)
$section1
$section2
```

The $section1 variable contains values from 1 to 50, and the $section2 variable contains values from 51 to 100.

> Avoid pipelines as much as you can. Use appropriately, because in larger script we may end up having a performance issue.
>
> Use Measure-Command and analyze the performance of commands using pipelines.

Here is a table comparing commands using pipeline with those that don't use a pipeline:

With pipeline	Result in milliseconds	Without pipeline	Result in milliseconds
65..90 | %{[char] [int]$_}	4	(65..90).ForEach({ [char] [int]$_})	1
1..10 | ? {$_ -ge 5} | Select -First 3	42	(1..10).Where({$_ -ge 5}, 'First' , 3)	2

PowerShell formatting

Windows PowerShell has a set of cmdlets that allows us to format the output. To find the cmdlets to format, use Verb Format to search, as shown in the following code:

```
Get-Command -Verb Format
```

Let's take a look at the default formatting of Windows PowerShell by executing the following the cmdlet:

```
Get-Process | Select -First 5
```

The output of this code is as follows:

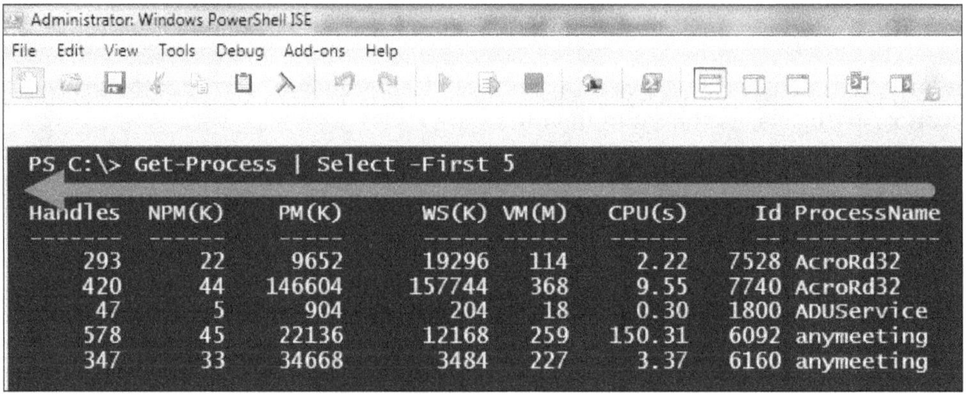

The headers are not exactly property names. This formatting is done using the file name, DOTNETTYPES.FORMAT.PS1XML.

The location of the file is $PSHome. Take a look at the following image:

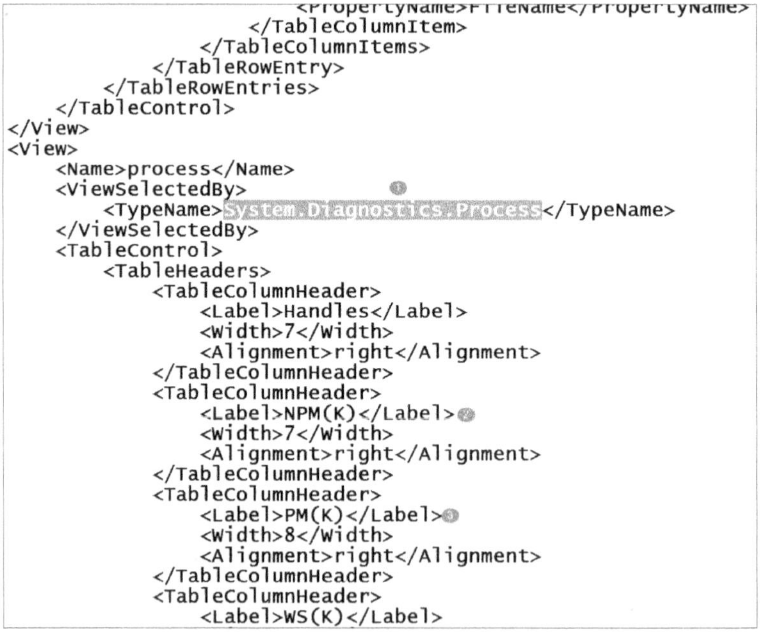

```
                    <PropertyName>FileName</PropertyName>
                </TableColumnItem>
            </TableColumnItems>
        </TableRowEntry>
    </TableRowEntries>
</TableControl>
</View>
<View>
    <Name>process</Name>
    <ViewSelectedBy>
        <TypeName>System.Diagnostics.Process</TypeName>
    </ViewSelectedBy>
    <TableControl>
        <TableHeaders>
            <TableColumnHeader>
                <Label>Handles</Label>
                <Width>7</Width>
                <Alignment>right</Alignment>
            </TableColumnHeader>
            <TableColumnHeader>
                <Label>NPM(K)</Label>
                <Width>7</Width>
                <Alignment>right</Alignment>
            </TableColumnHeader>
            <TableColumnHeader>
                <Label>PM(K)</Label>
                <Width>8</Width>
                <Alignment>right</Alignment>
            </TableColumnHeader>
            <TableColumnHeader>
                <Label>WS(K)</Label>
```

The following list explains the points marked in the preceding image:

- **1**: The type name of `Get-Process` is `System.Diagnostics.Process`
- **2**: For `NPM(K)`, refer to the image preceding the previous image
- **3**: For `PM(K)`, refer to the image preceding the previous image

The first thing we see in the `XML` file is the following warning:

```
Do not edit or change the contents of this file directly. Please see
the Windows PowerShell documentation or type.
```

Use the following command to obtain more information:

```
Get-Help Update-TypeData
```

So, let's not make any kind of modifications. Instead, let's take a look at the cmdlets to make minor modifications as desired, as shown in the following image:

```
PS C:\> Get-Command –Verb Format

CommandType     Name                Version     Source
-----------     ----                -------     ------
Function        Format-Hex          3.1.0.0     Microsoft.PowerShell.Utility
Cmdlet          Format-Custom       3.1.0.0     Microsoft.PowerShell.Utility
Cmdlet          Format-List         3.1.0.0     Microsoft.PowerShell.Utility
Cmdlet          Format-Table        3.1.0.0     Microsoft.PowerShell.Utility
Cmdlet          Format-Wide         3.1.0.0     Microsoft.PowerShell.Utility
```

In the following example, we will use the `Where` method to select *n* items required to keep the output precise and short.

The `help` command to format the table is as follows:

```
help Format-Table -ShowWindow
```

Let's select the first five running services and format them as follows:

```
(Get-Service).Where({$_.Status -eq 'Running'},'First',5) | Format-Table
```

This code outputs the default formatting.

Using the `Format-Table` cmdlet, we can hide the headers, auto size the table, use the expression, and much more. Let's consider the following command:

```
(Get-Service).Where({$_.Status -eq 'Running'},'First',5) | Format-Table
  -HideTableHeaders
```

The output of the command we just discussed is shown in the following image:

```
PS C:\> (Get-Service).Where({$_.Status -eq 'Running'},'First',5) | Format-Table -HideTableHeaders
                                                                                              1
Running  AdobeARMservice      Adobe Acrobat Update Service
Running  ADUServiceNSRT       ADU Service (Nokia Software Recover...
Running  AppHostSvc           Application Host Helper Service
Running  Appinfo              Application Information
Running  AudioEndpointBu...   Windows Audio Endpoint Builder
```

The default formatting of Windows PowerShell is not great, but it allows us to customize the format as required. The report we deliver to IT Management should be precise and readable. Using Windows PowerShell, we can achieve this.

Reports can be in the HTML, XML, CSV, or other desired formats.

Using an expression is allowed in `Format-Table` inside the {} script block token. Run the following command:

```
Get-WmiObject -Class Win32_LogicalDisk -Filter "DriveType=3" |
Format-Table Name,@{n="Freespace(byte)";e={"{0:N0}" -f
  $_.FreeSpace};a="center"}
```

The following image shows all three alignments: left, right, and center:

```
PS C:\> Get-WmiObject -Class Win32_LogicalDisk -Filter "DriveType=3" | Format-Table Name,
                @{n="Freespace(byte)";e={"{0:N0}" -f $_.FreeSpace};a="right"}

Name Freespace(byte)              Right
---- ---------------           Alignment
C:    32,858,230,784


PS C:\> Get-WmiObject -Class Win32_LogicalDisk -Filter "DriveType=3" | Format-Table Name,
                @{n="Freespace(byte)";e={"{0:N0}" -f $_.FreeSpace};a="left"}

Name Freespace(byte)              Left
---- ---------------           Alignment
C:    32,858,161,152


PS C:\> Get-WmiObject -Class Win32_LogicalDisk -Filter "DriveType=3" | Format-Table Name,
                @{n="Freespace(byte)";e={"{0:N0}" -f $_.FreeSpace};a="center"}

Name Freespace(byte)             Center
---- ---------------          Alignment
C:    32,856,981,504
```

Here is another example of a command to format the date in the day/month/year format using a format operator:

```
"Custom Date Format: {0},{1},{2}" -F (Get-Date).Day , (Get-Date).Month ,
  (Get-Date).Year
```

To view the `LastWriteTime.DayOfWeek` file, run the following command:

```
Get-ChildItem C:\Temp | Ft name , @{n="Day of Week" ; E =
  {$_.LastWriteTime.DayOfWeek}}
```

The following is the command to custom format using the `Format-Custom` cmdlet:

```
Get-Service | Format-Custom
```

The default output of the command we just discussed is as follows:

```
class ServiceController
{
    Status = Running                Type Name
    Name = wudfsvc
    DisplayName = Windows Driver Foundation - User-mode Driver Framework
}

class ServiceController
{                                   Properties
    Status = Stopped
    Name = WwanSvc
    DisplayName = WWAN AutoConfig
}

class ServiceController
{
    Status = Stopped
    Name = Zoho Assist-Remote Support
    DisplayName = Zoho Assist-Remote Support
}
```

Use the `Get-FormatData` cmdlet to view the formatting data from the `Format.
ps1xml` formatting files. In this demo, we will try to customize the default format in the current session, as follows:

```
help Get-FormatData -ShowWindow
```

```
help Export-FormatData -ShowWindow
```

```
help Update-FormatData -ShowWindow
```

Perform the following steps:

 In this demo, we will change the column header to test. This will break the output ONLY in the current session.

1. Identify the type name of the command. For example, here, we will use the `Get-Process | GM` command.

2. The `TypeName` parameter is `System.Diagnostics.Process`, as shown in the following command:

```
Get-FormatData -TypeName System.Diagnostics.Process |
Export-FormatData -Path C:\Temp\TestView.Format.PS1XML
```

3. Now, append the text of the column header in the `PS1XML` file in the `Temp` folder, as shown in the following command:

```
Update-FormatData -PrependPath C:\Temp\TestView.Format.PS1XM1
```

4. The `Get-Process` command returns the output as shown in the following image:

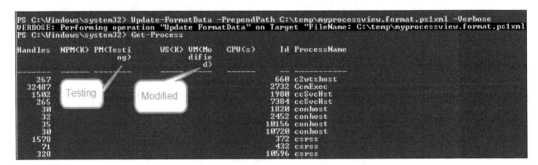

Exploring snippets in the PowerShell ISE

There is a cool way in the PowerShell ISE to reduce typing; however, before discussing PowerShell scripting, let's take a look at snippets.

Snippets are nothing but commonly used code. In PowerShell, we very often use functions, advanced functions, comment blocks, and so on.

Using an ISE, we don't type out the structure of the function. Instead, we can right-click on **Script Pane** and select **Start Snippets** or press *Ctrl + J*. This shows a menu of the available snippets.

The following image illustrates the snippets in the PowerShell ISE:

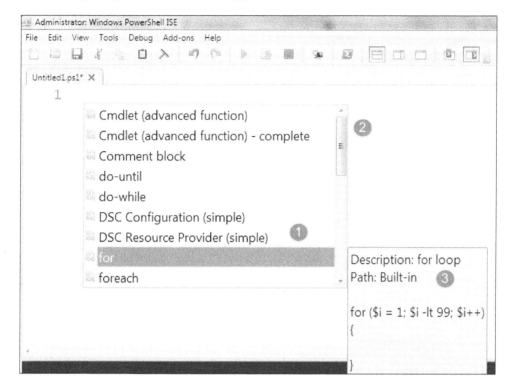

We need not be limited to only the available snippets; we can create our own snippets. In this demo, we will try to create a snippet. This is a simple snippet to add a mandatory parameter, which we can reuse in any of our functions.

This helps developers and IT professionals do the scripting faster.

There is no need for more typing; we just need to add a snippet wherever we need reusable codes, as shown in the following code:

```
$m = @'
Param(
[Parameter(Mandatory=$true)]
[String]
$String
)
'@
New-IseSnippet -Text $m -Title Mandatory -Description 'Adds a Mandatory
    function parameter' -Author "Chen V" -Force
```

Let's take a look at how this works:

- The $m variable holds the skeleton code
- The New-IseSnippet command is the one available in the module's ISE
- We used a few parameters with Text , which is the skeleton code; Title, which can be any friendly name; Description, which describes the snippet in short; and Author, which is the author's name
- After the code is executed, it creates a PS1XML file in the location, $home\ Documents\WindowsPowerShell\Snippets\
- The file name will be your title — in this case it's Mandatory.Snippets.PS1XML

We can copy and place it any machine — pressing *Ctrl* + *J* will show Mandatory in the snippets.

The following image illustrates the output of the newly created snippet:

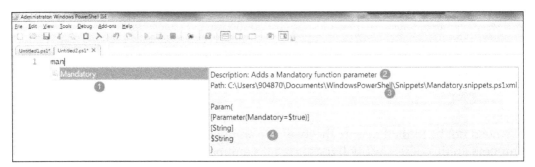

The following are the steps that explain the points marked in the preceding image:

- **1**: The name Mandatory is the title of our new snippet
- **2**: The **Description** field is shown in the pop-up box
- **3**: The **Path** field is the path of the PS1XML file
- **4**: This is the snippet code or skeleton code

Getting started with PowerShell scripting

Let's take a look at scripting in the cmdlet style.

We've arrived at a place from where we can explore PowerShell scripting with the knowledge of the previous topics. Wait! We haven't covered all that we need for scripting in PowerShell. Before we begin discussing scripting, we should know more about the scripting principles, using variables, commenting, writing help, and so on.

Here are a few principles of scripting:

If you want to deliver scripts to your organization or community, it's good to create the variables and follow the standard naming conventions. Do not use plain text passwords in the scripts, and avoid technical jargon in the comment blocks. Ensure that the script is readable for others.

Using Windows PowerShell scripting, we can perform complex tasks with the help of imperative commands. The scripting language supports branching, variables, and functions.

From now on, we will use the PowerShell ISE for its ease of use and benefits.

In this section, we will cover the following topics:

- Using variables
- The basics of Windows PowerShell scripting
- Writing the functions and advanced functions

Let's now discuss using variables.

A variable is used to store information, and it is the result of a running script.

Here's an example:

```
$value = Read-Host "Enter Value 1"
```

This script prompts for user input; once the value is entered, it stores it in the `$value` variable, as shown in the following image:

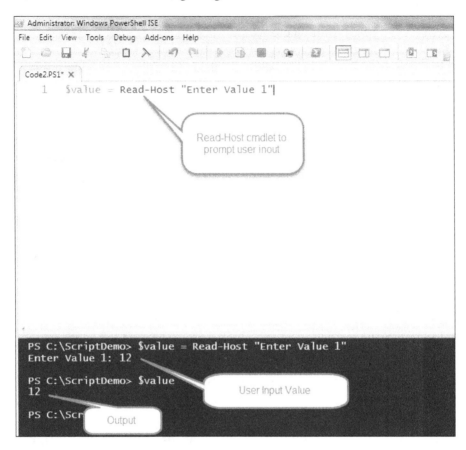

Following are a few points to note about variables:

- They can be string or integer, and they allow special characters
- They should be used precisely – don't use special characters in their name
- You need to use the standard naming conventions that are easily understandable
- You can use the automatic, preference, and environment variables
- You should modify the preference variables only if required

Using the `New-Variable` cmdlet, a variable can be created along with a scope definition. In the following example, let's create a variable name, `ws`, which holds the value of the Windows service, and sets the scope to `Global`:

```
New-Variable -Name 'ws' -Value (Get-Service) -Scope Global
```

Using `Remove-Variable`, it can be removed, as shown in the following code:

```
Remove-Variable -Name ws -Verbose
```

Windows PowerShell scripting is used to automate your daily tasks. It may be anything such as reporting, server health checkup, performing tasks such as restarting services, stopping services, deploying solutions, installing Windows features, and much more.

The following points need to be considered while creating PowerShell scripting:

- Keep the PowerShell code simple and neat.
- Follow the same indentation throughout the code.
- Make a clear, comments-based help.
- Comment on your parameters with descriptions. This allows others to get help about the parameters.

Let's write a simple script that prints hello world on the screen:

```
#Windows PowerShell Script to Retrieve Windows Services
Write-Host "Hello, World!" -ForegroundColor Green
```

To run the PowerShell script, you need to call the script using a dot (.) operator followed by backward (\) slash.

The extension of the PowerShell script file should be `.PS1`.

The output of the preceding code is illustrated in the following image:

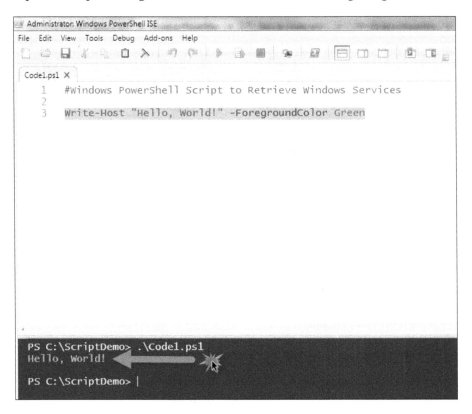

Let's create a script that does a basic system inventory.

This PowerShell script will create a CSS file for styles, query the basic system information, convert to an HTML file, and open up after the script is completely executed, as shown in the following code:

```
$UserName = (Get-Item  env:\username).Value
$ComputerName = (Get-Item env:\Computername).Value
$filepath = (Get-ChildItem env:\userprofile).value
Add-Content  "$Filepath\style.CSS"  -Value " body {
font-family:Calibri;
 font-size:10pt;
}
th {
```

```
background-color:black;
color:white;
}
td {
 background-color:#19fff0;
color:black;
}"
Write-Host "CSS File Created Successfully... Executing Inventory
  Report!!! Please Wait !!!" -ForegroundColor Yellow
#ReportDate
$ReportDate = Get-Date | Select -Property DateTime |ConvertTo-Html
  -Fragment
#General Information
$ComputerSystem = Get-WmiObject -Class Win32_ComputerSystem |
Select -Property Model , Manufacturer , Description , PrimaryOwnerName ,
  SystemType |ConvertTo-Html -Fragment
#Boot Configuration
$BootConfiguration = Get-WmiObject -Class Win32_BootConfiguration |
Select -Property Name , ConfigurationPath | ConvertTo-Html -Fragment
#BIOS Information
$BIOS = Get-WmiObject -Class Win32_BIOS | Select -Property
  PSComputerName , Manufacturer , Version | ConvertTo-Html -Fragment
#Operating System Information
$OS = Get-WmiObject -Class Win32_OperatingSystem | Select -Property
  Caption , CSDVersion , OSArchitecture , OSLanguage | ConvertTo-Html
  -Fragment
#Time Zone Information
$TimeZone = Get-WmiObject -Class Win32_TimeZone | Select Caption ,
  StandardName |
ConvertTo-Html -Fragment
#Logical Disk Information
$Disk = Get-WmiObject -Class Win32_LogicalDisk -Filter DriveType=3 |
Select SystemName , DeviceID , @{Name="size(GB)";Expression={"{0:N1}"
  -f($_.size/1gb)}}, @{Name="freespace(GB)";Expression={"{0:N1}"
  -f($_.freespace/1gb)}} |
```

```powershell
ConvertTo-Html -Fragment
#CPU Information
$SystemProcessor = Get-WmiObject -Class Win32_Processor  |
Select SystemName , Name , MaxClockSpeed , Manufacturer , status
  |ConvertTo-Html -Fragment
#Memory Information
$PhysicalMemory = Get-WmiObject -Class Win32_PhysicalMemory |
Select -Property Tag , SerialNumber , PartNumber , Manufacturer ,
  DeviceLocator , @{Name="Capacity(GB)";Expression={"{0:N1}" -f
  ($_.Capacity/1GB)}} | ConvertTo-Html -Fragment
#Software Inventory
$Software = Get-WmiObject -Class Win32_Product |
Select Name , Vendor , Version , Caption | ConvertTo-Html -Fragment
ConvertTo-Html -Body "<font color = blue><H4><B>Report Executed
  On</B></H4></font>$ReportDate
<font color = blue><H4><B>General
  Information</B></H4></font>$ComputerSystem
<font color = blue><H4><B>Boot
  Configuration</B></H4></font>$BootConfiguration
<font color = blue><H4><B>BIOS Information</B></H4></font>$BIOS
<font color = blue><H4><B>Operating System
  Information</B></H4></font>$OS
<font color = blue><H4><B>Time Zone Information</B></H4></font>$TimeZone
<font color = blue><H4><B>Disk Information</B></H4></font>$Disk
<font color = blue><H4><B>Processor
  Information</B></H4></font>$SystemProcessor
<font color = blue><H4><B>Memory
  Information</B></H4></font>$PhysicalMemory
<font color = blue><H4><B>Software Inventory</B></H4></font>$Software"
  -CssUri  "$filepath\style.CSS" -Title "Server Inventory" | Out-File
  "$FilePath\$ComputerName.html"
Write-Host "Script Execution Completed" -ForegroundColor Yellow
Invoke-Item -Path "$FilePath\$ComputerName.html"
```

The output of this code is illustrated in the following image:

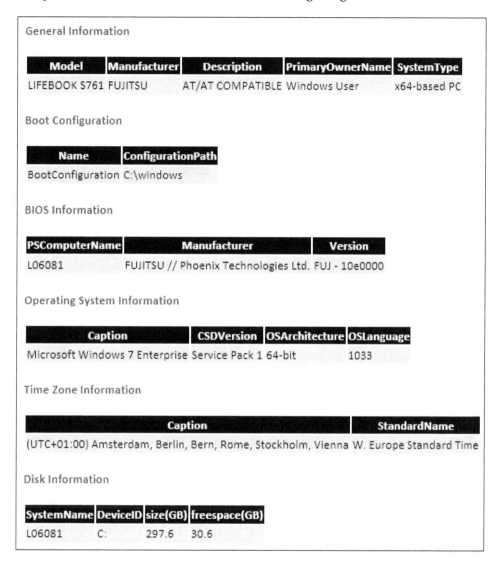

Let's take a look at how to write PowerShell functions with comments:

```
<#
.Synopsis
  To add two integer values
.DESCRIPTION
  Windows PowerShell Script Demo to add two values
  This accepts pipeline values
.EXAMPLE
  Add-Values -Param1 20 -Param2 30
.EXAMPLE
  12,23 | Add-Values
#>
function Add-Values
{
    [CmdletBinding()]
    [Alias()]
    [OutputType([int])]
    Param
    (
        # Param1 help description
        [Parameter(Mandatory=$true,
            ValueFromPipeline = $true,
            ValueFromPipelineByPropertyName=$true,
            Position=0)]
        #Accepts Only Integer
        [int]$Param1,
        #Accepts only integer
        [Parameter(Mandatory=$true,
            ValueFromPipeline = $true,
            ValueFromPipelineByPropertyName=$true,
            Position=0)]
        [int]$Param2
    )
    Begin
    {
```

```
    "Script Begins"

}

Process

{

    $result = $Param1 + $Param2

}

End

{

    $result

}

}
```

This is not a good script, but I will use this to demonstrate a PowerShell function with comments in order to help explore the use of help.

The following is an explanation of how this code works:

1. The most important part is the comment block. Let's take a look at the following code snippet:

```
<#
.Synopsis
    To add two integer values
.DESCRIPTION
    Windows PowerShell Script Demo to add two values
    This accepts pipeline values
.EXAMPLE
    Add-Values -Param1 20 -Param2 30
.EXAMPLE
    12,23 | Add-Values
#>
```

2. We need to provide a short description and synopsis of the script, as we did in this example. This will help others explore and know the usage of the script.

3. Then, we used the `Function` keyword and followed the standard *Verb-Noun* naming convention. In this example, we used `Add-Values`.

4. We parameterized our script using the `Param` block.

5. We named the parameter as applicable and added a comment/help description on top of the parameter.

6. We used the `Begin`, `Process`, and `End` blocks. I inserted the addition code in the `Process` block.

> To simplify all of these steps, open the ISE, press *Ctrl + J*, and select CMDLET (advanced function).

To execute this script, we need to use the `.\Filename.PS1` command. Take a look at the following image:

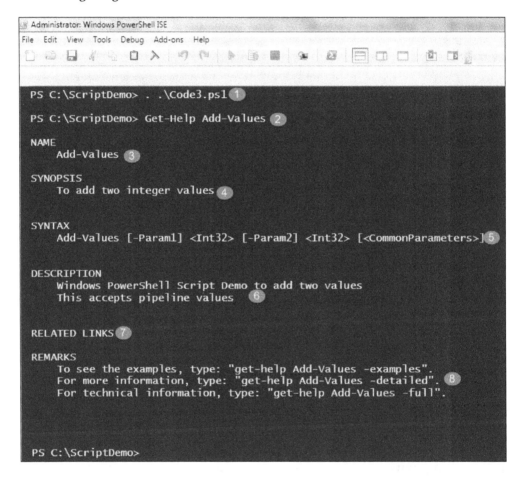

The following is an explanation of the steps marked in the image we just considered:

- **1**: We executed the `Code3` script
- **2**: We used the `Get-Help` cmdlet to read about the custom function
- **3**: This is the name of the command
- **4**: This is the customized synopsis
- **5**: The SYNTAX field is autogenerated
- **6**: This is the customized description
- **7**: The RELATED LINKS field is empty because we haven't included it in our comment block
- **8**: The REMARKS field is default

To view only the examples, we will use the following command:

```
Get-Help Add-Values -Examples
```

The output of this code is illustrated in the following image:

The following is an explanation of the points marked in the preceding image:

- **1**: The `Get-Help` cmdlet is used to get help of the custom function or script
- **2**: This is the name of the cmdlet/function
- **3**: This shows EXAMPLE 1
- **4**: This shows EXAMPLE 2

Similarly, we can view only parameters. The help description given above each parameter appears using the following code:

```
Get-Help Add-Values -Parameter *
```

Take a look at the following image:

```
PS C:\ScriptDemo> Get-Help Add-Values -Parameter *

-Param1 <Int32>
    Param1 help description  ①
    Accepts Only Integer

    Required?                          true
    Position?                          1
    Default value                      0
    Accept pipeline input?             true (ByValue, ByPropertyName)
    Accept wildcard characters?        false


-Param2 <Int32>
    Accepts only interger  ②

    Required?                          true
    Position?                          1
    Default value                      0
    Accept pipeline input?             true (ByValue, ByPropertyName)
    Accept wildcard characters?        false
```

The following are a few commands that use the `help` command:

```
help about_Functions
```

```
help about_Functions_Advanced_Methods
```

```
help about_Functions_Advanced_Parameters
```

```
help about_Functions_CmdletBindingAttribute
```

```
help about_Functions_OutputTypeAttribute
```

Let's take a look at how to write advanced functions.

Advanced functions are similar to compiled cmdlets but not exactly the same.

Here is a table comparing advanced functions and compiled cmdlets:

Advanced functions	Compiled cmdlets
These are designed using the PowerShell script.	These are designed using a .NET framework, such as C#, and compiled as DLL.
The actual work will be done in the process blocks.	The actual work will be done in the process records.

Advanced functions	Compiled cmdlets
An advanced function can be created easily using the PowerShell ISE.	A compiled cmdlet can be created easily using the Visual Studio class library.
The performance of advanced functions is slower compared to a compiled cmdlet.	Compiled cmdlets are faster.

In this section, we will discuss both writing an advanced function code using the PowerShell ISE and a compiled cmdlet using the Visual Studio C# class library.

Let's take a look at how to create a compiled cmdlet using the Visual Studio C# class library. Execute the following code:

```
using System;
using System.Collections.Generic;
using System.Linq;
using System.Text;
using System.Management;
using System.Management.Automation;
using System.IO;
namespace Windows_Management
{
    [Cmdlet(VerbsCommon.Clear, "TemporaryInternetFiles")]
    public class WindowsManagement : PSCmdlet
    {
        protected override void ProcessRecord()
        {
            //Delete Internet Cache Files and Folders
            string path = Environment.GetFolderPath(
              Environment.SpecialFolder.InternetCache);
            Console.ForegroundColor = ConsoleColor.DarkYellow;
            Console.WriteLine("Clearing Temporary Internet Cache Files
                and Directories....." + path);
            System.IO.DirectoryInfo folder = new DirectoryInfo(path);
            foreach (FileInfo files in folder.GetFiles())
            {
                try
                {
                    files.Delete();
```

```
            }
            catch (Exception ex)
            {
                System.Diagnostics.Debug.WriteLine(ex);
            }
        }
        foreach (DirectoryInfo Directory in folder.GetDirectories())
        {
            try
            {
                Directory.Delete();
            }
            catch (Exception ex)
            {
                System.Diagnostics.Debug.WriteLine(ex);
            }
        }
        Console.WriteLine("Done Processing!!!");
        Console.ResetColor();
        }
    }
}
namespace clearInternetexplorerHistory
{
    [Cmdlet(VerbsCommon.Clear, "IEHistory")]
    public class clearInternetexplorerHistory : PSCmdlet
    {
        protected override void ProcessRecord()
        {
            // base.ProcessRecord();
            string path = Environment.GetFolderPath(
              Environment.SpecialFolder.History);
            Console.ForegroundColor = ConsoleColor.DarkYellow;
            Console.WriteLine("Clearing Internet Explorer History....."
              + path);
            System.IO.DirectoryInfo folder = new DirectoryInfo(path);
```

```
        foreach (FileInfo files in folder.GetFiles())
        {
            try
            {
                files.Delete();
            }
            catch (Exception ex)
            {
                System.Diagnostics.Debug.WriteLine(ex);
            }
        }
        foreach (DirectoryInfo Directory in folder.GetDirectories())
        {
            try
            {
                Directory.Delete();
            }
            catch (Exception ex)
            {
                System.Diagnostics.Debug.WriteLine(ex);
            }
        }
        Console.WriteLine("Done Processing!!!");
        Console.ResetColor();
    }
}
}
namespace UserTemporaryFiles
{
    [Cmdlet(VerbsCommon.Clear, "UserTemporaryFiles")]
    public class UserTemporaryFiles : PSCmdlet
    {
        protected override void ProcessRecord()
        {
            //base.ProcessRecord();
```

```
        string temppath = System.IO.Path.GetTempPath();

        System.IO.DirectoryInfo usertemp = new
          DirectoryInfo(temppath);

        Console.WriteLine("Clearing Your Profile Temporary Files..."
          + temppath);

        foreach (FileInfo tempfiles in usertemp.GetFiles())

        {

            try

            {

                tempfiles.Delete();

            }

            catch (Exception ex)

            {

                System.Diagnostics.Debug.WriteLine(ex);

            }

        }

        Console.WriteLine("Done Processing!!!");

        foreach (DirectoryInfo tempdirectory in
          usertemp.GetDirectories())

        {

            try

            {

                tempdirectory.Delete();

            }

            catch (Exception ex)

            {

                System.Diagnostics.Debug.WriteLine(ex);

            }

        }

    }

  }

}
```

Once the DLL is compiled, we can import it as a module in Windows PowerShell.

The output of the command we just discussed is illustrated in the following image:

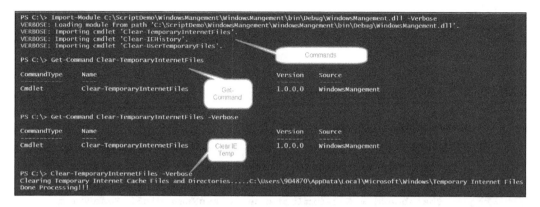

Now, let's consider the advanced functions in Windows PowerShell.

Advanced functions are more robust, can handle errors, support verbose and dynamic parameters, and so on.

Let's take a look at the small advanced functions used to retrieve system information, as follows:

```
function Get-SystemInformation
{
    [CmdletBinding()]
    [Alias()]
    [OutputType([int])]
    Param
    (
        # Param1 help description
        [Parameter(Mandatory=$true,
                    ValueFromPipelineByPropertyName=$true,
                    ValueFromPipeline = $true,
                    HelpMessage = "Enter Valid Host Names",
                    Position=0)]
        [Alias('Host')]
        [ValidateCount(0,15)]
        [String[]]$ComputerName,
        # Param2 help description
        [int]
```

```
        $Param2
    )
    Begin
    {
    }
    Process
    {
        foreach($cn in $ComputerName)
        {
            $cs = Get-CimInstance -ClassName Win32_ComputerSystem
-ComputerName $cn
            $baseboard = Get-CimInstance -ClassName Win32_BaseBoard
-ComputerName $cn
            $properties = New-Object psobject -Property @{
            ComputerName = $cs.Caption
            Model = $cs.Model
            ComputerOwner = $cs.PrimaryOwnerName
            Bootupsate = $cs.BootupState
            BaseBoardSerialNumber = $baseboard.SerialNumber
            BaseBoardManufacturer = $baseboard.Manufacturer
            }
            $properties
        }
    }
    End
    {
    }
}
'localhost' , 'localhost' | %{Get-SystemInformation -ComputerName $_}
```

The output of the code we just discussed is illustrated in the following image:

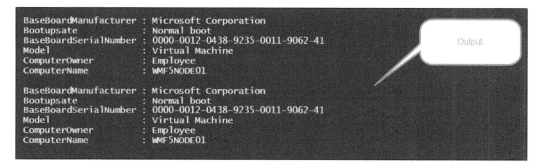

As we have already covered the topic of adding help for PowerShell functions, I ignored it in the advanced functions section. Remember, we do have snippets in the ISE to create advanced functions. It's simple; just right-click on the script pane, select **Start snippet**, and then choose the **Advanced function complete** option.

Start documenting the synopsis, description, and help for parameters and build your code in the process block. This is very easy and handy to build advanced scripts using PowerShell.

Before building scripts, use the `Measure-Command` cmdlet and think about optimization. This will help in performance.

Summary

So far, we covered the very basics of Windows PowerShell. We now know the importance of an object-based shell and how an ISE helps us in building scripts. We explored the Windows PowerShell consoles and ISE snippets. After completing this chapter, you know the power of an interactive shell, how to use cmdlets effectively, how to use help, and the fundamentals of PowerShell along with building standard functions and creating cmdlets using the Visual Studio class library.

In the next chapter, we will cover **Common Information Model (CIM)**, **Windows Management Instrumentation (WMI)**, Extensible Markup Language, COM, .NET objects, modules, and a more exciting section, *Exploring Windows PowerShell 5.0*.

2
Unleashing Development Skills Using Windows PowerShell 5.0

Windows PowerShell 5.0 is a dynamic and object-oriented scripting language. Compared to any other scripting language, it provides more benefits, such as reliability, security, managed code environments, and so on. Windows PowerShell has a strong connection with **Windows Management Instrumentation (WMI)**, **Common Information Model (CIM)**, **Extensible Markup Language (XML)**, and so on. Using this, we can develop solutions to automate our tasks.

PowerShell has the ability to manage different technologies. Using the PowerShell API, we can manage custom-built applications as well.

In this section, we will cover the following topics:

- Basics of WMI and CIM
- Exploring the XML and COM automation
- Exploring .NET objects for admins and development tasks
- Building advanced scripts and modules
- An insight into Windows PowerShell 5.0
- Script debugging

Basics of WMI and CIM

WMI – Windows Management Instrumentation – is the Microsoft implementation of WBEM – Web Based Enterprise Management – which allows us to access management information from any environment. PowerShell makes access to WMI easy and consistently deliverable using an object-based technique.

Let's explore a few PowerShell cmdlets of WMI.

WMI is a part of the `Microsoft.PowerShell.Management` module. You can run the following command to explore the WMI cmdlets:

```
Get-Command -Module Microsoft.PowerShell.Management -Name '*WMI*'
```

The output is illustrated in the following image:

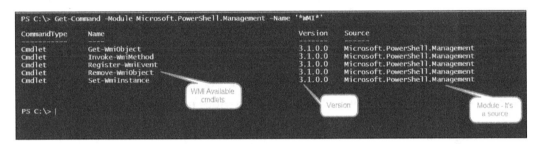

There are many tools available to explore all the WMI classes available in the WMI repository. You can use the following links to do so:

```
https://wmie.codeplex.com/
```

```
https://www.sapien.com/software/wmiexplorer
```

Using these tools, we can explore and view the classes, instances, properties, and qualifiers easily. It's a GUI tool, so it makes our job easy as well. As we are focusing more on PowerShell, let's do it the PowerShell way, on the fly and explore.

The `Get-WmiObject` cmdlet has a switch parameter to list all the classes. The `Get-WmiObject -List` command will retrieve all the classes from the `Root\CIMV2` namespace by default. However, we can explicitly mention the namespace using the `NameSpace` parameter to identify the specified WMI class location, as shown in the following command:

```
#Retrieves WMI Class from Root\Security NameSpace
Get-WmiObject -List -Namespace 'Root\Security'
#Retrieves WMI Class from Root\CIMV2 - Default
Get-WmiObject -List
```

To know more about WMI cmdlets, use the `help about_WMI_Cmdlets` command.

PowerShell supports the `WMIClass` type accelerators, which is a shortcut for using .NET classes in PowerShell.

- **[WMI]**: This is the type accelerator for the `ManagementObject` class
- **[WMIClass]**: This is the type accelerator for the `ManagementClass` class
- **[WMISearcher]**: This is the type accelerator for the `ManagementObjectSearcher` class

These make PowerShell richer and more useful; therefore, system administrators can use WMI in PowerShell very easily.

Let's query a service named `WinRM` using the WMI type accelerator. Run the following command:

```
[wmi]"root\cimv2:Win32_Service.Name='WinRM'"
```

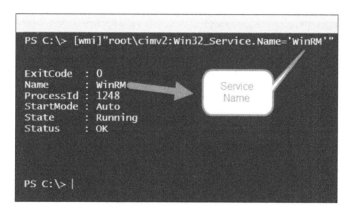

The same can be achieved using the following Windows PowerShell commands:

```
Get-WmiObject -Class Win32_Service -Filter "Name='WinRM'"
Get-WmiObject -Class Win32_Service | ? {$_.Name -eq 'WinRM'}
(Get-WmiObject -Class Win32_Service).Where({$_.Name -eq 'WinRM'})
```

All of the preceding commands provide the same result, and it depends upon the usage and optimization. The `Get-WMIObject` cmdlet has a parameter named `Query`, which allows us to use **WMI Query Language (WQL)**, as in the following command:

```
Get-WmiObject -Query "Select * from Win32_Service where Name='WinRM'"
```

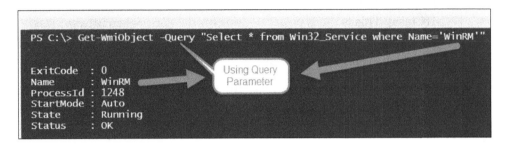

Using the `WMIClass` type accelerator, we can invoke any method easily, as shown in the following command:

```
$Obj = [wmiclass]"Win32_Process"
$Obj.Create('NotePad.exe')
```

The output of this command is as shown in the following image:

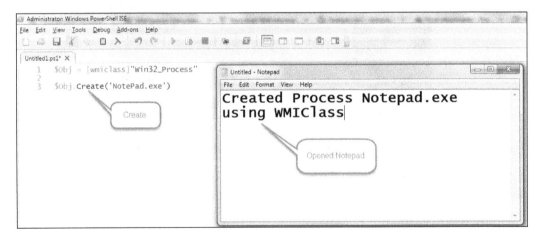

The WMI provider consists of the **Managed Object Format (MOF)** file, which defines the data, classes, and associated events. Using the `WMIClass` type accelerator method, it's possible to explore the MOF file. Consider the following commands:

```
$Obj = [wmiclass]"Win32_OperatingSystem"
$Obj.GetText('MOF')
```

The preceding commands would output the MOF file as shown in the following image — you can use the Out-GridView cmdlet for look and feel:

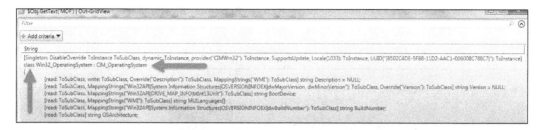

The same MOF file can be found at $ENV:Windir\SYSTEM32\WBEM. Use the following command:

```
Get-ChildItem  C:\windows\System32\wbem -Filter *.MOF
```

Windows PowerShell has a command named Invoke-WMIMethod, which is used to invoke methods without using type accelerators.

Note that in the following code, we have used | Out-Null, which deletes the output instead of sending it to the pipeline:

```
Invoke-WmiMethod -Class Win32_process -Name Create -ArgumentList
  Notepad.exe | Out-Null
```

This is similar to casting to Void type, as shown in the following command:

```
[Void] (Invoke-WmiMethod -Class Win32_process -Name Create
  -ArgumentList Notepad.exe)
```

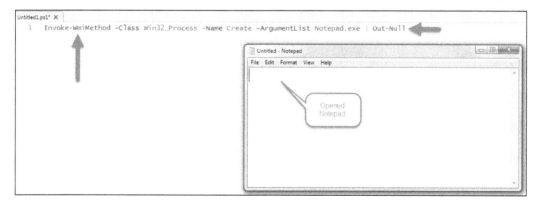

Using the `WMISearcher` type accelerator, we can explore the WMI data. Now, let's try the following code:

```
$Obj = [wmisearcher]"Select * from Win32_Process Where Name =
  'Notepad.exe'"

$Obj
```

```
PS C:\> $Obj = [wmisearcher]"Select * from Win32_Process Where Name = 'Notepad.exe'"
$Obj

                                                           Not useful result?

Scope      : System.Management.ManagementScope
Query      : System.Management.ObjectQuery
Options    : System.Management.EnumerationOptions
Site       :
Container  :
```

Let's consider what this is. This outputs `Scope`, `Query`, `Options`, `Site`, and `Container`, which are the properties. To get the result collections we need to invoke `GetMethod()` method.

```
$Obj = [wmisearcher]"Select * from Win32_Process Where Name =
  'Notepad.exe'"

$Obj.Get()
```

Using pipelines, we can select the properties we need to view, as in the following command:

```
$Obj = [wmisearcher]"Select * from Win32_Process Where Name =
  'Notepad.exe'"

$Obj.Get() | Select Caption , ExecutablePath , UserModeTime
```

The output is illustrated in the following image:

```
PS C:\> $Obj = [wmisearcher]"Select * from Win32_Process Where Name = 'Notepad.exe'"
$Obj.Get() | Select Caption , ExecutablePath , UserModeTime  ①

Caption       ExecutablePath  ②                      UserModeTime
-------       -------------                          ------------
notepad.exe   C:\windows\SYSTEM32\notepad.exe            1560010
notepad.exe   C:\windows\system32\notepad.exe            6708043
notepad.exe   C:\windows\system32\Notepad.exe             312002
notepad.exe   C:\windows\system32\Notepad.exe             624004


PS C:\> |
                                              Output
```

The points marked in the figure are explained in the following list:

- **1**: Here, we have used the pipeline to select the information required
- **2**: This shows the output `Caption`, `ExecutablePath`, and `UserModeTime`

Let's consider a demo of a tiny PowerShell function using WMI.

We will need to retrieve the BIOS, computer system, and operating system information from the given servers in the environment.

We will use the `WIN32_BIOS`, `Win32_ComputerSystem`, and `Win32_OperatingSystem` classes to get the information.

Execute the following code:

```
Function Get-SystemInformation {
  param(
  [parameter(Mandatory = $true)]
  [String] $computername
  )
  $OS = Get-WmiObject -Class Win32_OperatingSystem -ComputerName
    $computername
  $BIOS = Get-WmiObject -Class Win32_BIOS -ComputerName $computername
  $CS = Get-WmiObject -Class Win32_ComputerSystem -ComputerName
    $computername
  $properties = New-Object psobject -Property @{
    "OSName" = $os.Caption
```

```
    "ServicePack" = $os.CSDVersion

    "SerialNumber" = $BIOS.SerialNumber

    "Manufacturer" = $BIOS.Manufacturer

    "Bootupstate" = $cs.BootupState

  }

  $properties

}

Get-SystemInformation -computername localhost
```

```
Function Get-SystemInformation {
param(
[parameter(Mandatory = $true)]
[String]$computername
)
$OS = Get-WmiObject -Class Win32_OperatingSystem -ComputerName $computername
$BIOS = Get-WmiObject -Class Win32_BIOS -ComputerName $computername
$CS = Get-WmiObject -Class Win32_ComputerSystem -ComputerName $computername
$properties = New-Object psobject -Property @{
"OSName" = $os.Caption
"ServicePack" = $os.CSDVersion
"SerialNumber" = $BIOS.SerialNumber
"Manufacturer" = $BIOS.Manufacturer
"Bootupstate" = $cs.BootupState
}
$properties
}

Get-SystemInformation -computername localhost
```

Let's consider how this works. Perform the following steps:

1. Use the `Function` keyword to create a function.

2. You can name the function `Get-SystemInformation` as this is a friendly name, but ensure that you follow the verb-noun combination for easy understanding.

3. Use the `Param` block to declare a variable.

4. Declare a variable and name it `$ComputerName` (For now, we will use a localhost).

5. Use `Win32_BIOS`, `Win32_ComputerSystem`, and `Win32_OperatingSystem` and assign each a variable.

6. Create an object using the `PSObject` class and collect all information in `$Properties` object.

7. Get the required properties.

8. Output the result.

9. Call the function.

The output is illustrated in the following image:

```
SerialNumber  : DSCC007780
ServicePack   : Service Pack 1
Manufacturer  : FUJITSU // Phoenix Technologies Ltd.
BootUpState   : Normal boot
OSName        : Microsoft Windows 7 Enterprise
           1                    2
```

WMI uses **Distributed COM (DCOM)** to connect to a remote computer. However, in certain environments, this may be blocked by a firewall. In this scenario, we can retrieve the information using the PowerShell remoting feature or using the **WSMan** object.

To explore the WSMan commands, you can execute the following command:

```
Get-Command -Module Microsoft.WSMan.Management
```

The output is illustrated in the following image:

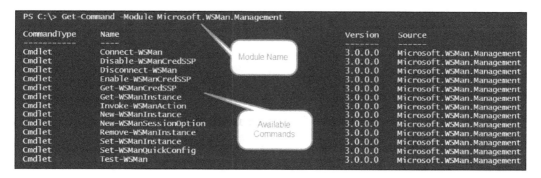

As we are discussing the basics of WMI here, we are not covering all the topics. However, we will discuss more about WMI and CIM in further topics.

CIM is defined by **Distributed Management Task Force (DMTF)** and is an object-oriented data model. In WMI, developers can use CIM to create classes. Using CIM, it's easy to manage the different elements of an environment.

CIM cmdlets are introduced in PowerShell 3.0, and these are vendor independent. Considering the recent Cloud operating system, we will have to work with different manufacturers. So, using CIM is the best option because WMI is Windows-based; it implements the DMTF standards in CIM and also allows us to query non-Windows operating systems.

The advantages of CIM in PowerShell are its usability and ability to run quite faster than WMI. PowerShell facilities such as tab completion make CIM cmdlets very rich. In other words, CIM is a superset of WMI.

To know the available CIM cmdlets, we can simply run the following code:

```
(Get-Command -Noun CIM*).Name
```

It will return the following output:

```
Get-CimAssociatedInstance
Get-CimClass
Get-CimInstance
Get-CimSession
Invoke-CimMethod
New-CimInstance
New-CimSession
New-CimSessionOption
Register-CimIndicationEvent
Remove-CimInstance
Remove-CimSession
Set-CimInstance
```

Let's query the basic OS and BIOS information as follows:

```
Function Get-SystemInformation {
  param(
  [Parameter(Mandatory = $true,ValueFromPipeline = $true)]
  [string[]]$ComputerName
  )
  Begin{}
  Process{
    foreach($computer in $ComputerName) {
      $OS = Get-CimInstance -ClassName CIM_OperatingSystem -
        ComputerName $computer
```

```
    $BIOS = Get-CimInstance -ClassName Win32_BIOS -ComputerName
      $computer
    $props = New-Object psobject -Property @{
      OSName = $os.Caption
      ServicePack = $OS.CSDVersion
      BIOSSerialNumber = $BIOS.SerialNumber
      BIOSReleaseDate = $BIOS.ReleaseDate
    }
  }
  $props
}
End{}
}
#Demo
"localhost" ,"Localhost" | %{
  Get-SystemInformation -ComputerName $_
}
```

Note that every time you run the function, the output order is different. To get an ordered output, we can make a minor change in the code, as shown in the following:

```
$props = [Ordered] @{
  OSName = $os.Caption
  ServicePack = $OS.CSDVersion
  BIOSSerialNumber = $BIOS.SerialNumber
  BIOSReleaseDate = $BIOS.ReleaseDate
}
New-Object psobject -Property $props
```

The preceding code returns an ordered output, as shown in the following image:

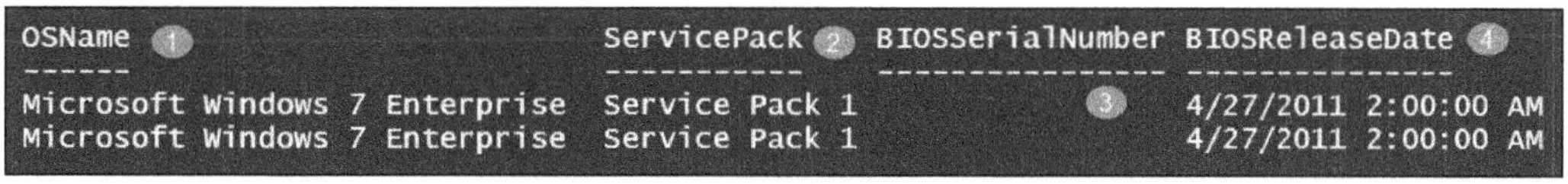

The points marked in the figure are explained in the following list:

- **1**: `OSName` lists the names of operating systems
- **2**: `ServicePack` gives service pack information
- **3**: `BIOSSerialNumber` gives BIOS serial number information
- **4**: `BIOSReleaseDate` lists the release date of operating systems

What does `[Ordered]` do here? It simply makes an ordered dictionary. Let's take a look at another example of this.

The following code creates a hash table; the output order will be random:

```
$props = @{A='1'
  B='2'
  C='3'

}
```

To identify the type name, we use the `GetType()` method, which returns a hash table as names. Following is the command:

```
$props.GetType()
```

The following code will return an output in the same order (A, B, and C). This is an ordered dictionary type:

```
$props = [Ordered]@{A='1'
  B='2'
  C='3'

}
```

CIM cmdlets are introduced in PowerShell 3.0; so, before using CIM to query devices, we should ensure that it complies with the CIM and **WSMan** standards defined by DMTF. You may wonder, how can we use CIM while querying in a mixed environment, where we may have Windows Server 2012 and 2008 R2 with PowerShell 2.0? The CIM class works on the devices that have PowerShell version 3.0. What happens if we try to use the `Invoke-Command` cmdlet? It will fail with an error message, `'Get-CimInstance' is not recognized as the name of a cmdlet, function, script file, or operable program.`

The solution is to use a CIM session. Let's take a look at how to use the CIM session in this example. Execute the following code:

```
Test-WSMan -ComputerName RemoteServer
```

The output is illustrated in the following image—the version used here is 2.0:

```
wsmid             : http://schemas.dmtf.org/wbem/wsman/identity/1/wsmanidentity.xsd
ProtocolVersion  : http://schemas.dmtf.org/wbem/wsman/1/wsman.xsd
ProductVendor    : Microsoft Corporation
ProductVersion   : OS: 0.0.0 SP: 0.0 Stack: 2.0
```
Version 2.0

All we need to know in the two CIM cmdlets are their parameters, which are as follows:

- The New-CimSessionOption cmdlet
- The Get-CimInstance cmdlet

Execute the following code:

```
$dcom = New-CimSessionOption -Protocol Dcom

$Remote = New-CimSession -ComputerName 'RemoteServer' -SessionOption
  $dcom

(Get-CimInstance -CimSession $Remote -ClassName
  CIM_OperatingSystem).InstallDate
```

Let's take a look at how this works.

We used the DCOM protocol, which is New-CimSessionOption, and assigned it to a $dcom variable. Then, we used the New-CIMSession cmdlet to create a session with the -SessionOption parameter (we used $dcom, which is nothing but a DComSessionOptions type). Finally, we used the Get-CimInstance cmdlet and consumed $Remote, which is the CimSession type, with the DCOM protocol.

To remove the CIM session, we will simply use the following snippet:

```
Get-CimSession | Remove-CimSession
```

The benefits of using CIM cmdlets are as follows:

- There are loads of improvements while working with WMI association
- We can use Get-CimClass to explore a WMI class
- CIM session is beneficial to the query devices included with version 2.0
- There are no more DCOM errors

Working with XML and COM

We explored the basics of WMI and CIM; and yes, that was just the basics. After completing the XML topic, we will discuss **cmdlet definition XML (CDXML)**, which is used to map the PowerShell cmdlets, and the CIM class operations or methods.

I have seen most developers create XML files using Visual Studio and use some tools to compare XML. It's not a wrong method, but we have a much more convenient way to play with XML using PowerShell.

XML is the type accelerator for `System.Xml.Document`.

 To explore all the type accelerators in Windows PowerShell, use the following code:

```
[psobject].Assembly.GetType("System.Management.
Automation.TypeAccelerators")::get
```

Let's take a look at the basic structure of an XML document:

```
<?xml version="1.0" encoding="utf-8"?>
<Custom>
<Computers>
  <Manufacturers>Fujitsu</Manufacturers>
  <Model>Lifebook S 700 Series</Model>
</Computers>
<Computers>
  <Manufacturers>Fujitsu</Manufacturers>
  <Model>Lifebook S 800 Series</Model>
</Computers>
</Custom>
```

XML is case-sensitive, so it's always better to use some tools to create XML documents. I used Visual Studio 2013 to create this demo XML document.

Now, let's use the `Get-Content` cmdlet to call the XML document in PowerShell, as shown in the following image:

```
$XML
<?xml version="1.0" encoding="utf-8"?>
<Custom>
<Computers>
    <Manufacturers>Fujitsu</Manufacturers>
    <Model>Lifebook S 700 Series</Model>
</Computers>
<Computers>
    <Manufacturers>Fujitsu</Manufacturers>
    <Model>Lifebook S 800 Series</Model>
</Computers>
</Custom>
```

Output of XML Content

Yeah! We can read this, but let's do in the XML way. So, let's use a type accelerator and perform our tasks, such as XML document manipulations, as in the following command:

```
[XML]$XML = Get-Content .\File1.XML
$XML
```

This outputs as shown in the following image:

```
xml  1                                    Custom  2
---                                       ------
version="1.0" encoding="utf-8" Custom


PS C:\windows\system32> |
```

The points marked in the figure are explained in the following list:

- **1**: This is the XML property
- **2**: This is our element; it's the `XMLElement` property

We can quickly read the XML document with PowerShell using the following code:

```
[XML]$XML = Get-Content .\File1.xml
$XML.Custom.Computers
```

The output we need is illustrated in the following image:

The points marked in the figure are explained in the following list:

- The $XML variable contains the XML document information, and now it is an object

- Manufacturers is a property that can be get and set

- Model is a property that can be get and set

Using PowerShell, we can read and manipulate the output as we need.

Now, let's take a look at the available properties, methods, and so on. Run the following command:

$XML.Custom.Computers | GM

This will output all the methods, properties, code methods, and parameterized properties, as shown in the following image:

```
PS C:\windows\system32> $XML | Get-Member –MemberType Methods


    TypeName: System.Xml.XmlDocument

Name                        MemberType Definition
----                        ---------- ----------
ToString                    CodeMethod static string XmlNode(psobject instance)
AppendChild                 Method     System.Xml.XmlNode AppendChild(System.Xml.XmlNode newChild)
Clone                       Method     System.Xml.XmlNode Clone(), System.Object ICloneable.Clone()
CloneNode                   Method     System.Xml.XmlNode CloneNode(bool deep)
CreateAttribute             Method     System.Xml.XmlAttribute CreateAttribute(string name), System.Xml.XmlAttribute
CreateCDataSection          Method     System.Xml.XmlCDataSection CreateCDataSection(string data)
CreateComment               Method     System.Xml.XmlComment CreateComment(string data)
CreateDocumentFragment      Method     System.Xml.XmlDocumentFragment CreateDocumentFragment()
CreateDocumentType          Method     System.Xml.XmlDocumentType CreateDocumentType(string name, string publicId, s
CreateElement               Method     System.Xml.XmlElement CreateElement(string name), System.Xml.XmlElement Creat
CreateEntityReference       Method     System.Xml.XmlEntityReference CreateEntityReference(string name)
CreateNavigator             Method     System.Xml.XPath.XPathNavigator CreateNavigator(), System.Xml.XPath.XPathNavi
CreateNode                  Method     System.Xml.XmlNode CreateNode(System.Xml.XmlNodeType type, string prefix, str
CreateProcessingInstruction Method     System.Xml.XmlProcessingInstruction CreateProcessingInstruction(string target
CreateSignificantWhitespace Method     System.Xml.XmlSignificantWhitespace CreateSignificantWhitespace(string text)
```

Before we use methods, let's do an exercise using the XML file as the configuration file that passes the parameters to the PowerShell scripts. The reason we need this is to simplify automation in environments. Based on our requirements, we can customize and code the script.

In this exercise, let's send an e-mail, where the parameters are preconfigured in an XML file, and the script reads the XML file to do the task.

The XML code is shown as follows:

```
<?xml version="1.0" encoding="utf-8"?>
<Settings>
  <SMTP>SMTP NAME</SMTP>
  <MailFrom>From Address</MailFrom>
  <MailTO>To Address</MailTO>
  <Subject>XML Demo</Subject>
</Settings>
```

Using the following PowerShell code we can trigger emails:

```
[XML]$email = Get-Content .\File2.XML
$mail = @{
  FROM = $email.Settings.MailFrom
  TO = $email.Settings.MailTO
  SMTP = $email.Settings.SMTP
  Subject = $email.Settings.Subject
}
Send-MailMessage @mail
```

PowerShell has a few commands to use XML; to find them, you can simply try the following code:

```
Get-Command *XML
```

The output is as shown in the following image:

The points marked in the figure are explained in the following list:

- **1**: `Microsoft.PowerShell.Utility` is the name of the module
- **2**: Starting from PowerShell 5.0, the version appears in the output
- **3**: Name shows all the available commands for XML
- **4**: Command types, here shown as cmdlet

The `ConvertTo-Xml` cmdlet creates an XML-based representation of an object, and its a .NET-based object. Try the following code in your system:

```
$hash = @{
  ServiceName = (Get-Service -Name Bits).Name
  Status = (Get-Service -Name Bits).Status
  CanStop = (Get-Service -Name Bits).CanStop
  CanPauseandContinue = (Get-Service -Name Bits).CanPauseAndContinue
}
$value = New-Object PSOBject -Property $hash
($value | Convertto-xml -NoTypeInformation).save("C:\Temp\Data.xml")
[xml]$xml = Get-Content C:\Temp\Data.xml
$xml.Objects.Object.Property
```

In the preceding code, we created a hash table using the `$hash` variable; then, we created a `PSObject` object and converted it to XML using the `ConvertTo-XML` command. The output is illustrated in the following image:

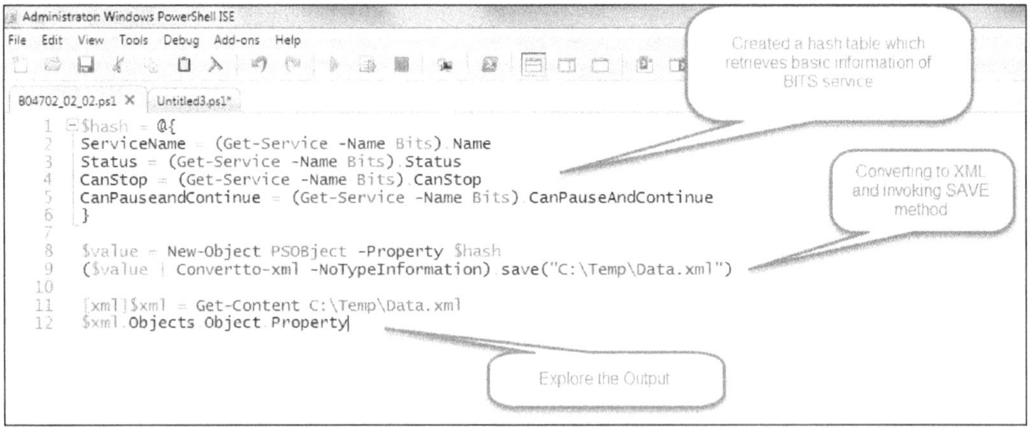

This is similar to `ConvertTo-XML`; we can use the `Export-CliXml` command, and this does more or less the same job, except that this saves the results as an XML file. To import, we will use the `Import-CliXml` command. The `Export-CliXml` command is very helpful when we use credentials in the scripts, while exporting the credentials as XML and importing it to use in the scripts.

 Note that this is a secure way because `Export-CliXml` encrypts the password using the **Windows Data Protection API**. So, decryption works only with the user account that has encrypted the credentials.

Before we start our next exercise, we need to set up the `MSOnline` module in our machine. The installation involves just clicking on next and finish—we need to follow the installation wizard.

Perform the following steps:

1. First and foremost, download and install **Microsoft Online Services Sign-In Assistant** from `http://go.microsoft.com/fwlink/?linkid=236300`.

2. Then, download and install **Microsoft Online Services Module for Windows PowerShell** from `http://go.microsoft.com/fwlink/?linkid=236297`.

As we are done with the installation, let's connect to the **Exchange Online** session using PowerShell. Perform the following steps:

1. Export the credential using the `Export-CliXml` command, as follows:

```
$credentials = Get-Credential
$credentials | Export-Clixml C:\Temp\SeccureString.xml
```

2. Import the credential using the `Import-CliXml` command, as follows:

```
$o365Cred = Import-Clixml C:\Temp\SeccureString.xml
```

3. Connect to the Exchange Online session using the following code:

```
$o365Cred = Import-Clixml C:\Temp\SeccureString.xml
Import-Module MSOnline
$O365Session = New-PSSession –ConfigurationName
  Microsoft.Exchange -ConnectionUri
  https://outlook.office365.com/powershell-
  liveid/?proxymethod=rps `
-Credential $O365Cred -Authentication Basic -AllowRedirection
Import-PSSession $O365Session
Connect-MsolService –Credential $O365Cred
```

As we passed the XML file as the value for the credential parameter, we don't need to enter the credential every time we connect to the Exchange Online session. Try to save the credential in a secured location.

It's really very handy and easy to create XML on the fly. For example, using the following code, we can create simple user XML:

```
[xml]$xmlUsers='<Configuration Description="Users">
<Customers>
<user surname="V" firstname="Chen"></user>
<user surname="Venkatesan" firstname="Chendrayan"></user>
</Customers>
</Configuration>'
$xmlUsers.Configuration.Customers.user
```

Take a look at the following image:

Here, we can see that `Surname` and `FirstName` are the properties of `User`. `User` is the property of `Customers` and `Customers` is the property of `Configuration`.

Exploring COM and Automation

Component Object Model (COM) is a binary interface used by developers to create reusable software components. The .NET framework and COM interfaces allow us to perform many admin tasks. `New-Object` is a magical command we use to create an instance of the COM object; similarly, we can create an instance of the Microsoft .NET Framework.

Windows PowerShell 5.0 includes a new COM implementation, which offers significant performance improvements.

Over the internet, we come across many COM Automation examples for Internet Explorer. So, in this exercise, we will explore MS Excel and MS Word Automation using PowerShell, which is also popular. IT managers need data in an Excel or Word format. Indeed, we can export to CSV and manipulate it as required. However, here, we need to exercise the usage of the COM object. So, let's use an Excel COM object for the same.

Perform the following steps:

1. Use `New-Object` to create an Excel COM object, this is a Program ID. Run the following command:

   ```
   $Excel = New-Object -ComObject Excel.Application
   ```

2. Now, let's take a look at the events, methods, properties, and parameterized properties. Run the following command:

   ```
   $Excel = New-Object -ComObject Excel.Application
   ```
   ```
   "Excel Object has {0} events , {1} methods , {2} properties
      and {3} parameterizedproperty" -f (($Excel | GM -MemberType
      Event).Count ,
   ```
   ```
   ($Excel | GM -MemberType Method).Count , ($Excel | GM -
      MemberType Property).Count , ($Excel | GM -MemberType
      ParameterizedProperty).Count)
   ```

   The output is illustrated in the following image:

   The points marked in the figure are explained in the following list:
   - **1**: This shows that there are 43 events
   - **2**: This shows that there are 171 methods
   - **3**: This shows that there are 225 properties
   - **4**: This shows that there are 9 parameterized properties

3. Simply pipe and get members such as in the following command:

   ```
   $Excel | GM
   ```

4. Invoke the `Speak` method from the `Speech` property. Run the following command:

   ```
   $Excel = New-Object -ComObject Excel.Application
   ```
   ```
   $Excel.Speech.Speak("Opening Excel please wait!")
   ```

This will not open Excel for now, but we can listen to the audio—just for the purpose of this demo.

5. Now, set the visible property to `$true` to open Excel. Run the following command:

```
$Excel = New-Object -ComObject Excel.Application
$Excel.Visible
```

This returns `False`. Run the following command:

```
$Excel = New-Object -ComObject Excel.Application
$Excel.Visible = $true
```

This opens Excel in your localhost, as shown in the following screenshot:

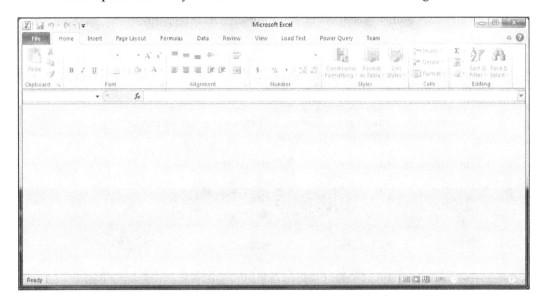

Here, we opened Excel using the PowerShell `ComObject` property.

6. Now, let's add a workbook. Run the following command:

```
$Excel = New-Object -ComObject Excel.Application
$Excel.Visible = $true
$Wb = $Excel.Workbooks.Add()
```

7. After this, name the Work Sheet through the following command:

```
$Excel = New-Object -ComObject Excel.Application
$Excel.Visible = $true
$Wb = $Excel.Workbooks.Add()
$worksheet = $Wb.Worksheets.Item(1)
$worksheet.Name = "System Information"
```

The output is illustrated in the following image:

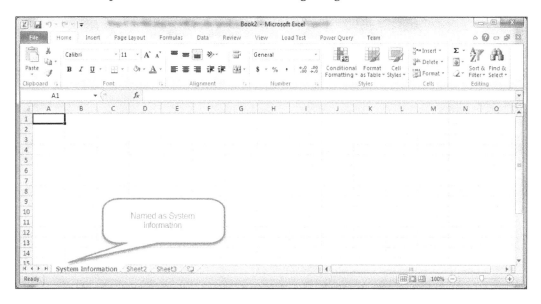

8. Insert some values in the cells. Run the following command:

```
$Excel = New-Object -ComObject Excel.Application
$Excel.Visible = $true
$Wb = $Excel.Workbooks.Add()
$worksheet = $Wb.Worksheets.Item(1)
$worksheet.Cells.Item(1,1) = "ComputerName"
$worksheet.Cells.Item(2,1) = $env:COMPUTERNAME
$worksheet.Cells.Item(1,2) = "DomainName"
$worksheet.Cells.Item(2,2) = $env:USERDOMAIN
```

The output is illustrated in the following image:

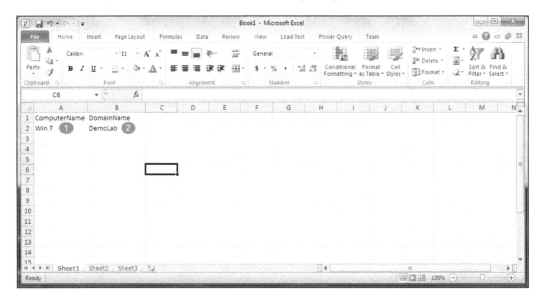

Now that we have inserted some names for the localhost and domain name in the Excel sheet, let's change the color of this text. Run the following command:

```
$Excel = New-Object -ComObject Excel.Application
$Excel.Visible = $true
$Wb = $Excel.Workbooks.Add()
$worksheet = $Wb.Worksheets.Item(1)
$worksheet.Cells.Item(1,1) = "ComputerName"
$worksheet.Cells.Item(1,1).Font.Bold = $true
$worksheet.Cells.Item(1,1).Font.ColorIndex = 53
$worksheet.Cells.Item(2,1) = $env:COMPUTERNAME
$worksheet.Cells.Item(1,2) = "DomaiName"
$worksheet.Cells.Item(1,2).Font.Bold = $true
$worksheet.Cells.Item(1,2).Font.ColorIndex = 53
$worksheet.Cells.Item(2,2) = $env:USERDOMAIN
```

The output is illustrated in the following image:

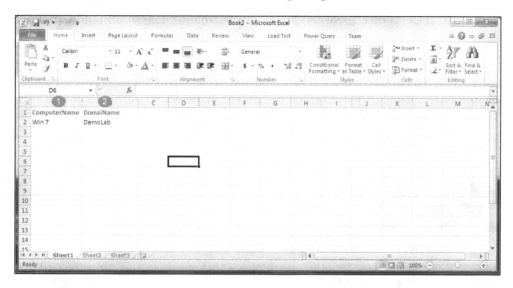

The points marked in the figure are explained in the following list:

- ○ **1**: This shows that background color is set to index 53, which is brown color, and font weight is bold
- ○ **2**: This shows that same styles are applied as **1**

9. Invoke the `SaveAs` method to save the Excel file through the following command:

```
$Excel = New-Object -ComObject Excel.Application
$Excel.Visible = $false
$Wb = $Excel.Workbooks.Add()
$worksheet = $Wb.Worksheets.Item(1)
$worksheet.Cells.Item(1,1) = "ComputerName"
$worksheet.Cells.Item(1,1).Font.Bold = $true
$worksheet.Cells.Item(1,1).Font.ColorIndex = 53
$worksheet.Cells.Item(2,1) = $env:COMPUTERNAME
$worksheet.Cells.Item(1,2) = "DomaiName"
$worksheet.Cells.Item(1,2).Font.Bold = $true
$worksheet.Cells.Item(1,2).Font.ColorIndex = 53
$worksheet.Cells.Item(2,2) = $env:USERDOMAIN

$Wb.SaveAs('C:Temp\Output.xlsx')
```

In the preceding code, we have set the Excel visible property to false.

Using an Excel COM object, we can insert graphs, manipulate information, merge cells, and so on. Explore all the objects and create your code as required.

Now, let's explore the Microsoft Word object. This is similar to an Excel COM object exercise, so we will not cover each step. Instead, let's consider a sample code using the Word COM object. Always remember to release the COM object because it runs in the background. Before we begin, let's discuss the steps to release the COM object.

This is how the background chunk appears in your system:

```
PS C:\> Get-Process -Name WINWORD

Handles  NPM(K)    PM(K)     WS(K) VM(M)    CPU(s)     Id ProcessName
-------  ------    -----     ----- -----    ------     -- -----------
    754      96    83284    101928   572      4.80   1832 WINWORD
    749      74    69424    105144   555      1.78   3380 WINWORD
    737      76    69704    106948   565      1.90   4664 WINWORD
    740      76    66452    103424   565      1.83   6748 WINWORD
    718      68    60880     82180   521      1.33   8148 WINWORD
    853     112   122976     97560   714  1,085.77  11228 WINWORD
    717      68    61188     82636   521      1.65  12024 WINWORD
    714      68    61324     82872   521      2.11  12924 WINWORD
    712      67    61084     55032   518      1.45  13108 WINWORD
    740      76    69216    106416   562      2.31  13440 WINWORD
    719      67    61312     55640   519      1.86  13884 WINWORD
```

Background chunks!

Let's kill this process using the `Stop-Process` command. The result is illustrated in the following image:

```
PS C:\> Stop-Process -Name WINWORD -Verbose  1
VERBOSE: Performing the operation "Stop-Process" on target "WINWORD (1832)".
VERBOSE: Performing the operation "Stop-Process" on target "WINWORD (3380)".
VERBOSE: Performing the operation "Stop-Process" on target "WINWORD (4664)".
VERBOSE: Performing the operation "Stop-Process" on target "WINWORD (6748)".
VERBOSE: Performing the operation "Stop-Process" on target "WINWORD (8148)".
VERBOSE: Performing the operation "Stop-Process" on target "WINWORD (10044)".  2
VERBOSE: Performing the operation "Stop-Process" on target "WINWORD (12024)".
VERBOSE: Performing the operation "Stop-Process" on target "WINWORD (12924)".
VERBOSE: Performing the operation "Stop-Process" on target "WINWORD (13108)".
VERBOSE: Performing the operation "Stop-Process" on target "WINWORD (13440)".
VERBOSE: Performing the operation "Stop-Process" on target "WINWORD (13884)".
```

While exploring the members, I observed that it uses the `Quit` method, so I used it to close Word. Take a look at the following image:

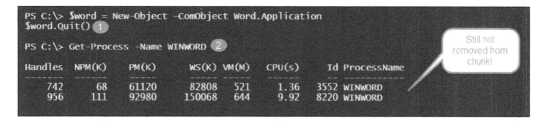

Here, we can see that nothing's turned up, and there are still two Word processes running. One of the processes is running in the background, and the other has opened up because I am writing this book in MS Word.

With reference to the MSDN documentation, I tried to use the following method:

```
$word = New-Object -ComObject Word.Application
[System.Runtime.Interopservices.Marshal]::ReleaseComObject($word)
Remove-Variable -Name word -Verbose
```

As expected, it didn't turn up. The result is illustrated in the following image:

```
PS C:\> Stop-Process -Name WINWORD

PS C:\> $word = New-Object -ComObject Word.Application
[System.Runtime.Interopservices.Marshal]::ReleaseComObject($word)
0  1

PS C:\> Get-Process -Name WINWORD  2

Handles   NPM(K)     PM(K)      WS(K) VM(M)    CPU(s)      Id ProcessName
-------   ------     -----      ----- -----    ------      -- -----------
   829       73     66844      83664   551      1.40   11368 WINWORD
```

Finally, the following code worked as we expected it to:

```
$Word = New-Object -ComObject Word.Application
[System.Runtime.InteropServices.Marshal]::ReleaseComObject(
  [System.ComObject]$Word) | out-null
[System.GC]::Collect()
[System.GC]::WaitForPendingFinalizers()
```

Now, let's try to create a Word document that has a report executed date, computer name, and domain name. Run the following command:

```
$word = New-Object -ComObject "Word.application"
$word.visible = $true
$doc = $word.Documents.Add()
$doc.Activate()
$word.Selection.Font.Name = "Calibri"
$word.Selection.Font.Size = "10"
$word.Selection.TypeText("Report Executed on " +
   (Get-Date).ToShortDateString())
$word.Selection.TypeParagraph()
$word.Selection.TypeText("Computer Name is $env:computerName")
$word.Selection.TypeParagraph()
$word.Selection.TypeText("Domain Name is $env:USERDOMAIN")
$word.Selection.TypeParagraph()
$word.Quit()
```

The output of the preceding code output is shown in the following image:

The points marked in the figure are explained in the following list:

- **1**: The date is converted to short date string format
- **2**: The $env:computerName variable is used to get the computer name
- **3**: The $env:USERDOMAIN variable is used to get the domain name

Let's create a small Word document that will retrieve information from active directory and build a Word document. The desired output will be similar to the following screenshot:

Venkatesan, C. (Chendrayan)

Department: ICT, Office Phone: +31xxxxxxxxxx, Email: <Email Address>

Objective

Skills

Education

Projects

I hereby declare that the above written particulars are true to the best of my knowledge and belief.

Name : Venkatesan, C. (Chendrayan)

Date : 06/22/2015 14:45:12

Let's take a look at how this works. Perform the following steps:

1. Create a variable to save the username and filename as required. Run the following command:

```
$FileName = $Env:USERNAME
$savepath="C:\$FileName.docx"
```

2. Create an instance of a Word application using the `Word.Application` command. Add the document using the `Add()` property and select the document using the `Selection` property. Run the following command:

```
$word = New-object -ComObject "Word.Application"
$doc=$word.documents.Add()
$Resume=$word.Selection
```

3. Set the style and use the `Get-ADUser` command to fetch the AD properties. Run the following command:

```
$Resume.Style="Title"

$UserName = Get-ADUser -Identity $ENV:USERNAME -Properties *

$Picture = Get-ADUser -Identity $ENV:USERNAME -Properties
   thumbnailphoto
```

4. Save the picture in the desired location with the following command:

```
$Picture.thumbnailphoto | Set-Content "C:\Photo.jpg" -Encoding
   Byte

$Resume.TypeText("$($UserName.Name)")

$Resume.InlineShapes.AddPicture("C:\Photo.jpg")
```

5. Retrieve the required information from AD using the following command:

```
$Resume.TypeParagraph()

$Resume.Style="Normal"

$Resume.TypeText("Department: $($UserName.Department), Office
   Phone: $($UserName.OfficePhone), Email: $($UserName.mail)")
```

6. Type out the text as required using the following code:

```
$Resume.TypeParagraph()

$Resume.Style="SubTitle"

$Resume.TypeText(("Objective"))

$Resume.TypeParagraph()

$Resume.Style="SubTitle"

$Resume.TypeText(("Skills"))

$Resume.TypeParagraph()

$Resume.Style="SubTitle"

$Resume.TypeText(("Education"))

$Resume.TypeParagraph()

$Resume.Style="SubTitle"

$Resume.TypeText(("Projects"))

$Resume.TypeParagraph()

$Resume.TypeParagraph()

$Resume.TypeParagraph()

$Resume.Style="SubTitle"

$Resume.TypeText(("I hereby declare that the above written
   particulars are true to the best of my knowledge and
   belief."))
```

```
$Resume.TypeParagraph()
$Resume.TypeParagraph()
$Resume.TypeParagraph()
$Resume.Style="Strong"
$Resume.TypeText("Name       :      $($UserName.Name)")
$Resume.TypeParagraph()
$Date = Get-Date
$Resume.TypeText("Date       :      $($Date)")
```

7. Save the file. Run the following command:

```
$doc.SaveAs([ref]$savepath)
$doc.Close()
```

8. Run the following command to quit Word and open the file:

```
$word.quit()
Invoke-Item $savepath
```

You can use the complete code, which is as follows:

```
$FileName = $Env:USERNAME
$savepath="C:\$FileName.docx"
$word = New-object -ComObject "Word.Application"
$doc=$word.documents.Add()
$Resume=$word.Selection
$Resume.Style="Title"
$UserName = Get-ADUser -Identity $ENV:USERNAME -Properties *
$Picture = Get-ADUser -Identity $ENV:USERNAME -Properties
  thumbnailphoto
$Picture.thumbnailphoto | Set-Content "C:\Photo.jpg" -Encoding
  Byte
$Resume.TypeText("$($UserName.Name)")
$Resume.InlineShapes.AddPicture("C:\Photo.jpg")
$Resume.TypeParagraph()
$Resume.Style="Normal"
$Resume.TypeText("Department: $($UserName.Department), Office
  Phone: $($UserName.OfficePhone), Email: $($UserName.mail)")
$Resume.TypeParagraph()
$Resume.Style="SubTitle"
$Resume.TypeText(("Objective"))
$Resume.TypeParagraph()
```

```
$Resume.Style="SubTitle"

$Resume.TypeText(("Skills"))

$Resume.TypeParagraph()

$Resume.Style="SubTitle"

$Resume.TypeText(("Education"))

$Resume.TypeParagraph()

$Resume.Style="SubTitle"

$Resume.TypeText(("Projects"))

$Resume.TypeParagraph()

$Resume.TypeParagraph()

$Resume.TypeParagraph()

$Resume.Style="SubTitle"

$Resume.TypeText(("I hereby declare that the above written
    particulars are true to the best of my knowledge and
    belief."))

$Resume.TypeParagraph()

$Resume.TypeParagraph()

$Resume.TypeParagraph()

$Resume.Style="Strong"

$Resume.TypeText("Name    :     $($UserName.Name)")

$Resume.TypeParagraph()

$Date = Get-Date

$Resume.TypeText("Date    :     $($Date)")

$doc.SaveAs([ref]$savepath)

$doc.Close()

$word.quit()

Invoke-Item $savepath
```

Exploring .NET objects

An object is nothing but a combination of methods and properties in PowerShell. Using Windows PowerShell, we can store a reference to an object to a variable and use it in the current shell as required.

We discussed in *Chapter 1, Getting Started with Windows PowerShell* that PowerShell takes advantage of the underlying .NET framework. So, the objects are a representation of the parts and actions to use it. An object is a combination of the properties and methods (*Objects = Properties + Methods*).

For example, a Windows service object has properties and methods. The properties are Get and Set, and the methods are invoked to perform a meaningful operation.

Consider the following image:

```
PS C:\> $service = New-Object System.ServiceProcess.ServiceController -ArgumentList BITS

#Invoking Start Method
$service.Start()        ①


PS C:\> $Service.Status
Running    ②

PS C:\>
```

Creating .NET objects

We have discussed objects in a few of the preceding examples as well. In this section, we will explore the .NET objects in PowerShell. In order to create a .NET object, we will use the same New-Object cmdlet, but instead of the COM object, we will use different types of objects.

To create a .NET object for the system version, we will use the following code:

```
$Version = New-Object -TypeName System.Version -ArgumentList 1.2.3.4
$Version
```

The output is illustrated in the following image:

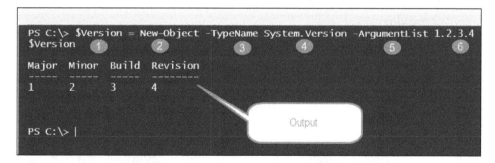

The points marked in the figure are explained in the following list:

- **1**: Here, we created a variable $Version
- **2**: Here, we used the New-Object cmdlet
- **3**: Here, we are using the parameter -TypeName to call the .NET framework class

- **4**: Here, we are calling the `System.Version` .NET framework class
- **5**: Here, we are using `-ArgumentList` to pass values to the constructor of the class
- **6**: The passed values are `1.2.3.4`.

As we have discussed a little about typecasting in the previous topics, we can do the same here as well. Run the following command:

```
[System.Version]"1.2.3.4"
```

The result is the same, as shown in the following image:

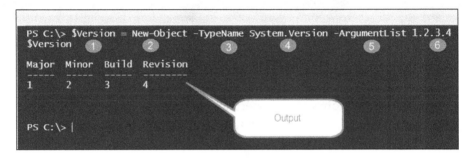

Extending .NET objects for Administrations and Development tasks

Using PowerShell, we can extend the instance of the .NET object. To do this, we will use the `Add-member` cmdlet. In the following example, we will discuss extending the `System.String` class:

```
$string = New-Object -TypeName System.String -ArgumentList
  "PowerShell Rocks!"
```

```
($string).GetType()
```

The output of the code we just saw is illustrated in the following image:

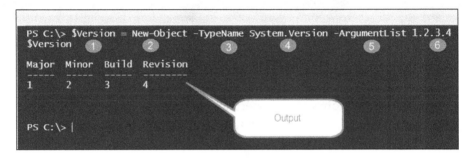

The points marked in the figure are explained in the following list:

- **1**: In the above code, we use GetType() method to explore the type name. It's a string.
- **2**: Here, the argument passed for the constructor of System.String class is PowerShell Rocks!
- **3**: Here, the value returned is String
- **4**: The base objects in System.Object (Note: If we do $var = 123 ; $var. GetType() the base objects returns System.Value). In the above code we have created a String object. So, the base type shows the ultimate base class of all classes in the .NET Framework

Now, let's add NoteProperty. This will return the total character counts from the value passed through, which is ArgumentList. Run the following command:

```
$string = New-Object -TypeName System.String -ArgumentList
  "PowerShell Rocks!"
$String | Add-Member -MemberType NoteProperty "TotalCharacters"
  -Value $string.Length
$string.TotalCharacters
```

The output is illustrated in the following image:

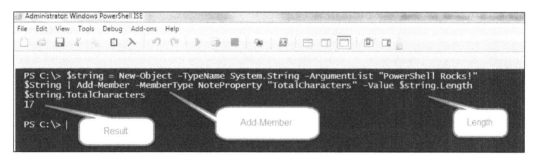

Let's consider another example where we concatenate the ScriptMethod object to a string object. Run the following command:

```
$string = New-Object -TypeName System.String -ArgumentList
  "PowerShell Rocks!"
$String | Add-Member -MemberType ScriptMethod -Name "ConcatCustom"
  -Value { [String]::Concat($this , " Demo") }
$string.ConcatCustom()
```

The preceding code appended the Demo string to the ArgumentList string, PowerShell Rocks!.

The output is illustrated in the following image:

```
PS C:\> $string = New-Object -TypeName System.String -ArgumentList "PowerShell Rocks!"
$String | Add-Member -MemberType ScriptMethod -Name "ConcatCustom" -Value {[String]::Concat($this , " Demo")}

$string.ConcatCustom()  8
PowerShell Rocks! Demo
                    9
PS C:\> |
```

The points marked in the figure are explained in the following list:

- **1**: This shows that the member type of the Add-Member cmdlet is ScriptMethod
- **2**: Here, I named the script as CustomConcat just for demo purposes — You can choose any custom name
- **3**: Here, the Value parameter defines the script
- **4**: Here, we used the [String]::Concat method just for simple demo purposes
- **5**: Here, we see that the Concat method accepts two string parameters (string1, string2)
- **6**: Here, we can see that the value parameter accepts the $this automatic variable as well
- **7**: Here, we see that Demo is a string we need to concatenate
- **8**: Here, we invoke our script method
- **9**: Here, we see the output as PowerShell Rocks! Demo

Extending the .NET Framework types

Using Windows PowerShell, we can define a Windows .NET Framework class in the session and instantiate the object using New-Object. PowerShell allows us to use the inline C# code using a **here-string**. To define a here-string in Windows PowerShell, we should use @" and close it with "@ — anything between these marks is a here-string, as shown in the following snippet:

```
@"

"here strings"

"@
```

From Windows PowerShell 5.0 onward, we can write the class in Windows PowerShell. The `Class` keyword is supported only in PowerShell version 5.0. For now, let's take a look at how the `Add-Type` cmdlet works. In the following example, we will take a look at code with the inline C# code:

```
$sourcecode = @"
public class Calculator
{
  public static int Add(int a, int b)
  {
    return (a + b);
  }
}
"@
Add-Type -TypeDefinition $sourcecode
[Calculator]
```

The output is illustrated in the following image:

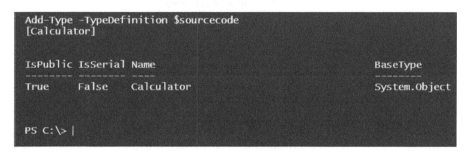

Now, we can call the `Add` method directly without using the `New-Object` cmdlet. Run the following command:

```
$sourcecode = @"
public class Calculator
{
  public static int Add(int a, int b)
  {
    return (a + b);
  }
}
```

```
"@
```

```
Add-Type -TypeDefinition $sourcecode
```

```
[Calculator]::Add(10,5)
```

PowerShell allows us to execute the static methods of a class directly in PowerShell. `System.Math` has a static method called `sqrt`, which can be used as shown in the following command:

```
[System.Math]::Sqrt(4)
```

In the following example, we will create a simple class using the `Class` keyword:

```
Class Demo
{
  #Properties
  [string]$FirstName = "Chen"
  [string]$surname = "V"
  #Methods - This will print the values and just for demo
  [string]GetInformation() {
    return "$($this.FirstName) $($this.surname)"
  }
}
```

Following is the alternate method to instantiate the class:

- We have used the keyword `Class` and named it as `Demo`
- `$FirstName` and `$surname` are properties
- `GetInformation` is a method and `$this` is an automatic variable used
- Used `$var` variable and instantiating the class using `New-Object` cmdlet. With the same code the class can instantiated using `$var = [Demo]::new();$var.GetInformation()`

The output is shown in the following image:

Let's explore the property, as shown in the following image:

The class `Demo` we created in the preceding section has properties and methods, but we practically don't need the `GetInformation` method because it just prints the property values. Let's create another class with the `SetInformation` method which updates the property values. Run the following command:

```
Class Demo
{
  #Properties
  [string]$FirstName = "Chen"
  [string]$surname = "V"
  #Methods - This will print the values and just for demo
  GetInformation() {
    $this.FirstName
    $this.surname
  }
```

```
  SetInformation([string]$fn,[string]$sn) {
  $this.FirstName = $fn
  $this.surname = $sn
  }
}
$var = New-Object -TypeName Demo
$var.SetInformation("Chendrayan" , "Venkatesan")
$var
```

The preceding code returns the following output:

We will cover more information about the classes in the *Exploring Windows PowerShell 5.0* section.

Building advanced scripts and modules

Windows PowerShell scripting is used imperatively to perform complex operations using cmdlets. Windows PowerShell supports variables, functions, branching, loops, structured exception handling and, as we all know, .NET integration.

The PowerShell script file has a PS1 extension. For example, let's save the following file as PS1 and execute it:

```
Function Get-Information
{
  (Get-Service).Where({$_.Status -eq 'Stopped'})
}
Get-Information
```

The preceding script is a very basic code to retrieve all the running services. Consider the following image:

```
Status  1  Name   2              DisplayName  3
------     ----                  -----------
Stopped    AdobeFlashPlaye...    Adobe Flash Player Update Service
Stopped    AeLookupSvc           Application Experience
Stopped    ALG                   Application Layer Gateway Service
Stopped    AppIDSvc              Application Identity
Stopped    aspnet_state          ASP.NET State Service
Stopped    AxInstSV              ActiveX Installer (AxInstSV)
Stopped    BDESVC                BitLocker Drive Encryption Service
Stopped    Blackberry Devi...    Blackberry Device Manager
Stopped    Browser               Computer Browser
Stopped    c2wts                 Claims to Windows Token Service
Stopped    clr_optimizatio...    Microsoft .NET Framework NGEN v2.0....
Stopped    clr_optimizatio...    Microsoft .NET Framework NGEN v2.0....
Stopped    clr_optimizatio...    Microsoft .NET Framework NGEN v4.0....
Stopped    clr_optimizatio...    Microsoft .NET Framework NGEN v4.0....
Stopped    COMSysApp             COM+ System Application
Stopped    cphs                  Intel(R) Content Protection HECI Se...
Stopped    defragsvc             Disk Defragmenter
Stopped    dot3svc               Wired AutoConfig
Stopped    ehRecvr               Windows Media Center Receiver Service
Stopped    ehSched               Windows Media Center Scheduler Service
```

Before taking a look at the advanced functions, let's consider the fundamentals of PowerShell scripting.

A PS1 file is nothing but a text file that contains a sequence of PowerShell cmdlets to perform certain complex tasks. Before you execute a PowerShell script, ensure that the script execution policy is set as required. There are different types of execution policies; to know them, simply execute the following help cmdlet:

```
help about_Execution_Policies -Detailed
```

Before creating PowerShell scripts, ensure that you plan and document the synopsis. Using the Measure-Command cmdlet, ensure that you optimize the performance of the code as required.

Now, let's take a look at the advanced function and save it as PS1 file. For this demo, I have used the PowerShell ISE, which has a snippet for advanced functions and advanced function complete.

The structure of the advanced function is shown in the following image:

The points marked in the figure are explained in the following list:

- **1**: This is a comment block
- **2**: Using synopsis, description, examples, and notes makes the script readable and easy to understand
- **3**: Name of the function — always a Verb-Noun Combination is the best practice
- **4**: The `CmdletBinding` attribute is an attribute of functions, which makes a function work similarly to a compiled cmdlet that is written in C#
- **5**: Here, the param block is used to define parameters
- **6**: Here, the begin block is used to provide optional onetime pre-processing
- **7**: Here, the process block is used to provide record by record processing
- **8**: Here, the end block is used to provide optional one time post-processing

Let's take the example of a PowerShell script that retrieves system information and saves the output as an HTML file, which uses the CSS style sheet. Run the following code:

```
<#
 .SYNOPSIS
 Windows Machine Inventory Using PowerShell.
 .DESCRIPTION
  This script is to document the Windows machine. This script will work
only for Local Machine.
```

```
.EXAMPLE

  PS C:\> .\System_Inventory.PS1

.OUTPUTS

  HTML File OutPut ReportDate , General Information , BIOS Information
etc.

#>

#Set-ExecutionPolicy RemoteSigned -ErrorAction SilentlyContinue

$UserName = (Get-Item  env:\username).Value

$ComputerName = (Get-Item env:\Computername).Value

$filepath = (Get-ChildItem env:\userprofile).value

Add-Content  "$Filepath\style.CSS"  -Value " body {

  font-family:Calibri;

  font-size:10pt;

}

th {

  background-color:black;

  color:white;

}

td {

  background-color:#19fff0;

  color:black;

}"

Write-Host "CSS File Created Successfully... Executing Inventory
  Report!!! Please Wait !!!" -ForegroundColor Yellow

#ReportDate

$ReportDate = Get-Date | Select -Property DateTime |ConvertTo-Html
  -Fragment

#General Information

$ComputerSystem = Get-WmiObject -Class Win32_ComputerSystem |

Select -Property Model , Manufacturer , Description ,
  PrimaryOwnerName , SystemType |ConvertTo-Html -Fragment

#Boot Configuration

$BootConfiguration = Get-WmiObject -Class Win32_BootConfiguration |

Select -Property Name , ConfigurationPath | ConvertTo-Html -Fragment

#BIOS Information
```

```powershell
$BIOS = Get-WmiObject -Class Win32_BIOS | Select -Property
  PSComputerName , Manufacturer , Version | ConvertTo-Html -Fragment

#Operating System Information

$OS = Get-WmiObject -Class Win32_OperatingSystem | Select -Property
  Caption , CSDVersion , OSArchitecture , OSLanguage | ConvertTo-Html
  -Fragment

#Time Zone Information

$TimeZone = Get-WmiObject -Class Win32_TimeZone | Select Caption ,
  StandardName |

ConvertTo-Html -Fragment

#Logical Disk Information

$Disk = Get-WmiObject -Class Win32_LogicalDisk -Filter DriveType=3 |

Select SystemName , DeviceID , @{Name="size(GB)";Expression={"{0:N1}"
  -f($_.size/1gb)}}, @{Name="freespace(GB)";Expression={"{0:N1}"
  -f($_.freespace/1gb)}} |

ConvertTo-Html -Fragment

#CPU Information

$SystemProcessor = Get-WmiObject -Class Win32_Processor   |

Select SystemName , Name , MaxClockSpeed , Manufacturer ,
  status |ConvertTo-Html -Fragment

#Memory Information

$PhysicalMemory = Get-WmiObject -Class Win32_PhysicalMemory |

Select -Property Tag , SerialNumber , PartNumber , Manufacturer ,
  DeviceLocator , @{Name="Capacity(GB)";Expression={"{0:N1}"
  -f ($_.Capacity/1GB)}} | ConvertTo-Html -Fragment

#Software Inventory

$Software = Get-WmiObject -Class Win32_Product |

Select Name , Vendor , Version , Caption | ConvertTo-Html -Fragment

ConvertTo-Html -Body "<font color = blue><H4><B>Report Executed
  On</B></H4></font>$ReportDate

<font color = blue><H4><B>General
  Information</B></H4></font>$ComputerSystem

<font color = blue><H4><B>Boot
  Configuration</B></H4></font>$BootConfiguration

<font color = blue><H4><B>BIOS Information</B></H4></font>$BIOS

<font color = blue><H4><B>Operating System
  Information</B></H4></font>$OS

<font color = blue><H4><B>Time Zone
  Information</B></H4></font>$TimeZone
```

```
<font color = blue><H4><B>Disk Information</B></H4></font>$Disk

<font color = blue><H4><B>Processor
   Information</B></H4></font>$SystemProcessor

<font color = blue><H4><B>Memory
   Information</B></H4></font>$PhysicalMemory

<font color = blue><H4><B>Software
   Inventory</B></H4></font>$Software" -CssUri  "$filepath\style.CSS"
   -Title "Server Inventory" | Out-File "$FilePath\$ComputerName.html"

Write-Host "Script Execution Completed" -ForegroundColor Yellow

Invoke-Item -Path "$FilePath\$ComputerName.html"
```

Note that the preceding code is not a function—it's just a script. Save this as PS1 and execute the script.

The sample output is shown in the following image:

The script has the following elements:

- Comment block
- Parameter declared for computer name and file path
- Creates CSS file in `C:\` drive for styling
- Report executed date
- General system information
- Boot configuration information

- BIOS information
- OS information
- Time zone settings
- Logical disk information
- CPU information
- Memory information
- Software inventory
- Converts to HTML and outputs in HTML file
- Invoke the HTML file in default browser

Consider the following image:

```
 1 ⊞ <# ··· #>  1
15
16 ⊞ #region - param ...  2
21
22 ⊞ #region - Create CSS...  3
37    Write-Host "CSS File Created Successfully... Executing Inventory Report!!! Please Wait !!!" -ForegroundColor Yellow
38 ⊞ #region ReportDate ...  4
41
42 ⊞ #region General Information ..  5
46
47 ⊞ #region Boot Configuration ...  6
51
52 ⊞ #region BIOS Information ..  7
55
56 ⊞ #region Operating System Information ..  8
59
60 ⊞ #region Time Zone Information ..  9
64
65 ⊞ #region Logical Disk Information ..  10
70
71 ⊞ #region CPU Information ..  11
75
76 ⊞ #region Memory Information ..  12
80
81 ⊞ #region Software Inventory ..  13
85
86 ⊞ #region HTML Body ..  14
98
99 ⊞ #region Invoke the HTML file..  15
```

Let's take an example where we will create an advanced function. Advanced functions include help, parameters, accepting pipelines, and so on.

> Note that, to do this easily, you can open PowerShell ISE, press *CTRL + J*, and choose the **Cmdlet (advanced function)**.

Perform the following steps:

1. Write a simple help block for a function:

    ```
    <#
    .Synopsis
      A script to retrieve OS information.
    .DESCRIPTION
      This PowerShell script will retrieve OS information like Name ,
    OS Architecture, Serial Number and Last Bootup time.
      This script use CIM instance.
    .EXAMPLE
      Get-OSInformation -ComputerName localhost
    .EXAMPLE
      Get-OSInformation -ComputerName localhost , remotecomputer
    .EXAMPLE
      localhost , remotecomputer | Get-OSInformation
    #>
    ```

    The help block has synopsis, description, and three examples.

2. Create a function using the keyword `function` and name it in the
    Verb-Noun form. In our example, this is `Get-OSInformation`, as
    shown in the following command:

    ```
    function Get-OSInformation { #Code goes here}
    ```

3. Use `CmdletBinding`. Take a look at the following code:

    ```
    [CmdletBinding(ConfirmImpact = 'Low', HelpUri =
      'http://chen.about-powershell.com')]
    ```

    I have set the `ConfirmImpact` to low, and I have used `HelpUri` from
    my blog post—just for this example. You can use any valid site that has
    some information. You may wonder, why do we use `CmdletBinding`?
    It is to ease our function creation and to make additional validation for
    our parameters. For more information execute `help about_Functions_
    CmdletBindingAttribute`

4. Declare the parameters. In this example, we will use a single parameter, as shown in the following code:

```
Param
(
    # Param1 help description
    [Parameter(Mandatory=$true,
        HelpMessage = "Please enter valid host
            name",
        ValueFromPipelineByPropertyName=$true,
        ValueFromPipeline = $true,
        Position=0)]
    [String[]]$ComputerName
)
```

Use the following code:

```
Begin
{
    #Intentionally left blank
}
Process
{
    foreach($computer in $ComputerName)
    {
        $params = @{'ComputerName' = $Computer
            'Class' = 'CIM_OperatingSystem'}
        Get-CimInstance @Params |
        Select Caption , OSArchitecture , SerialNumber ,
            LastBootUptime
    }
}
End
{
    #Intentionally left blank
}
```

5. Save the PS1 file in the desired location and call it using a dot sourcing operator. Take a look at the following image:

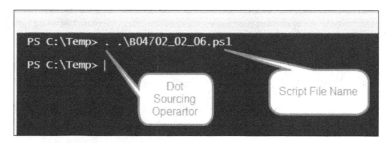

Now, let's call the function using `Get-OSInformation` by skipping the mandatory parameter, as shown in the following image:

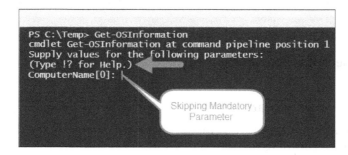

Type `!?` to see the help text, as shown in the following image:

```
PS C:\Temp> Get-OSInformation
cmdlet Get-OSInformation at command pipeline position 1
Supply values for the following parameters:
(Type !? for Help.)
ComputerName[0]: !?
Please enter valid host name
ComputerName[0]: |
```

That's cool! Now, we can see the help message in the parameter block.

Using the help command, we can obtain more information about the command.

The output is illustrated in the following image:

```
PS C:\Temp> help Get-OSInformation
NAME  1
    Get-OSInformation

SYNOPSIS  2
    A script to retrieve OS information.

SYNTAX  3
    Get-OSInformation [-ComputerName] <String[]> [<CommonParameters>]

DESCRIPTION  4
    This PowerShell script will retrieve OS information like Name , OS Architecture, Serial Number and Last Bootup time.
    This script use CIM instance.

RELATED LINKS  5

REMARKS  6
    To see the examples, type: "get-help Get-OSInformation -examples".
    For more information, type: "get-help Get-OSInformation -detailed".
    For technical information, type: "get-help Get-OSInformation -full".
```

The points marked in the figure are explained in the following list:

- **1**: Name of the command appears here.
- **2**: Whatever we enter in the synopsis appears here.
- **3**: Here, syntax appears automatically and it shows the datatype as well.
- **4**: Description is again customized — what we entered in the description section appears here.
- **5**: RELATED LINKS — appears by default if you have included .LINK in the comment block. Used for external web site links.
- **6**: REMARKS — appears by default.

Note that here, the help command will not show the input and output parameters, and so on.

Use the help Get-OSInformation -Full command to explore more.

We used the blog post URL in the help message URI in cmdlet binding; so, to make use of this, we can use the following code:

```
help Get-OSInformation -Online
```

The complete code is available here:

```
<#
.Synopsis
  A script to retrieve OS information.
.DESCRIPTION
```

```
    This PowerShell script will retrieve OS information like Name , OS
      Architecture, Serial Number and Last Bootup time.
    This script use CIM instance.
.EXAMPLE
  Get-OSInformation -ComputerName localhost
.EXAMPLE
  Get-OSInformation -ComputerName localhost , remotecomputer
.EXAMPLE
  localhost , remotecomputer | Get-OSInformation
#>
function Get-OSInformation {
  [CmdletBinding(ConfirmImpact = 'Low', HelpUri =
  'http://chen.about-powershell.com')]
Param(
# Param1 help description
[Parameter(Mandatory=$true,
    HelpMessage = "Please enter valid host name",
    ValueFromPipelineByPropertyName=$true,
    ValueFromPipeline = $true,
    Position=0)]
    [String[]]$ComputerName)
Begin{<#Intentionally left blank#>}
    Process
    {
        foreach($computer in $ComputerName)
        {
            $params = @{'ComputerName' = $Computer
                'Class' = 'CIM_OperatingSystem'}
            Get-CimInstance @Params |
            Select Caption , OSArchitecture , SerialNumber ,
              LastBootUptime
        }
    }
    End
    {
        #Intentionally left blank
    }
}
```

In this section, we will explore Windows PowerShell modules.

Windows PowerShell modules are packages that contain the PowerShell commands. Using modules, we can organize our commands and share them with others.

In this example, we will create a simple module as a demo and this will be a script module. We will discuss all types of modules and demos in the *Understanding PowerShell Modules* section.

A script module is a file (`.psm1`) that contains valid Windows PowerShell code. Script developers and administrators can use this type of module to create modules whose members include functions, variables, and more.

In this example, we have two functions — `Get-OSInformation` and `Get-DiskInformation`. Let's save this as `Sysinformation.PSM1` in the `temp` folder for now.

```
Function Get-SystemInformation
{
    param(
    [Parameter(Mandatory = $true)]
    [String]
    $ComputerName
    )
    $OS = Get-WmiObject -Class Win32_OperatingSystem
    $BIOS = Get-WmiObject -Class Win32_Bios
    $CS = Get-WmiObject -Class Win32_ComputerSystem
    $Properties = New-Object psobject -Property @{

    "OSName" = $OS.Caption
    "ServicePack" = $OS.CSDVersion
    "SerialNumber" = $BIOS.SerialNumber
    "Manufacturer" = $BIOS.Manufacturer
    "BootUpState" = $CS.BootupState
    }
    $Properties
}
Get-SystemInformation -ComputerName localhost
```

Now, we need to import a module; to do this we need to use the `Import-Module` command. In the following code the `-Verbose` and `-Force` parameters are used for a clear output. Take a look at the following image:

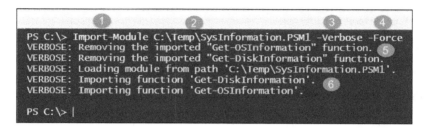

The points marked in the figure are explained in the following list:

- **1**: Here, we use the `Import-Module` cmdlet to import the script module we created. The module name is `SysInformation.PSM1`.

- **2**: Here, we explicitly mention the path—we have saved the script in `C:\Temp\`.

- **3**: `-Verbose` is used to see the verbose data.

- **4**: `-Force` parameter is used to remove the existing script and import it newly.

- **5**: Since we use the force parameter we can see here that the function is being removed.

- **6**: Here, the function is being imported again.

Now, let's call the functions as cmdlet. Take a look at the following image:

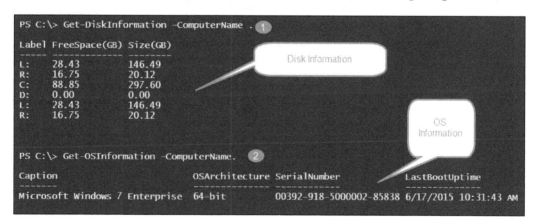

Note that each `Get-OSInformation` and `Get-DiskInformation` cmdlet has its own help information.

Exploring Windows PowerShell 5.0

In this section, we will cover the following topics:

- Basics of Desired State Configuration
- Parsing structured objects using PowerShell
- Exploring Package Management
- Exploring PowerShellGet
- Exploring other enhanced features

Windows PowerShell 5.0 has many significant benefits; to know more about them, refer to the following link:

`http://go.microsoft.com/fwlink/?LinkID=512808`

Here are a few highlights of Windows PowerShell 5.0:

- Improved usability
- Backward compatibility
- `Class` and `enum` keywords are introduced
- Parsing structured objects is easy using the `ConvertFrom-String` command
- We have a few new modules introduced in Windows PowerShell 5.0, such as `Archive`, `Package Management` (formerly known as `OneGet`), and so on
- ISE supports transcriptions
- Using `PowerShellGet`, we can find, install, and publish modules
- Debugging at runspace is possible using the `Microsoft.PowerShell.Utility` module

The basics of Desired State Configuration

Desired State Configuration, also known as DSC, is a new management platform in Windows PowerShell. Using DSC, we can deploy and manage the configuration data for software servicing and can also manage the environment. DSC can be used to streamline a datacenter. This was introduced along with Windows Management Framework 4.0 and was heavily extended in Windows Management Framework 5.0.

Here are a few highlights of DSC in the April 2015 Preview:

- New cmdlets are introduced in WMF 5.0
- A few of the DSC commands are updated, which has made remarkable changes to the configuration management platform in PowerShell 5.0
- The DSC resources can be built using class, so there is no need for a MOF file

It's not mandatory to know PowerShell or to learn DSC, but it adds a great advantage.

This is similar to function, as we can use a configuration keyword; however, there is a huge difference because in DSC everything is declarative. This is a cool feature of Desired State Configuration. So, before beginning this exercise, I created a DSCDemo lab machine in the Azure cloud with Windows Server 2012, and it's available out of the box. So, the default PowerShell version we will use is 4.0.

For now, let's create and define a simple configuration that creates a file in the localhost. Yeah! A simple `New-Item` command can do this, but it's an imperative cmdlet, and we need to write a program to tell the computer to create it if it does not exist.

Let's execute the following code:

Structure of DSC configuration is as follows:

```
Configuration Name
{
    Node ComputerName
    {
        ResourceName <String>
        {

        }
    }
}
```

So now to create a simple text file with contents, we use the following code:

```
Configuration FileDemo
{
    Node $env:COMPUTERNAME
    {
        File FileDemo
        {
            Ensure = 'Present'
            DestinationPath = 'C:\Temp\Demo.txt'
            Contents = 'PowerShell DSC Rocks!'
            Force = $true
        }
    }
}
```

Take a look at the following image:

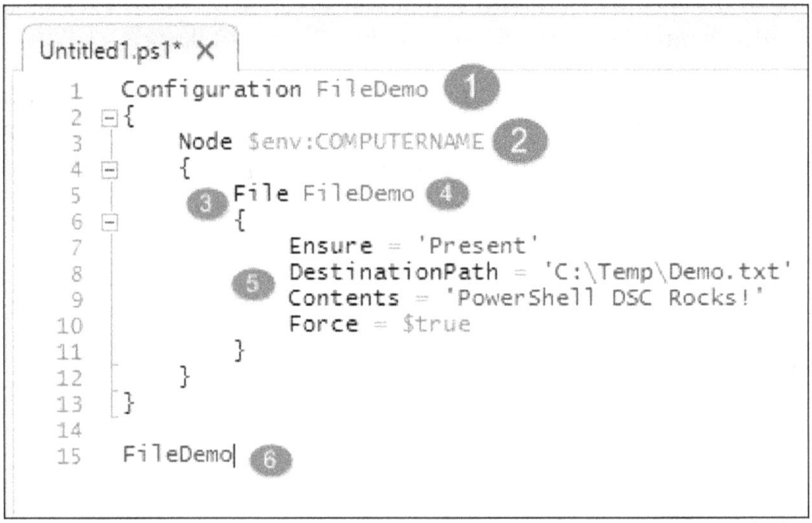

The points marked in the figure are explained in the following list:

- **1**: Here, using the `Configuration` keyword, we are defining a configuration with a name `FileDemo`—it's a friendly name
- **2**: Inside the `Configuration` block, we created a `Node` block and created a file on localhost

- **3**: Here, `File` is the resource name

- **4**: Here, `FileDemo` is a friendly name of the resource, which is a string.

- **5**: These are the properties of the file resource

- **6**: This creates a MOF File—we called this similar to function; but wait, a file is not yet created here. We just created a MOF file.

Look at the MOF file structure in the following image:

```
/*
@TargetNode='DSCDEMOLAB'
@GeneratedBy=ChenV
@GenerationDate=06/23/2015 12:09:02          1
@GenerationHost=DSCDEMOLAB
*/

instance of MSFT_FileDirectoryConfiguration as $MSFT_FileDirectoryConfiguration1ref   2
{
ResourceID = "[File]FileDemo";
 Ensure = "Present";
 Contents = "PowerShell DSC Rocks!";
 DestinationPath = "C:\\Temp\\Demo.txt";
 Force = True;
 ModuleName = "PSDesiredStateConfiguration";
 SourceInfo = "::5::9::File";
 ModuleVersion = "1.0";

};

instance of OMI_ConfigurationDocument   3
{
 Version="1.0.0";
 Author="ChenV";
 GenerationDate="06/23/2015 12:09:02";
 GenerationHost="DSCDEMOLAB";
};
```

We can manually edit the MOF file and use it on other machines that have PS 4.0 installed. It's not mandatory to use PowerShell to generate a MOF, but if you are comfortable with PowerShell, you can directly write the MOF file.

To explore the available DSC Resources, you can execute the following command:

```
Get-DscResource
```

The output is illustrated in the following image:

The points marked in the figure are explained in the following list:

- **1**: This shows how the resources are implemented, which can be `Binary`, `Composite`, `PowerShell`, and so on. In the preceding example, we created a DSC configuration, that is `FileDemo` and that is listed as `Composite`.

- **2**: This is the name of the resource.

- **3**: This is the module name the resource belongs to.

- **4**: These are the properties of resources.

To know the syntax of a particular DSC resource we can try the following code:

```
Get-DscResource -Name Service -Syntax
```

The output is illustrated in the following image which shows the resource syntax in detail:

Now, let's take a look at how DSC works and its three different phases, which are as follows:

- The Authoring phase
- The Staging phase
- The "Make it so" phase

The Authoring phase

In this phase, we will create a DSC configuration using PowerShell, and this will output a MOF file. We have seen a `FileDemo` example for creating a configuration. This is considered to be the Authoring phase.

The Staging phase

In this phase, the declarative MOF file will be staged as per its node (a MOF file will be created for each computer). DSC has the push and pull model, where push simply pushes configuration to the target nodes. The custom providers need to be manually placed in the target machines. On the other hand, in the pull model, we need to build an IIS server that will have the MOF files as the target nodes. This is well defined by the OData interface. In the pull model, the custom providers are downloaded to target system.

The "Make it so" phase

This is the phase used to enact the configuration. In other words, here we will apply the configuration on the target nodes.

We will cover the multinode configuration and the other DSC topic details in *Chapter 3*, *Exploring Desired State Configuration*.

Before we summarize the basics of DSC, let's take a look at a few more DSC commands. We can do this by executing the following command:

```
Get-Command -Noun DSC*
```

The output is as shown in the following image:

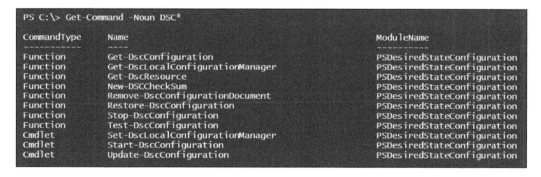

 Note that we are using the PowerShell 4.0 stable release and not 5.0; so, the version property for the cmdlet will not be listed.

Local Configuration Manager (**LCM**) is the engine for DSC, and this runs on all the nodes. LCM is responsible for calling the configuration resources that are included in a DSC configuration script. Try executing the `Get-DscLocalConfigurationManager` cmdlet to explore its properties. To apply the LCM settings on the target nodes, we can use the `Set-DscLocalConfigurationManager` cmdlet.

Use case of classes in WMF 5.0

Using classes in PowerShell gets IT professionals, system administrators, and system engineers to start learning development.

Okay, it's time for us to switch back to Windows PowerShell 5.0 because the `Class` keyword is supported in the versions from 5.0 onward. You may wonder, why do we need to write class in PowerShell? Is it specially needed? Perhaps in this section, we will answer this, but this is one reason for which I would say that PowerShell is far better than scripting language.

When the class keyword was introduced, it was mainly focused at creating DSC resources. However, using class, we can create objects as we would with any other object-oriented programming language. The class we will create in Windows PowerShell is truly a .NET framework type.

You may now wonder, how do we create a PowerShell class? It's easy: just use the `Class` keyword! The following steps will help you to create a PowerShell class:

1. Create a class using the command `Class ClassName {}` — This is an empty class.

2. Define properties in the class using the command `Class ClassName {$Prop1 , $prop2}`

3. Instantiate the class using the command `$var = [ClassName]::New()`

4. Now, take a look at the output of `$var`:

```
Class ClassName {
  $Prop1
  $Prop2
}
$var = [ClassName]::new()
$var
```

In this example, we will take a look at how to create a class and what its advantages are.

Define `Properties` in `Class`; run the following command:

```
Class Catalog
{
  #Properties
  $Model = 'Fujitsu'
  $Manufacturer = 'Life Book S Series'
}


$var = New-Object Catalog
$var
```

The following image shows the output of class, its members, and setting of the property value:

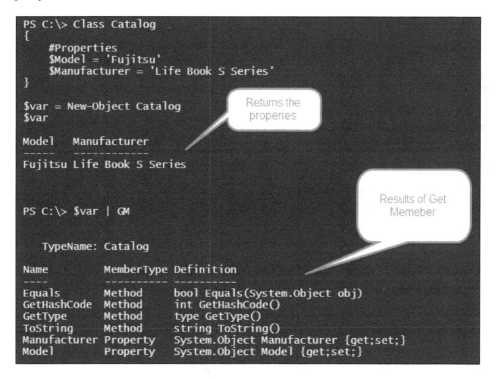

If we change the property value, the output will be as shown in the following image:

Now, let's create a method with the overloads. In the following example, we will create a method named SetInformation that will accept two arguments, $mdl and $mfgr, and these are of the String type.

Using $var.SetInformation, and with no parentheses, we will take a look at the overload definitions of the method.

Execute the following code:

```
Class Catalog
{
  #Properties
  $Model = 'Fujitsu'
  $Manufacturer = 'Life Book S Series'
  SetInformation([String]$mdl,[String]$mfgr)
  {
    $this.Manufacturer = $mfgr
    $this.Model = $mdl
  }
}
$var = New-Object -TypeName Catalog
$var.SetInformation
#Output
OverloadDefinitions
-------------------
void SetInformation(string mdl, string mfgr)
```

Let's set Model and Manufacturer using Set information, as follows:

```
Class Catalog
{
  #Properties
```

```
    $Model = 'Fujitsu'
    $Manufacturer = 'Life Book S Series'
    SetInformation([String]$mdl,[String]$mfgr)
    {
        $this.Manufacturer = $mfgr
        $this.Model = $mdl
    }
}
$var = New-Object -TypeName Catalog
$var.SetInformation('Surface' , 'Microsoft')
$var
```

The output is illustrated in the following image:

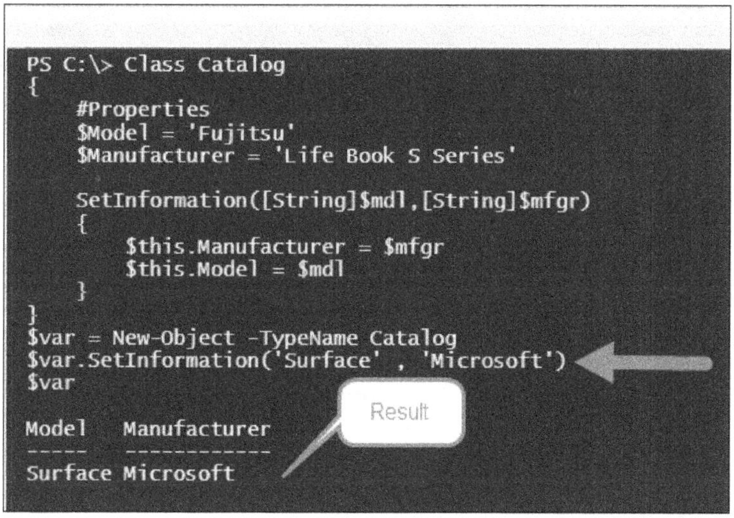

In PowerShell class, we can use the PowerShell cmdlets as well. The following code is just a demo of using the PowerShell cmdlet.

Class allows us to validate the parameters as well. Let's take a look at the code in the following example:

```
Class Order
{
    [ValidateSet("Red" , "Blue" , "Green")]
    $color
    [ValidateSet("Audi")]
```

```
$Manufacturer
Book($Manufacturer , $color)
{
   $this.color = $color
   $this.Manufacturer = $Manufacturer
}
}
```

The $Color and $Manufacturer parameters have a ValidateSet attribute, which has a set of values. Now, let's use New-Object and set property with an argument that doesn't belong to this set. Run the following command:

```
$var = New-Object Order
$var.color = 'Orange'
```

Now, we will get the following error:

```
Exception setting "color": "The argument "Orange" does not belong to
   the set "Red,Blue,Green" specified by the ValidateSet attribute.
   Supply an argument that is in the set and then try the command
   again."
```

Let's set the argument values correctly to get the result using the Book method:

```
$var = New-Object Order
$var.Book('Audi' , 'Red')
$var
```

The output is illustrated in the following image:

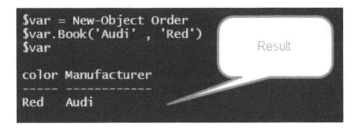

Constructors

A constructor is a special type of method that creates new objects. It has the same name as the class, and the return type is `void`. Multiple constructors are supported, but each one has to take different numbers and types of parameters. In this exercise, let's take a look at the steps to create a simple constructor in PowerShell that will create a user in the active directory. Execute the following code:

```
Class ADUser {
  $identity
  $Name
  ADUser($Idenity , $Name) {
    New-ADUser -SamAccountName $Idenity -Name $Name
    $this.identity = $Idenity
    $this.Name = $Name
  }
}
$var = [ADUser]::new('Dummy' , 'Test Case User')
$var
```

The output of the code we just saw is illustrated in the following image:

We can also hide the properties in a PowerShell class; as an example, let's create two properties and hide one. In theory, it hides the property but we can still use it. Execute the following code:

```
Class Hide {
  [String] $Name
  Hidden $ID
}
$var = [Hide]::new()
$var
```

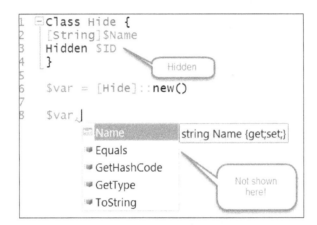

However, we can perform operations such as Get and Set, as shown in the following code:

```
Class Hide {
  [String] $Name
  Hidden $ID
}
$var = [Hide]::new()
$var.Id = '23'
$var.Id
```

This will return the output as 23.

To know more about the class, use help about_Classes -Detailed.

Parsing structured objects using PowerShell

In Windows PowerShell 5.0, a new cmdlet, `ConvertFrom-String`, has been introduced, and this is available in the `Microsoft.PowerShell.Utility` module.

Using this command, we can parse structured objects from any given string content. For more information, use `help ConvertFrom-String -Detailed`.

 Note that the help has an incorrect parameter, `PropertyName`. Copying and pasting will not work, so you need to use the `ConvertFrom-String -Parameter *` help command and read the parameter—it's actually `PropertyNames`.

Now, let's consider an example where we will use `ConvertFrom-String`.

The scenario is such that a team has custom code that generates a log file to create a daily health checkup report of its environment. Unfortunately, the tool delivered by the vendor is an EXE file, and there is no source code available. The log file format is as follows:

```
"Error 4356 Lync" , "Warning 6781 SharePoint" , "Information 5436
  Exchange",
"Error 3432 Lync" , "Warning 4356 SharePoint" , "Information 5432
  Exchange"
```

There are many ways to manipulate this record, but let's take a look at how the PowerShell cmdlet, `ConvertFrom-String`, can help us. Using the following code, we will simply extract `Type`, `EventID`, and `Server`:

```
"Error 4356 Lync" , "Warning 6781 SharePoint" , "Information 5436
  Exchange",
"Error 3432 Lync" , "Warning 4356 SharePoint" , "Information 5432
  Exchange" |
ConvertFrom-String -PropertyNames Type , EventID, Server
```

So what's interesting in this? It's cool because now your output is a `PSCustomObject` object, which you can manipulate as required. Take a look at the following image:

```
PS C:\> "Error 4356 Lync" , "Warning 6781 SharePoint" , "Information 5436 Exchange",
"Error 3432 Lync" , "Warning 4356 SharePoint" , "Information 5432 Exchange" |
ConvertFrom-String -PropertyNames Type  , EventID, Server  | GM

    TypeName: System.Management.Automation.PSCustomObject

Name         MemberType   Definition
----         ----------   ----------
Equals       Method       bool Equals(System.Object obj)
GetHashCode  Method       int GetHashCode()
GetType      Method       type GetType()
ToString     Method       string ToString()
EventID      NoteProperty int16 EventID=4356
Server       NoteProperty string Server=Lync
Type         NoteProperty string Type=Error
```

Following is the output we just saw in the image:

```
"Error 4356 Lync" , "Warning 6781 SharePoint" , "Information 5436
  Exchange",
```

```
"Error 3432 SharePoint" , "Warning 4356 SharePoint" , "Information
  5432 Exchange" |
```

```
ConvertFrom-String -PropertyNames Type , EventID, Server | ?
  {$_.Type -eq 'Error'}
```

One of the outputs is `Lync`, and SharePoint has some error logs that need to be looked at as a priority. As your requirements may vary, you can use this cmdlet in whichever way you need.

`ConvertFrom-String` has a delimiter parameter that helps us to manipulate the strings as well. In the following example, let's use the `-Delimiter` parameter, which removes white spaces and returns the properties:

```
"Chen V" | ConvertFrom-String -Delimiter "\s" -PropertyNames
  "FirstName" , "SurName"
```

This outputs `FirstName` and `SurName` as the result—`FirstName` as `Chen` and `SurName` as `V`.

In this example, we will walk you through using the template file to manipulate the string as we need. To do this, we need to use the `TemplateContent` parameter. You can use `help ConvertFrom-String –Parameter TemplateContent`.

Before we begin, we need to create a template file; to do this, let's ping a website, `www.microsoft.com`, which will return the outputs as follows:

```
Pinging e10088.dspb.akamaiedge.net [2.21.47.138] with 32 bytes of
  data:
Reply from 2.21.47.138: bytes=32 time=37ms TTL=51
Reply from 2.21.47.138: bytes=32 time=35ms TTL=51
Reply from 2.21.47.138: bytes=32 time=35ms TTL=51
Reply from 2.21.47.138: bytes=32 time=36ms TTL=51
Ping statistics for 2.21.47.138:
  Packets: Sent = 4, Received = 4, Lost = 0 (0% loss),
Approximate round trip times in milli-seconds:
  Minimum = 35ms, Maximum = 37ms, Average = 35ms
```

Now that we have the information in some structure, let's extract the IP and the bytes to do this. I replaced the IP and the bytes with {IP*:2.21.47.138}, as follows:

```
Pinging e10088.dspb.akamaiedge.net [2.21.47.138] with 32 bytes of
  data:
Reply from {IP*:2.21.47.138}: bytes={[int32]Bytes:32} time=37ms
  TTL=51
Reply from {IP*:2.21.47.138}: bytes={[int32]Bytes:32} time=35ms
  TTL=51
Reply from {IP*:2.21.47.138}: bytes={[int32]Bytes:32} time=36ms
  TTL=51
Reply from {IP*:2.21.47.138}: bytes={[int32]Bytes:32} time=35ms
  TTL=51
Ping statistics for 2.21.47.138:
  Packets: Sent = 4, Received = 4, Lost = 0 (0% loss),
Approximate round trip times in milli-seconds:
  Minimum = 35ms, Maximum = 37ms, Average = 35ms
```

The output is illustrated in the following figure:

```
PS C:\> ping www.microsoft.com | ConvertFrom-String -TemplateFile C:\Temp\Template.txt

IP            Bytes
--            -----
2.21.47.138      32
2.21.47.138      32
2.21.47.138      32
2.21.47.138      32
```

`ConvertFrom-String` has a debug parameter. Using this, we can debug our template file. In the following example, let's consider the debugging output:

```
ping www.microsoft.com | ConvertFrom-String -TemplateFile
  C:\Temp\Template.txt -Debug
```

```
PS C:\> ping www.microsoft.com | ConvertFrom-String -TemplateFile C:\Temp\Template.txt -Debug
DEBUG: Property: IP
Program: <SequenceProgram symbol="Nl" score="5481" ><NonterminalNode symbol="$Nl" rule="LinesMap">
  <NonterminalNode symbol="$l1" rule="SingleLinePositionPair">
    <VariableNode symbol="$v" />
    <NonterminalNode symbol="$Pl" rule="RegPos1">
      <VariableNode symbol="$s1" />
      <NonterminalNode symbol="$RR" rule="RegexPair">
        <LiteralNode symbol="$r">
          <RegularExpression />
        </LiteralNode>
        <LiteralNode symbol="$r">
          <RegularExpression>
            <Token name="Date" score="109" isSymbol="true"><![CDATA[((?<!\d)(\d?\d)([-\/\.])(\d?\d)\3(19|20)?\d\d(?!\d)|(?<!\d)(19|20)?\d\d
([-\/\.])(\d?\d)\/(\d?\d)(?!\d))]]></Token>
          </RegularExpression>
        </LiteralNode>
      </NonterminalNode>
      <LiteralNode symbol="$k"><![CDATA[1]]></LiteralNode>
    </NonterminalNode>
    <NonterminalNode symbol="$Pl" rule="RegPos1">
      <VariableNode symbol="$s1" />
      <NonterminalNode symbol="$RR" rule="RegexPair">
        <LiteralNode symbol="$r">
          <RegularExpression>
            <Token name="IP" score="109" isSymbol="true"><![CDATA[(?<!\d)(?:(?:25[0-5]|2[0-4][0-9]|[01]?[0-9][0-9]?)\.){3}(?:25[0-5]|2[0-4]
[0-9]|[01]?[0-9][0-9]?)(?!\d))]]></Token>
```

 Note that as we mentioned earlier, PowerShell 5.0 is a preview release and has a few bugs. Let's ignore these for now and focus on the features that work fine and can be utilized in our environment.

Exploring Package Management

In this topic, we will walk you through the features of Package Management. This is another great feature of Windows Management Framework 5.0. This is introduced in Windows 10, and formerly, Package Management was known as OneGet.

Using Package Management, we can automate software discovery, installation of software, and inventorying. Do not think about **Software Inventory Logging** (SIL) for now; we will cover that later in *Chapter 3, Exploring Desired State Configuration.*

As we know, the Windows software installation technology has its own way of installing, for example MSI, MSU and so on. It is a real challenge for IT professionals and DevOps to think about unique automation of software installation / deployments. Now, we can do it using the Package Management module.

To begin with, let's take a look at the Package Management module using the following code:

```
Get-Module -Name PackageManagement
```

The output is illustrated in the following image:

Well, we've got an output showing that it's a binary module. So, how do we find the available cmdlets and their usage? PowerShell always has the simplest way of doing things! Execute the following code:

```
Get-Module -Name PackageManagement
```

The available cmdlets are shown in the following image:

CommandType	Name	Version	Source
Cmdlet	Find-Package	1.0.0.0	PackageManagement
Cmdlet	Get-Package	1.0.0.0	PackageManagement
Cmdlet	Get-PackageProvider	1.0.0.0	PackageManagement
Cmdlet	Get-PackageSource	1.0.0.0	PackageManagement
Cmdlet	Install-Package	1.0.0.0	PackageManagement
Cmdlet	Register-PackageSource	1.0.0.0	PackageManagement
Cmdlet	Save-Package	1.0.0.0	PackageManagement
Cmdlet	Set-PackageSource	1.0.0.0	PackageManagement
Cmdlet	Uninstall-Package	1.0.0.0	PackageManagement
Cmdlet	Unregister-PackageSource	1.0.0.0	PackageManagement

Package providers are nothing but providers connected to Package Management (OneGet), and package sources are registered for the providers. To view the list of providers and sources, we will use the following cmdlets:

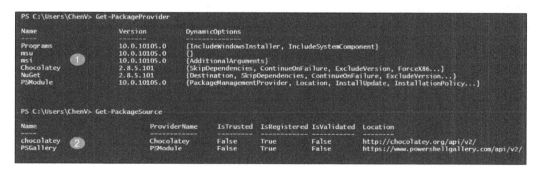

Now, let's take a look at the packages available. In the following example, I will select the first 20 packages just for an easy view:

```
PS C:\> Find-Package | Select -First 20

Name                            Version     Source        Summary
----                            -------     ------        -------
GallioBundle                    3.4         chocolatey    The Gallio platform seeks to facilitate the creation of a rich ecosystem of interoperabl
scummvm                         1.7.0       chocolatey    scummvm
residualvm                      0.1.1       chocolatey    residualvm
WindowsAzurePowershell_0871     0.8.7.1     chocolatey
Leechcraft                      0.6.70.2    chocolatey    LeechCraft is a free open source cross-platform modular live environment.
AzureBuildSDKvs2013             2.4.0       chocolatey    Azure SDK for build servers and Visual Studio 2013
XSockets.PerformanceCounters    0.1         chocolatey    Installs Performance Monitor counters for XSockets.NET v4
GoCiAgent                       14.2.0      chocolatey    Installs Go Agent
linqpad4.AnyCPU.portable        4.51.03     chocolatey    LINQPad 4 (Portable, AnyCPU build for "massive" queries)
poshpuppetreports               0.9.55      chocolatey
ceed                            0.8.0       chocolatey    ceed
simply-weather                  0.2.2       chocolatey    Weather without all the fuss
OrchardCms                      1.8.1.2     chocolatey    Installs an instance of the Orchard Cms
frozenbytes.dev.essentials      1.01        chocolatey    frozenbytes.dev.essentials
csved                           2.3.2       chocolatey    CSVed is an easy and powerful CSV file editor, you can manipulate any CSV file, separate
dtksneak                        1.0.0.1     chocolatey    The DTK Barcode Reader SDK _loves_ to pop up a licensing dialog when running in debug. I
jpegoptim                       1.2.4.4     chocolatey    Utility to optimize jpeg files. Provides lossless optimization (based on optimizing the
resourcesextract                1.18        chocolatey    Extract resource files (bitmaps, icons, html files, and more) from dll files
xbox-one-controller             1.0.0.0     chocolatey    PC Drivers for the Xbox One Controller Now Available
tfsSidekicks                    2.4.0       chocolatey    Team Foundation Sidekicks is a suite of tools for Microsoft Team Foundation Server admin
```

Now, we have 20 packages; using the `Install-Package` cmdlet, let's install `WindowsAzurePowerShell` on our Windows 2012 Server.

We need to ensure that the source is available prior to any installations. To do that, simply execute the `Get-PackageSource` cmdlet. If the source, **chocolatey**, doesn't show up in the output, simply execute the following code; however, do not change any values. This code will install chocolatey in your machine. Once the installation is done, we need to restart PowerShell:

```
Invoke-Expression ((New-Object
  System.Net.WebClient).DownloadString(
  'https://chocolatey.org/install.ps1'))
```

```
Find-Package -Name WindowsAzurePowerShell | Install-Package -Verbose
```

The preceding command shows the confirmation dialog for chocolatey, which is the package source, as shown in the following screenshot:

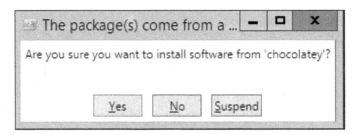

Click on **Yes** to install the package.

```
PS C:\> Find-Package -Name WindowsAzurePowerShell | Install-Package -Verbose
VERBOSE: Performing the operation "Install Package" on target "Package 'WindowsAzurePowershell' version '0.8.8' from 'chocolatey'".
VERBOSE: NuGet: GET http://chocolatey.org/api/v2/Packages(Id='DotNet4.5',Version='4.5')
VERBOSE: NuGet: GET http://chocolatey.org/api/v2/package/DotNet4.5/4.5
VERBOSE: NuGet: Installing 'DotNet4.5 4.5'.
VERBOSE: NuGet: Successfully installed 'DotNet4.5 4.5'.
VERBOSE:
VERBOSE: False
VERBOSE: NuGet: GET http://chocolatey.org/api/v2/Packages(Id='WindowsAzurePowershell',Version='0.8.8')
VERBOSE: NuGet: Attempting to resolve dependency 'DotNet4.5'.
VERBOSE: NuGet: GET http://chocolatey.org/api/v2/package/WindowsAzurePowershell/0.8.8
VERBOSE: NuGet: Installing 'WindowsAzurePowershell 0.8.8'.
VERBOSE: NuGet: Successfully installed 'WindowsAzurePowershell 0.8.8'.
VERBOSE: CreateFolder Success C:\Users\ChenV\AppData\Local\Temp\2\chocolatey\WindowsAzurePowershell
VERBOSE: GetChocolateyWebFile WindowsAzurePowershell => http://az412849.vo.msecnd.net/downloads03/azure-powershell.0.8.8.msi
VERBOSE: Package Successfully Installed WindowsAzurePowershell
VERBOSE: True

Name                          Version    Source        Summary
----                          -------    ------        -------
DotNet4.5                     4.5        chocolatey    The Microsoft .NET Framework 4.5
WindowsAzurePowershell        0.8.8      chocolatey
```

Installed .NET 4.5 and Windows Azure PowerShell

The points marked in the figure are explained in the following list:

- **1**: Here, the prerequisites are installed
- **2**: Here, a temp folder is created
- **3**: Here, the package is installed successfully

Windows Server 2012 has .NET 4.5 in the box by default, so the verbose will turn up as `False` for .NET 4.5. This means that .NET 4.5 will be skipped while enacting the configuration, but `WindowsAzurePowerShell` will be installed successfully. Take a look at the following image:

If you try to install the same package and the same version that is available in your system, the cmdlet will skip the installation. Execute the following code:

```
Find-Package -Name PowerShellHere | Install-Package -Verbose
VERBOSE: Skipping installed package PowerShellHere 0.0.3
```

Explore all the Package Management cmdlets and automate your software deployments.

Exploring PowerShellGet

PowerShellGet is a module available in the Windows PowerShell 5.0 preview. You can do the following using this:

- Search through the modules in the Gallery with `Find-Module`

- Save modules to your system from the Gallery with `Save-Module`

- Install modules from the Gallery with `Install-Module`

- Update your modules to the latest version with `Update-Module`

- Add your own custom repository with `Register-PSRepository`

The following screenshot shows the additional cmdlets that are available:

```
PS C:\> Import-Module 'C:\Program Files\WindowsPowerShell\Modules\PowerShellGet' -Verbose
VERBOSE: Loading module from path 'C:\Program Files\WindowsPowerShell\Modules\PowerShellGet\PowerShellGet.psd1'.
VERBOSE: Loading 'FormatsToProcess' from path 'C:\Program Files\WindowsPowerShell\Modules\PowerShellGet\PSGet.Format.ps1xml'.
VERBOSE: Loading module from path 'C:\Program Files\WindowsPowerShell\Modules\PowerShellGet\PSGet.psm1'.
VERBOSE: Importing function 'Find-Module'.
VERBOSE: Importing function 'Get-InstalledModule'.
VERBOSE: Importing function 'Get-PSRepository'.
VERBOSE: Importing function 'Install-Module'.
VERBOSE: Importing function 'Publish-Module'.
VERBOSE: Importing function 'Register-PSRepository'.
VERBOSE: Importing function 'Save-Module'.
VERBOSE: Importing function 'Set-PSRepository'.
VERBOSE: Importing function 'Uninstall-Module'.
VERBOSE: Importing function 'Unregister-PSRepository'.
VERBOSE: Importing function 'Update-Module'.
VERBOSE: Importing alias 'fimo'.
VERBOSE: Importing alias 'inmo'.
VERBOSE: Importing alias 'pumo'.
VERBOSE: Importing alias 'upmo'.
```

You can refer to this link for more information about PowerShell Gallery:

```
https://www.powershellgallery.com
```

This will allow us to find a module from PowerShell Gallery and install it in our environment. PSGallery is a repository of modules. Using the `Find-Module` cmdlet, we can obtain a list of the modules available in PS Gallery. Pipe and install the required module. Alternatively, we can save the module and examine it before installation; to do this, you need to use the `Save-Module` cmdlet.

The following image illustrates the installation and uninstallation of the xJEA module:

```
PS C:\> Find-Module -Name xJEA | Install-Module -Verbose
VERBOSE: The specified Location is 'https://www.powershellgallery.com/api/v2/' and PackageManagementProvider is 'NuGet'.
VERBOSE: Getting the provider object for the PackageManagement Provider 'NuGet'.
VERBOSE: The specified Location is 'https://www.powershellgallery.com/api/v2/' and PackageManagementProvider is 'NuGet'.
VERBOSE: Performing the operation "Install-Module" on target "Version '0.2.16.6' of module 'xJea'".
VERBOSE: The specified module will be installed in 'C:\Program Files\WindowsPowerShell\Modules'.
VERBOSE: The specified Location is 'NuGet' and PackageManagementProvider is 'NuGet'.
VERBOSE: Downloading module 'xJea' with version '0.2.16.6' from the repository 'https://www.powershellgallery.com/api/v2/'.
VERBOSE: NuGet: GET https://www.powershellgallery.com/api/v2/Packages(Id='xJea',Version='0.2.16.6')
VERBOSE: NuGet: GET https://www.powershellgallery.com/api/v2/package/xJea/0.2.16.6
VERBOSE: NuGet: Installing 'xJea 0.2.16.6'.
VERBOSE: NuGet: Successfully installed 'xJea 0.2.16.6'.
VERBOSE: Module 'xJea' was installed successfully.

PS C:\> Uninstall-Module -Name xJEA -Verbose
VERBOSE: Performing the operation "Uninstall-Module" on target "Version '0.2.16.6' of module 'xJea'".
VERBOSE: Successfully uninstalled the module 'xJea' from module base 'C:\Program Files\WindowsPowerShell\Modules\xJea\0.2.16.6'.

PS C:\> |
```

We can also publish a module in PSGallery, which will be available over the internet for others.

This is not a great module; all it does is get user information from active directory for the same given account name, so you can create a function and save it as PSM1 in the module folder. In order to publish the module in PSGallery, we need to ensure that the module manifests. We will take a look at the details of the modules in the next chapter.

Perform the following steps:

1. Create a PSM1 file.
2. Create a PSD1 file which is a Manifest Module—data file.
3. Get your NuGet API key from the PSGallery link shared before.
4. Publish your module using the Publish-Module cmdlet.

We get the following output:

Manage My Modules

Modules

These modules are currently published for the world to see.

	Module	Module ID	Description	Downloads
✏ 🗑	Testing	Testing	Just for Demo!	0
You have a total of 1 modules.				0

Following figure shows the published module:

Understanding PowerShell modules

Windows PowerShell modules present a simple way to organize and package our script so as to make it distributable and reusable.

In this section, we will cover the following topics:

- What is a module?
- Script modules
- Binary modules
- Manifest modules
- Dynamic modules

Introduction to modules

Windows PowerShell can be created dynamically or persisted to our disk. While discussing PowerShell modules, for a moment I thought about the old-style snap-ins in PowerShell version 1.0, which still exist. Yeah! SharePoint still has snap-ins and not modules.

Snap-ins only contain cmdlets and providers, whereas in modules, we can have functions, variables, aliases, and PowerShell drives.

Before we create a module, we need to know what a module should deliver and where it should be placed. Use this code to find the module path:

```
$env:PSModulePath -split ';'
```

You will see two different paths, where one is the system location and the other is the user profile location, as follows:

```
$ENV:Windir\System32\WindowsPowerShell\v1.0\Modules
```

```
$ENV:UserProfile\Documents\WindowsPowerShell\Modules
```

The folder name and module name should be the same. For example, if you create an `ADUserInformation` module, you need to save it under a folder named `ADUserInformation`.

Script modules

Any valid PowerShell code can be made as a script module. You can create a PowerShell script with a bunch of functions and save it as a PSM1 file, and that would be a script module.

Normally, we save the PowerShell script as PS1; if you save it as PSM1, you can't run the code as a script. Instead, we would need to use the `Import-Module` cmdlet, load the module to the disk, and make use of the cmdlets. The cmdlets here are nothing but your function name, as shown in the following code:

```
Function Get-RunningServices
{
   (Get-Service).Where({$_.Status -eq 'Running'})
}


Function Get-StoppedServices
{
   (Get-Service).Where({$_.Status -eq 'Stopped'})
}
New-Alias -Name grsv -Value Get-RunningServices
New-Alias -Name gssv -Value Get-StoppedServices
Export-ModuleMember -Function * -Alias *
```

Now, we will use the `Import-Module` command to load the module. Take a look at the following image:

The points marked in the figure are explained in the following list:

- 1: Here, all the functions are imported
- 2: Here, all the aliases are imported

The following code will show you the aliases and functions that we will create in the PSM1 file:

```
Get-Module WindowsService | Select ExportedAliases ,
  ExportedFunctions
```

Using Windows PowerShell 5.0, we can write a class, save it as PSM1, and explore the objects. In the following example, we can take a look at how this works:

```
Class Demo
{
    $FirstName
    $SurName
    GetInformation($ID)
    {
        $result = Get-ADUser -Identity $ID
        $this.FirstName = $result.GivenName
        $this.SurName = $result.SurName
    }
}
```

The preceding code will result as shown in the following image:

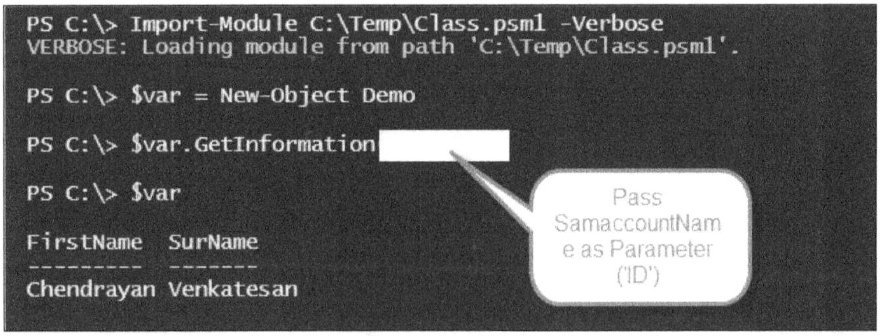

```
PS C:\> Import-Module C:\Temp\Class.psml -Verbose
VERBOSE: Loading module from path 'C:\Temp\Class.psml'.

PS C:\> $var = New-Object Demo

PS C:\> $var.GetInformation

PS C:\> $var

FirstName   SurName
---------   -------
Chendrayan  Venkatesan
```

Pass SamaccountName as Parameter ('ID')

Binary modules

A binary module is an assembly file (the DLL file). Inbuilt PowerShell modules are good examples of binary modules. Execute the following code:

```
Get-Module -Name Microsoft.PowerShell.*
```

Binary modules are faster and easier to build using a PowerShell reference. We can parameterize, validate the parameters, and perform many such functions in binary modules. A great feature in Visual Studio is that while parameterizing, we can get a syntax highlighter, which makes our job easier and faster.

The following exercise will guide us to creating a binary module. It's simple, and all this does is clear the temp files and the temp IE files. For this, we will create three cmdlets and compile them as DLL.

Perform the following steps to create a binary module:

1. Open Visual Studio.
2. Choose **Visual C#** and select **Class Library**.
3. Name your project.
4. Add `System.Management.Automation` DLL as a reference. This is available in your system's GAC assembly folder.
5. Add the code shared in the following section in `Class.cs`.
6. Create the solution, and now we will have the DLL file.
7. Import the DLL file and make use of the PowerShell cmdlet.

Let's take a look at the usage and explanation:

```
using System;
using System.Collections.Generic;
using System.Linq;
using System.Text;
using System.Management;
using System.Management.Automation;
using System.IO;


namespace Windows_Management
{
    [Cmdlet(VerbsCommon.Clear, "TemporaryInternetFiles")]
    public class WindowsManagement : PSCmdlet
    {
        protected override void ProcessRecord()
        {
            //Delete Internet Cache Files and Folders
```

```csharp
            string path = Environment.GetFolderPath(
              Environment.SpecialFolder.InternetCache);
            Console.ForegroundColor = ConsoleColor.DarkYellow;
            Console.WriteLine("Clearing Temporary Internet Cache
              Files and Directories....." + path);
            System.IO.DirectoryInfo folder = new DirectoryInfo(path);
            foreach (FileInfo files in folder.GetFiles())
            {
                try
                {
                    files.Delete();
                }
                catch (Exception ex)
                {
                    System.Diagnostics.Debug.WriteLine(ex);
                }
            }
            foreach (DirectoryInfo Directory in
              folder.GetDirectories())
            {
                try
                {
                    Directory.Delete();
                }
                catch (Exception ex)
                {
                    System.Diagnostics.Debug.WriteLine(ex);
                }
            }
            Console.WriteLine("Done Processing!!!");
            Console.ResetColor();
        }
    }
}
```

```
namespace clearInternetexplorerHistory
{
    [Cmdlet(VerbsCommon.Clear, "IEHistory")]
    public class clearInternetexplorerHistory : PSCmdlet
    {
        protected override void ProcessRecord()
        {
            // base.ProcessRecord();
            string path = Environment.GetFolderPath(
                Environment.SpecialFolder.History);
            Console.ForegroundColor = ConsoleColor.DarkYellow;
            Console.WriteLine("Clearing Internet Explorer
                History....." + path);
            System.IO.DirectoryInfo folder = new DirectoryInfo(path);
            foreach (FileInfo files in folder.GetFiles())
            {
                try
                {
                    files.Delete();
                }
                catch (Exception ex)
                {
                    System.Diagnostics.Debug.WriteLine(ex);
                }
            }
            foreach (DirectoryInfo Directory in
                folder.GetDirectories())
            {
                try
                {
                    Directory.Delete();
                }
                catch (Exception ex)
                {
                    System.Diagnostics.Debug.WriteLine(ex);
                }
            }
```

```
                Console.WriteLine("Done Processing!!!");
                Console.ResetColor();
            }
        }
}
namespace UserTemporaryFiles
{
    [Cmdlet(VerbsCommon.Clear, "UserTemporaryFiles")]
    public class UserTemporaryFiles : PSCmdlet
    {
        protected override void ProcessRecord()
        {
            //base.ProcessRecord();
            string temppath = System.IO.Path.GetTempPath();
            System.IO.DirectoryInfo usertemp = new
              DirectoryInfo(temppath);
            Console.WriteLine("Clearing Your Profile Temporary
              Files..." + temppath);
            foreach (FileInfo tempfiles in usertemp.GetFiles())
            {
                try
                {
                    tempfiles.Delete();
                }
                catch (Exception ex)
                {
                    System.Diagnostics.Debug.WriteLine(ex);
                }
            }
            Console.WriteLine("Done Processing!!!");
            foreach (DirectoryInfo tempdirectory in
              usertemp.GetDirectories())
            {
                try
                {
                    tempdirectory.Delete();
```

```
            }

            catch (Exception ex)

            {

                System.Diagnostics.Debug.WriteLine(ex);

            }

        }

    }

}
}
```

```
PS C:\> Import-Module C:\SystemManagement.dll -Verbose
VERBOSE: Loading module from path 'C:\SystemManagement.dll'. ①
VERBOSE: Importing cmdlet 'Clear-TemporaryInternetFiles'.
VERBOSE: Importing cmdlet 'Clear-IEHistory'.             ②
VERBOSE: Importing cmdlet 'Clear-UserTemporaryFiles'.

PS C:\> Clear-TemporaryInternetFiles   ③
Clearing Temporary Internet Cache Files and Directories.....C:\Users\ChenV\AppData\Local\Microsoft\Windows\INetCache
Done Processing!!!

PS C:\> Clear-IEHistory  ④
Clearing Internet Explorer History.....C:\Users\ChenV\AppData\Local\Microsoft\Windows\History
Done Processing!!!

PS C:\> Clear-UserTemporaryFiles  ⑤
Clearing Your Profile Temporary Files...C:\Users\ChenV\AppData\Local\Temp\2\
Done Processing!!!

PS C:\>
```

- **1**: Here, the DLL is loaded using the `Import-Module` cmdlet
- **2**: Here, the cmdlet is loaded that we coded in the C# class library
- **3**: The cmdlet `Clear-TemporaryInternetFiles` clears the temp IE files
- **4**: The cmdlet `Clear-IEHistory` clears the IE history
- **5**: The cmdlet `Clear-UserTemporaryFiles` clears the user temporary files

Manifest modules

A manifest module is nothing but a data file with a PSD1 extension. This file will describe the contents of the module and how the module process works.

The manifest module is used to export an assembly that is installed in the global assembly cache. A manifest module is also required for modules that support the **Updatable Help** feature. Updatable Help uses the `HelpInfoUri` key in the manifest module to find the help information (HelpInfo XML) file, which contains the location of the updated help files for the module.

A manifest module can be created using PowerShell cmdlets. You can even manually type and save the file as PSD1, but using PowerShell is quicker. In the following example, we will create a manifest module:

```
$Param = @{
  Author = "Chendrayan Venkatesan"
  CompanyName = "Contoso"
  ModuleVersion = "1.0"
  Description = "Module Manifest Demo"
  PowerShellVersion = "5.0"
  Path = "C:\Temp\ModuleManifestDemo.psd1"
}
New-ModuleManifest @Param
```

The preceding code creates a manifest module, as shown in the following image:

```
#
# Module manifest for module 'ModuleManifestDemo'
#
# Generated by: Chendrayan Venkatesan
#
# Generated on: 6/26/2015
#

@{

# Script module or binary module file associated with this manifest.
# RootModule = ''

# Version number of this module.
ModuleVersion = '1.0'

# ID used to uniquely identify this module
GUID = 'abfe91d1-ef13-4d24-8b0f-26642f28eedf'

# Author of this module
Author = 'Chendrayan Venkatesan'

# Company or vendor of this module
CompanyName = 'Contoso'

# Copyright statement for this module
Copyright = '(c) 2015 Chendrayan Venkatesan. All rights reserved.'

# Description of the functionality provided by this module
Description = 'Module Manifest Demo'

# Minimum version of the Windows PowerShell engine required by this module
PowerShellVersion = '5.0'
```

The remaining parameter that we missed will be commented in the manifest module. We can manually edit it using any text editor.

Dynamic modules

A dynamic module is a module that does not persist on the disk but in the memory; so, it will be lost once you close your PowerShell session. This type of modules can be created from the functions and script blocks within the same session, which is useful to developers for a better, object-oriented scripting. It is also useful to administrators at times when they want to execute certain modules on remote computers where they physically exist using PowerShell remoting. Dynamic modules are created using the New-Module cmdlet and with parameters such as -Function and –ScriptBlock, which specify the function and script blocks that are to be included in this module.

In the following example, let's create a dynamic module using the New-Module cmdlet:

```
New-Module -ScriptBlock {Function Print {"Dynamic Module Demo!"};
  Print}
```

This creates a dynamic module with the exported Print cmdlet, as follows:

```
PS C:\> Print
Dynamic Module Demo!
```

Script debugging

Debugging in PowerShell is similar to that in other programming languages. Script debugging is available in the console host as well as in the PowerShell ISE; ISE has both GUI and cmdlet-based debugging, whereas console has only cmdlets to debug your scripts.

The debugging feature in the PowerShell ISE is available under the **Debug** tab, which is self-explanatory. Let's take a look at the breakpoints and debug cmdlets:

```
(Get-Command -Name *Debug*).Where({$_.Source -ne 'Azure' -and
  $_.CommandType -eq 'cmdlet'})
Get-Command -Name *BreakPoint
```

Note that in the first snippet, I used the `where` method to ignore `Azure` and to get only the core cmdlets; the output is illustrated in the following image:

```
PS C:\> (Get-Command -Name *Debug*).where({$_.Source -ne 'Azure' -and $_.CommandType -eq 'cmdlet'})

CommandType     Name                            Version      Source
-----------     ----                            -------      ------
Cmdlet          Debug-Job                       3.0.0.0      Microsoft.PowerShell.Core
Cmdlet          Debug-Process                   3.1.0.0      Microsoft.PowerShell.Management
Cmdlet          Debug-Runspace                  3.1.0.0      Microsoft.PowerShell.Utility
Cmdlet          Disable-RunspaceDebug           3.1.0.0      Microsoft.PowerShell.Utility
Cmdlet          Enable-RunspaceDebug            3.1.0.0      Microsoft.PowerShell.Utility
Cmdlet          Get-RunspaceDebug               3.1.0.0      Microsoft.PowerShell.Utility
Cmdlet          Set-PSDebug                     3.0.0.0      Microsoft.PowerShell.Core
Cmdlet          Wait-Debugger                   3.1.0.0      Microsoft.PowerShell.Utility
Cmdlet          Write-Debug                     3.1.0.0      Microsoft.PowerShell.Utility


PS C:\> Get-Command -Name *BreakPoint

CommandType     Name                            Version      Source
-----------     ----                            -------      ------
Cmdlet          Disable-PSBreakpoint            3.1.0.0      Microsoft.PowerShell.Utility
Cmdlet          Enable-PSBreakpoint             3.1.0.0      Microsoft.PowerShell.Utility
Cmdlet          Get-PSBreakpoint                3.1.0.0      Microsoft.PowerShell.Utility
Cmdlet          Remove-PSBreakpoint             3.1.0.0      Microsoft.PowerShell.Utility
Cmdlet          Set-PSBreakpoint                3.1.0.0      Microsoft.PowerShell.Utility
```

Managing breakpoints

Windows PowerShell has three types of breakpoints. They are as follows:

Line breakpoints

In this, the script pauses when the designated line is reached during the operation of the script. For example, run the following command:

```
$line = Set-psbreakpoint -script C:\Temp\Scriptdemo.ps1 -Line 4
$line | fl
```

The output is as follows:

```
Id       : 6
Script   : C:\Temp\Scriptdemo.ps1
Line     : 4
Column   : 0
Enabled  : True
HitCount : 0
Action   :
```

```
$servers = @('localhost' , 'NotOnline' , 'localhost')
foreach($server in $servers)
{
    Get-WmiObject -Class Win32_OperatingSystem -ComputerName $server
}
```

> Line breakpoint
> enabled

Variable breakpoints

In this, the script pauses whenever the designated variable's value changes. Run the following command:

```
$Variable = Set-psbreakpoint -script C:\Temp\Scriptdemo.ps1 -Variable
  Server
```

```
$Variable
```

Command breakpoints

In this, the script pauses whenever the designated command is about to be run during the operation of the script. It can include parameters to further filter the breakpoint to only the operation that you want. The command can also be a function that you create. Run the following command:

```
$cmd = Set-PSBreakpoint -Command Get-Service
```

```
$cmd | Enable-PSBreakpoint
```

The output is illustrated in the following image:

```
PS C:\> Get-PSBreakpoint -id 13

ID Script                        Line Command                    Variable              Action
-- ------                        ---- -------                    --------              ------
13                                    Get-Service

PS C:\> Enable-PSBreakpoint -Id 13 -Verbose
PS C:\> Get-PSBreakpoint -id 13

ID Script                        Line Command                    Variable              Action
-- ------                        ---- -------                    --------              ------
13                                    Get-Service
```

The `Disable-PSBreakpoint` cmdlet disables the breakpoint temporarily, whereas the `Remove-PSBreakpoint` cmdlet removes the breakpoint permanently.

Debugging scripts

After setting up the required breakpoints, we can debug the scripts by simply executing the PS1 file. In this example, we have enabled only the variable breakpoint. Take a look at the following image:

```
PS C:\Temp> .\Scriptdemo.ps1
Hit Variable breakpoint on 'C:\Temp\Scriptdemo.ps1:$Server' (Write access) ①
Hit Variable breakpoint on 'C:\Temp\Scriptdemo.ps1:$Server' (Write access)
[DBG]: PS C:\Temp>>  ②

[DBG]: PS C:\Temp>>
PS C:\Temp> |
```

The points marked in the figure are explained in the following list:

- **1**: Here, the variable breakpoint is hit for $server. We see it twice because $server is used in two places. To step over use the short cut key *S*.

- **2**: Now, we are in debug mode.

When we do step over, the script in ISE looks like the following image:

```
$servers = @('localhost' , 'NotOnline' , 'localhost')
foreach($server in $servers)
{
    Get-WmiObject -Class Win32_OperatingSystem -ComputerName $server   ①
}
```

In Windows PowerShell 5.0, Wait-Debugger and Debug-Job are the two new debugging cmdlets.

- Debug-Job: This debugs a running background, remote machine, or Windows PowerShell Workflow job

- Wait-Debugger: This stops a script in the debugger before running the next statement in the script, as shown in the following image:

```
PS C:\> $Debug = Start-Job -Name DebugDemo -ScriptBlock {
$var = 1
Wait-Debugger
$var
$var + 10
}

PS C:\> Debug-Job -Job $Debug -Verbose
VERBOSE: Performing the operation "Debug" on target "DebugDemo".
Stopped at: $var
[DBG]: [Job42]: PS C:\Users\904870\Documents>> |
```

In the following example, we have used the `Set-PSBreakPoint` cmdlet instead of the `Wait-Debugger` cmdlet:

```
$job = Start-Job -ScriptBlock { Set-PSBreakpoint
  C:\Temp\Scriptdemo.ps1 -Line 4; C:\Temp\Scriptdemo.ps1 }
$job
```

In the figure we can see that the state is `AtBreakpoint`.

The following cmdlet will enter debug mode of the running job:

```
Debug-Job $job -Verbose
```

Windows PowerShell 5.0 makes it easy for us to debug the PowerShell scripts. Using the `Set-PSBreakPoint` cmdlet, we can pause the execution of the script at a particular line before we proceed further. Just to avoid the risk! Debugging is easy in Windows PowerShell!

Summary

Windows PowerShell 5.0 preview has got many more significant features, such as enhancement in PowerShell DSC, new cmdlets and improvements in existing cmdlets, the ISE supporting transcriptions, supporting Class, the ability to create Custom DSC resources and easy string manipulation using Class, the introduction of the new Network Switch module that helps automate and manage Microsoft-signed network switches, and so on.

In this chapter, we discussed a few great features of Windows PowerShell, such as exploring the basics of DSC, writing classes, PowerShell debugging, and so on.

In the next chapter, we will cover Windows PowerShell 5.0 Desired State Configuration, Remote Management, and more.

3
Exploring Desired State Configuration

In the previous chapter, we covered the basics of Desired State Configuration; this chapter is a continuation of the same.

To learn DSC, you would need to watch the video in Microsoft Virtual Academy.

Here are some useful links:

To get started with Windows PowerShell Desired State Configuration (DSC) – `http://www.microsoftvirtualacademy.com/training-courses/getting-started-with-powershell-desired-state-configuration-dsc-`

For advanced PowerShell Desired State Configuration (DSC) and custom resources – `http://www.microsoftvirtualacademy.com/training-courses/advanced-powershell-desired-state-configuration-dsc-and-custom-resources`

DSC – Desired State Configuration – is a Windows PowerShell extension released with Windows Management Framework 4.0. DSC is a fast-growing technology. Any IT professional or developer responsible for configuration management automation needs DSC. In this chapter, we will cover the following topics:

- The prerequisites for DSC
- Installing WMF 5.0 using DSC
- Imperative versus declarative programming
- Getting started with DSC
- Understanding MOF

- Exploring WinRM and CIM
- Creating and deploying a configuration
- Types of deployment modes

Prerequisites

DSC needs a supporting PowerShell version, which is version 4.0, and operating system from Windows 2008 R2 onwards. DSC is built on CIM and needs the WinRM listeners, service, and script execution policy.

Let's set up a machine to jump-start DSC. Here, we will use a machine working on the Windows Server 2008 R2 operating system with SP1, and the PowerShell version is 2.0. Perform the following steps:

- Download .NET Framework 4.5 using the URL: `http://www.microsoft.com/en-us/download/details.aspx?id=40855`

- Download WMF 4.0 from the following link: `http://www.microsoft.com/en-us/download/details.aspx?id=40855`

Let's take a look at the .NET framework version installed on the Windows 2008 R2 SP1 box from the registry using PowerShell. Run the following command for this:

```
Get-ItemProperty 'HKLM:\SOFTWARE\Microsoft\NET Framework Setup\NDP\v4\Client'
```

The output is illustrated in the following image:

You can also install the .NET Framework 4.5 first and then check the version after successful upgrade of .NET Framework by executing the code mentioned before, which shows the version as 4.5.50709. The machine we will use for this demo doesn't have Windows PowerShell ISE installed, so let's enable the feature using the following PowerShell code:

```
Import-Module ServerManager -Verbose

Get-WindowsFeature -Name '*ISE*' -verbose

Add-WindowsFeature -Name 'PowerShell-ISE' -Verbose
```

Yeah! It's done. Take a look at the following image:

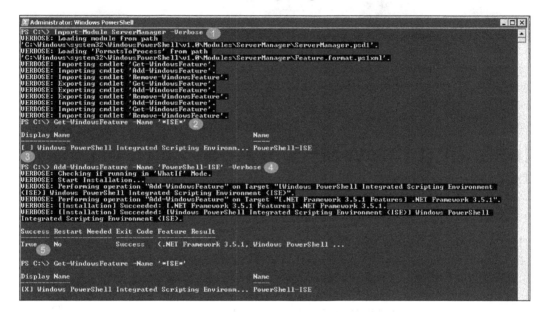

Install the WMF 4.0 MSU file; you can refer to the steps used for this in *Chapter 1, Getting Started with Windows PowerShell*. This installation requires a reboot, so plan according to your production environment. Take a look at the following image:

After the reboot, PS will be upgraded to version 4.0, and we can take a look at the `PSDesiredStateConfiguration` module, as shown in the following image:

```
PS C:\> Get-Module -ListAvailable


    Directory: C:\Windows\system32\WindowsPowerShell\v1.0\Modules


ModuleType Version   Name                                ExportedCommands
---------- -------   ----                                ----------------
Manifest   1.0.0.0   ADRMS                               {Update-ADRMS, Uninstall-ADRMS, Install-ADRMS}
Manifest   1.0.0.0   AppLocker                           {Set-AppLockerPolicy, Get-AppLockerPolicy, Test-AppLockerPolicy, Get-AppLockerFileInformation...}
Manifest   1.0       BestPractices                       {Get-BpaModel, Invoke-BpaModel, Get-BpaResult, Set-BpaResult}
Manifest   1.0.0.0   BitsTransfer                        {Add-BitsFile, Remove-BitsTransfer, Complete-BitsTransfer, Get-BitsTransfer...}
Manifest   1.0.0.0   CimCmdlets                          {Get-CimAssociatedInstance, Get-CimClass, Get-CimInstance, Get-CimSession...}
Script     1.0.0.0   ISE                                 {New-IseSnippet, Import-IseSnippet, Get-IseSnippet}
Manifest   3.0.0.0   Microsoft.PowerShell.Diagnostics    {Get-WinEvent, Get-Counter, Import-Counter, Export-Counter...}
Manifest   3.0.0.0   Microsoft.PowerShell.Host           {Start-Transcript, Stop-Transcript}
Manifest   3.1.0.0   Microsoft.PowerShell.Management      {Add-Content, Clear-Content, Clear-ItemProperty, Join-Path...}
Manifest   3.0.0.0   Microsoft.PowerShell.Security       {Get-Acl, Set-Acl, Get-PfxCertificate, Get-Credential...}
Manifest   3.1.0.0   Microsoft.PowerShell.Utility         {Format-List, Format-Custom, Format-Table, Format-Wide...}
Manifest   3.0.0.0   Microsoft.WSMan.Management           {Disable-WSManCredSSP, Enable-WSManCredSSP, Get-WSManCredSSP, Set-WSManQuickConfig...}
Binary     1.0       PSDesiredStateConfiguration         {Set-DscLocalConfigurationManager, Start-DscConfiguration, Configuration, Get-DscConfiguration...}
Script     1.0.0.0   PSDiagnostics                       {Disable-PSTrace, Disable-PSWSManCombinedTrace, Disable-WSManTrace, Enable-PSTrace...}
Binary     1.1.0.0   PSScheduledJob                      {New-JobTrigger, Add-JobTrigger, Remove-JobTrigger, Get-JobTrigger...}
Manifest   2.0.0.0   PSWorkflow                          {New-PSWorkflowExecutionOption, New-PSWorkflowSession, nwsn}
Manifest   1.0.0.0   PSWorkflowUtility                   Invoke-AsWorkflow
Manifest   1.0.0.0   ServerManager                       {Get-WindowsFeature, Add-WindowsFeature, Remove-WindowsFeature}
Manifest   1.0.0.0   TroubleshootingPack                 {Get-TroubleshootingPack, Invoke-TroubleshootingPack}
```

We have now successfully installed Windows Management Framework 4.0; in the next chapter, we will discuss the steps to upgrade WMF to version 5.0, the April 2015 preview, using DSC.

Installing the WMF 5.0 April 2015 preview

The latest released version of WMF 5.0 is the April 2015 preview. It's good to read the release document, refer the following link: `https://www.microsoft.com/en-us/download/details.aspx?id=46889`

The PowerShell team releases experimental DSC resources to configure an environment, and the latest DSC resource kit is **Wave 10**. Let's download this from the **TechNet Gallery** website (`https://gallery.technet.microsoft.com/scriptcenter/DSC-Resource-Kit-All-c449312d`) to install WMF 5.0 because we need the **xHotfix** resource to perform this action. We will discuss all about the DSC resources later in this chapter.

Note that from April 2015 onward, the DSC resource kit has been outsourced to **GitHub**.

The central repository for DSC resources can be found at `https://github.com/powershell/DscResources`.

In this example, we will install the MSU file for WMF 5.0 using DSC; to do this, we will use the `Configuration` keyword with the following script block:

```
Configuration WMF5
{
    Import-DscResource -ModuleName xWindowsUpdate
```

```
Node localhost
{
    xHotfix WMFInstall
    {
        Path = 'C:\Users\ChenV\Downloads\Windows6.1-KB2908075-x64.msu'
        Id = 'KB2908075'
        Ensure = 'Present'
    }
}
}
WMF5
```

How does this work? Take a look at the following image:

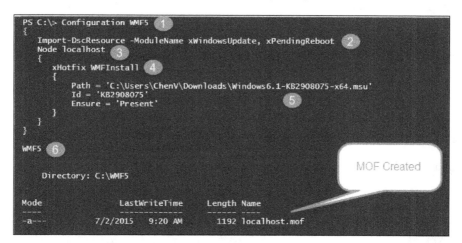

The points marked in the figure are explained in the following list:

- **1**: Here, we use the `Configuration` keyword and keyword and block.

- **2**: Here, we import the experimental DSC resource, `xWindowsUpdate`. `Import-DscResource` should be inside the configuration block.

- **3**: Here, we declare the node. We will use the localhost.

- **4**: Here, we use the xHotfix DSC resource and give it a friendly name.

- **5**: Here, we declare the DSC properties— `Path`, `ID`, and `Ensure`.

- **6**: Here, we call the configuration to create an MOF file. As you did with the function, use a friendly name.

- **MOF Created**: Here, we have successfully created our MOF file.

After creating the MOF file, we can apply the configuration using `Start-DscConfiguration`. Wait! First, let's do some additional setting up, such as updating the help, execution policy, WinRM services, and so on. Take a look at the following code. It will update the help files, modify the execution policy to `RemoteSigned`, and `Set-WSManQuickConfig` in it will do the following:

- It will check whether the WinRM service is running. If it is not running, the service will be started.
- It will set the WinRM service startup type to automatic.
- It will create a listener that will accept requests on any IP address. By default, the transport is HTTP.
- It will enable a firewall exception for the WinRM traffic.

By default, WinRM is enabled in Windows Server 2012 and Windows 8.1. We will perform this action here because we will be using Windows Server 2008 R2 SP1.

`Start-DscConfiguration` will apply the configuration on the target node, which is our localhost. Run the following command:

```
Update-Help -Verbose

Set-ExecutionPolicy -ExecutionPolicy RemoteSigned -Verbose

Set-WSManQuickConfig -Verbose

Start-DscConfiguration .\WMF5 -Wait -Force -WhatIf
```

Let's take a look at the output of `Start-DSConfiguration`:

The points marked in the figure are explained in the following list:

- **1**: Here, the configuration is started
- **2**: Here, a test is performed to check whether the hotfix is present
- **3**: Here, the path is validated
- **4**: Here, it shows the time consumed for validation
- **5**: Here, since we haven't provided the log path, DSC creates a log file in `C:\Windows\Temp`

- **6**: Here, the MSU installation happens using `wsusa.exe`
- **7**: Here, the installation is completed
- **8**: Here, it shows the total time consumed to apply the configuration

After a reboot, we can see that the updates are being installed, as in the following image:

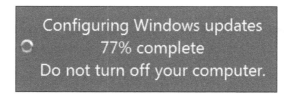

We have applied the configuration successfully; the box is in WMF 5.0, as shown in the following image:

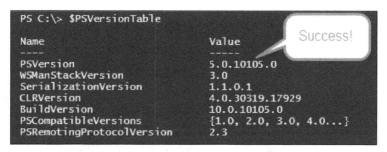

Imperative versus declarative programming

Imperative programming means describing the computations in terms of statements, as we do in procedural programming. In imperative programming, we instruct the computer on which operation to do and how to do it. It is an explicit sort of coding. For example, we use imperative programming to perform certain operations and catch all the exceptions that may occur, or to install software if it does not exist on a specific machine. PowerShell uses imperative programming style, except in the DSC feature. In the preceding topic, we installed the PowerShell ISE using the `ServerManager` module, which is an imperative programming practice. Let's revisit it—what we will do here is check whether the PowerShell ISE feature is installed; if not, we will proceed with the installation.

We removed the PowerShell ISE using the `Remove-WindowsFeature` cmdlet. Now, we will execute the following code to install the PowerShell ISE:

```
Import-Module ServerManager
If (-not (Get-WindowsFeature -Name "PowerShell-ISE").Installed) {
    try {
        Write-Host "Feature is not available....Installation begins...."
-ForegroundColor Green
        Add-WindowsFeature -Name "PowerShell-ISE" -ErrorAction Stop
-Verbose
    }
    catch {
        $_.Exception
    }
}
```

How does this work? Take a look at the following image:

- It imports the `ServerManager` module
- It checks the installation status; if this is true, no action is taken
- If the installation status returns false, the installation will begin
- Adding the PowerShell ISE feature doesn't need a reboot, but removing it requires one.

Let's take a look at how the same operation can be performed using PowerShell DSC.

In PowerShell DSC, we can do this using declarative syntax. For this, we will use the `Configuration` block, as shown in the following code:

```
Configuration InstallISE
{
    Node localhost
    {
        WindowsFeature ISE
        {
            Name =  'PowerShell-ISE'
            IncludeAllSubFeature = $true
            LogPath = 'C:\LogISE.txt'
            Ensure = 'Present'
        }
    }
}
InstallISE
```

Take a look at the verbose message in the following image—here, it skipped the installation because the feature is already installed:

By simply changing the `Ensure` property to `Absent`, we can uninstall the feature, as shown in the following code:

```
Configuration InstallISE
{
    Node $ENV:COMPUTERNAME
    {
        WindowsFeature ISE
        {
            Name =    'PowerShell-ISE'
            IncludeAllSubFeature = $true
            LogPath = 'C:\LogISE.txt'
            Ensure = 'Absent'
        }
    }
}
InstallISE
```

Take a look at the verbose message, which appears while applying the configuration, in the following image; it informs us about the reboot, so the action is not completed until we reboot the machine:

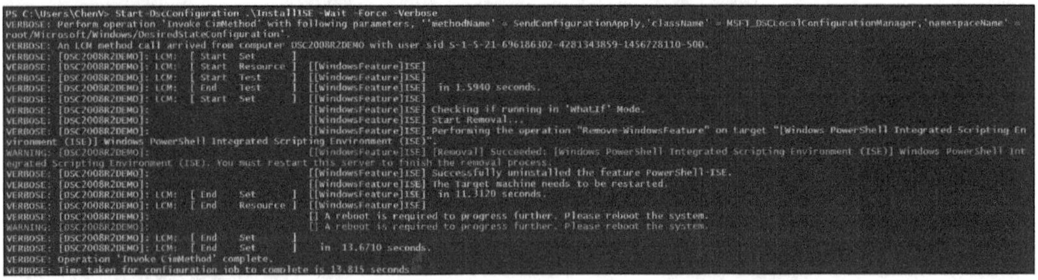

Here is a comparison of imperative and declarative programming:

Imperative	Declarative
This describes the task in statements.	This describes the action required.
A step-by-step procedure of execution is required in the code.	In this, we describe the requirement in the code, and the machine executes the task as required.

Let's review a few more declarative samples to study DSC's features and benefits.

Getting started with DSC

Using DSC, we can configure our environment through codes. As we know, PowerShell DSC is not a tool; it is a configuration management platform. DSC uses a `Configuration` keyword. If you are an IT professional or developer responsible for infrastructure compliance and automation, DSC will help you perform most of your tasks easily and swiftly.

DSC enables a consistent infrastructure, standardized configuration, and continuous deployments. Using DSC, we can remediate the drift in our environment. Following are a few of the most common use cases of DSC:

- Enabling or disabling server roles and features
- Managing registry settings
- Managing files and directories
- Starting, stopping, and managing processes and services
- Managing groups and user accounts
- Deploying new software
- Managing environment variables
- Running Windows PowerShell scripts
- Fixing a configuration that has drifted away from the desired state
- Discovering the actual configuration state on a given node

The architecture of DSC is illustrated in the following image:

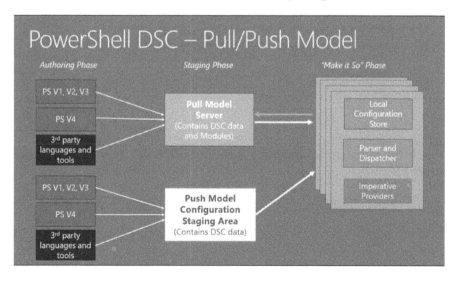

Now, it's time for us to explore all the three phases of DSC shown in the preceding image. This image is taken from `http://blogs.technet.com/b/ privatecloud/archive/2013/08/30/introducing-powershell-desired-state- configuration-dsc.aspx`.

The Authoring phase

DSC can be created using PowerShell or any other third-party extensions. We will stick to PowerShell because that's our scope. This is the phase where the configuration is authored using declarative scripting.

Configuration is the core component of DSC, and the base structure looks similar to the following:

```
Configuration <Identifier>
{

}
```

Here, `Configuration` is the keyword and `Identifier` is the string (or friendly name) of our configuration, followed by the { } block. Inside the configuration block, we will use `Node` and the resources as illustrated in the following code:

```
Configuration Test
{
    Node localhost
    {
        File Test
        {

        }
    }
}
```

Here, `Node` is the target node, and `File` is the built-in resource used to manage the file or directories.

Let's switch to Windows Server 2012 to continue the demo; there are a few differences in this, but the PS version remains the same. Execute the following code:

```
Configuration Test
{
    Node localhost
    {
        File Test
        {
            Ensure = 'Present'
            DestinationPath = 'C:\'
            Contents = 'PowerShell DSC'
        }
    }
}
Test
```

The configuration script creates a folder as Test (name of the configuration we created) in C:\ and saves the MOF file over there. Take a look at the following image, which shows the Test folder and the localhost.mof file:

```
    Directory: C:\Test    ①


Mode                LastWriteTime         Length Name        ②
----                -------------         ------ ----
-a----        8/24/2015  12:03 PM           1892 localhost.mof
```

The Staging phase

Once the configuration script is created and executed, the next phase is staging, which is nothing but generating the MOF file. We haven't discussed the Push and Pull modes yet, so we will save the MOF file in a local machine. The MOF file can be saved in a central location, **Server Message Block (SMB)**, with the appropriate access to write MOF.

The preceding image shows the generated MOF; this is not enacted yet. This is a staging phase.

The "Make it so" phase

The enactment of the configuration takes place in this phase, and then the configuration script applies the changes to the target nodes. The configuration is applied on the target node using **Local Configuration Manager** (**LCM**), which is an engine that comes with WMF versions from 4.0.

In PowerShell 5.0, the LCM version is 2.0, which is significantly improved. To see the meta configuration of LCM, we can execute the following codes; both return the same result:

```
Get-CimClass -ClassName MSFT_DscMetaConfiguration -Namespace root/
microsoft/Windows/DesiredStateConfiguration | Select -ExpandProperty
CimClassProperties | Select Name

Get-DscLocalConfigurationManager | GM -MemberType Properties | Select
Name
```

Now, let's push the configuration using the `Start-DscConfiguration` cmdlet, and take a look at the LCM state. This enacts the configuration in the localhost and changes are effected immediately, as shown in the following image:

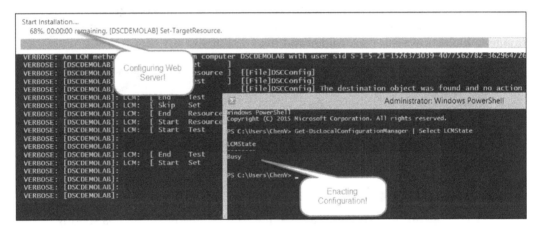

Local Configuration Manager

Local Configuration Manager is the engine of Windows PowerShell DSC. The configurations we push to the nodes are parsed using LCM, and it gets the required resources to keep the machine in the desired state.

To modify the LCM settings, you can use the following code:

```
[DscLocalConfigurationManager()]
Configuration LCM
{
    Node localhost
    {
        Settings
        {
            RebootNodeIfNeeded = $true
        }
    }
}
LCM
```

In the preceding example, we enacted the configuration using `Start-DscConfiguration`, but to apply the meta configuration changes, we need to use the `Set-DscLocalConfigurationManager` cmdlet.

If we execute the preceding code, it would create an MOF file such as `NodeName.Meta.MOF`. Running the following command changes the LCM settings:

```
PS C:\> Set-DscLocalConfigurationManager .\LCM -Verbose
VERBOSE: Performing the operation "Start-DscConfiguration: SendMetaConfigurationApply" on target "MSFT_DSCLocalConfigurationManager".
VERBOSE: Perform operation 'Invoke CimMethod' with following parameters, ''methodName' = SendMetaConfigurationApply,'className' = MSFT_DSCLocalConfigurationM
anager,'namespaceName' = root/Microsoft/Windows/DesiredStateConfiguration'.
VERBOSE: An LCM method call arrived from computer DSCDEMOLAB with user sid S-1-5-21-1526373039-4077562782-3629647265-500.
VERBOSE: [DSCDEMOLAB]: LCM:  [ Start  Set      ]
VERBOSE: [DSCDEMOLAB]: LCM:  [ Start  Resource ]  [MSFT_DSCMetaConfiguration]
VERBOSE: [DSCDEMOLAB]: LCM:  [ Start  Set      ]  [MSFT_DSCMetaConfiguration]
VERBOSE: [DSCDEMOLAB]: LCM:  [ End    Set      ]  [MSFT_DSCMetaConfiguration]  in 0.0160 seconds.
VERBOSE: [DSCDEMOLAB]: LCM:  [ End    Resource ]  [MSFT_DSCMetaConfiguration]
VERBOSE: [DSCDEMOLAB]: LCM:  [ End    Set      ]
VERBOSE: [DSCDEMOLAB]: LCM:  [ End    Set      ]  in  0.0620 seconds.
VERBOSE: Operation 'Invoke CimMethod' complete.
VERBOSE: Set-DscLocalConfigurationManager finished in 0.774 seconds.
```

Parameterizing the configuration script

For now, we have a basic understanding of DSC in PowerShell. Let's discuss parameterizing the configuration code. The following code is just an example, where we will create a folder in `C:\Temp` or whichever path is passed as the parameter value:

```
Configuration CreateFolder
{
    param([Parameter(Mandatory = $true)]
    $FolderName,
    [Parameter(Mandatory = $true)]
```

```
    $ComputerName,
    $Ensure = 'Present',
    $Type = 'Directory'
    )
    Node $ComputerName
    {
        File CreateFolder
        {
            DestinationPath =  $FolderName
            Ensure = $Ensure
            Type = $Type


        }
    }


}
CreateFolder -FolderName 'C:\Temp\PSDSC' -ComputerName localhost
Start-DscConfiguration .\CreateFolder -Wait -Verbose -Force
```

Really, this is cool stuff! We can do many more things easily using parameterizing which allows us to make the configuration script more dynamic. Execute the following code:

```
Configuration WebServer
{
    param([string[]]$NodeName)
    Node $NodeName
    {
        WindowsFeature WebServer
        {
            Name =   "Web-Server"
            Ensure = "Present"
            IncludeAllSubFeature = $true
        }
    }
}
WebServer -NodeName 'WMF05Node4' , 'WMF05Node5'
```

The preceding code generates two MOF files for their respective servers.

Understanding MOF

MOF stands for **Managed Object Format**. These files are compiled using `mofcomp.exe`. A WMI provider normally consists of an MOF file, which defines the data and the event classes for which the provider returns the data, and a DLL file, which contains the code that supplies the data.

To take a look at the MOF structure, we can execute the following code:

```
([wmiclass] "Win32_OperatingSystem").GetText("mof")
```

This returns the MOF structure of the `Win32_OperatingSystem` class.

Using MOF, we can perform tasks such as the following:

- Compiling MOF files
- Creating classes, instances, methods, and comments
- Adding a qualifier

> For more information about MOF and its supported operations, refer to the following link:
>
> https://msdn.microsoft.com/en-us/library/
> aa823192%28v=vs.85%29.aspx?f=255&MSPPError=-2147217396

So, using DSC, when we execute the following code, an MOF file with the name `Localhost` will be created:

```
Configuration TestMOF
{
    Node Localhost
    {
        Service BITS
        {
            Name =    'BITS'
            State = 'Stopped'
            StartupType = 'Automatic'
        }
    }
}
TestMof
/
```

```
@TargetNode='Localhost'
@GeneratedBy=ChenV
@GenerationDate=08/26/2015 15:33:19
@GenerationHost=ComputerName
*/


instance of MSFT_ServiceResource as $MSFT_ServiceResource1ref
{
ResourceID = "[Service]BITS";
 State = "Stopped";
 SourceInfo = "::5::9::Service";
 Name = "BITS";
 StartupType = "Automatic";
 ModuleName = "PsDesiredStateConfiguration";
 ModuleVersion = "0.0";
ConfigurationName = "TestMOF";
};
instance of OMI_ConfigurationDocument
                    {
 Version="2.0.0";
                    MinimumCompatibleVersion = "1.0.0";
                    CompatibleVersionAdditionalProperties= {"Omi_Base
Resource:ConfigurationName"};
                    Author="ChenV";
                    GenerationDate="08/26/2015 15:33:19";
                    GenerationHost="ChenVDSC";
                    Name="TestMOF";
                    };
```

If you are familiar with MOF, you can create an MOF file without using PowerShell.

Since we have an MOF file, which leads to BITS being in the Stopped state, we can simply edit the MOF file and get this status to Running; for example, we can set State from State = 'Stopped' to be changed to State = 'Running'.

Exploring Windows Remote Management and CIM

Every IT professional is interested in managing their servers remotely. It would be better if we can achieve our tasks on remote machines from our desk than having to travel to a data center (unless there's a physical failure).

Remoting is the key feature of Windows PowerShell. However, most security administrators consider this to be a security risk. This is not completely true; Windows PowerShell remoting works based on a two-way authentication (a mutual authentication), and this inherits the feature of the Active Directory Kerberos protocol. This applies only for domain-joined machines.

We will cover the following topics:

- Understanding WS-Management cmdlets
- The HTTP listener
- The HTTPS listener
- Exploring the CIM commands
- Exploring the CIM methods
- Querying the remote machines using CIM

Windows PowerShell remoting

The Windows PowerShell remoting feature makes it richer, and this works based on the WS-Management protocol and the **Windows Remote Management (WinRM)** service. From Windows PowerShell 3.0 onward, the WS-Management configurations can be manipulated using the PowerShell provider, which is the WSMan drive.

WS-Management is a SOAP-based protocol for servers and is according to the DMTF open-based standard. Following are the standard abilities of DMTF **Web Services Management (WSMan)**:

- It gets, puts (updates), creates, and deletes individual resource instances, such as settings and dynamic values
- It enumerates the contents of the containers and collections, such as large tables and logs
- It subscribes to the events emitted by the managed resources
- It executes the specific management methods with strongly typed input and output parameters

The WinRM service processes the request sent by WSMan over the network and the listening happens through the `HTTP.sys` driver.

Exploring WSMan cmdlets

WSMan cmdlets are used to manage WSMan protocols. These commands are organized in the `Microsoft.WSMan.Management` module. Run the following command:

```
Get-Command -Module Microsoft.WSMan.Management
```

The output is as shown in the following image:

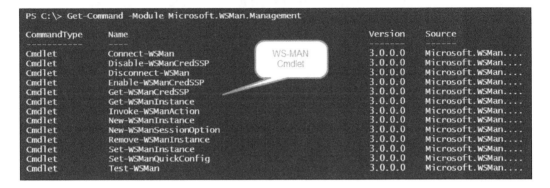

For more information, refer to the following link:

```
https://technet.microsoft.com/en-us/library/
hh849876.aspx
```

In this exercise, let's take a look at how we can change the maximum session configurations. Let's consider the current maximum allowed connections.

Using the native PowerShell `Get-Item` command, execute the following code and refer to the following image:

```
CD WSMAN:\WMF5Node03\Shell\MaxShellsPerUser
```

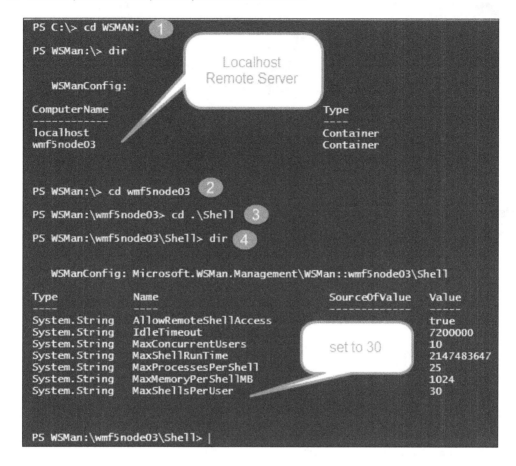

Let us see the result of the following code:

```
Set-Item WSMan:\wmf5node03\Shell\MaxShellsPerUser -Value 30
```

```
PS WSMan:\wmf5node03\Shell> ls


    WSManConfig: Microsoft.WSMan.Management\WSMan::wmf5node03\Shell

Type              Name                      SourceOfValue   Value
----              ----                      -------------   -----
System.String     AllowRemoteShellAccess                    true
System.String     IdleTimeout                               7200000
System.String     MaxConcurrentUsers                        10
System.String     MaxShellRunTime                           2147483647
System.String     MaxProcessesPerShell                      25
System.String     MaxMemoryPerShellMB                       1024
System.String     MaxShellsPerUser                          5
```

Using the WSMan cmdlets, we can manage the session's timeout period. Run the following command:

```
$Time = New-WSManSessionOption -operationtimeout 3000
```

```
Connect-WSMan -computer WMF5Node02 -sessionoption $Time
```

We can call `Disconnect-WSMan` to disconnect the client from the WinRM service. Once this is executed, we don't see the remote computer in the WSMan drive.

Now, let's establish a connection with the remote LYNC 2013 server using the `WSManConnectionInfo` class using C# and PowerShell. Following is a sample code:

```
using System;
using System.Collections.Generic;
using System.Linq;
using System.Management.Automation;
using System.Management.Automation.Remoting;
using System.Management.Automation.Runspaces;
using System.Security;
using System.Collections.ObjectModel;
using System.Text;

namespace Office365
{
    class Program
    {
```

```csharp
static void Main(string[] args)
{
    string username = "DSCDEMOLAB\\SKBAdminID";
    string password = "SecureString";
    System.Security.SecureString securepassword = new System.
Security.SecureString();
    foreach (char c in password)
    {
        securepassword.AppendChar(c);
    }
    PSCredential credential = new PSCredential(username,
securepassword);
    WSManConnectionInfo connectioninfo = new
WSManConnectionInfo(new Uri("https://RemoteServer/OcsPowershell"),
"http://schemas.microsoft.com/powershell/Microsoft.PowerShell",
credential);
    connectioninfo.AuthenticationMechanism =
AuthenticationMechanism.Default;
    connectioninfo.SkipCACheck = true;
    connectioninfo.SkipCNCheck = true;
    //connectioninfo.AuthenticationMechanism =
AuthenticationMechanism.Basic;
    connectioninfo.MaximumConnectionRedirectionCount = 2;
    //connectioninfo.MaximumConnectionRedirectionCount = 2;
    using (Runspace runspace = RunspaceFactory.
CreateRunspace(connectioninfo))
    {
        runspace.Open();
        using (PowerShell powershell = PowerShell.Create())
        {
            powershell.Runspace = runspace;
            //Create the command and add a parameter
            powershell.AddCommand("Get-CsUser");
            Collection<PSObject> results = powershell.Invoke();
            foreach (PSObject result in results)
            {
                Console.WriteLine(result.
Properties["SamaccountName"].Value.ToString());
```

```
                              Console.ReadLine();
                  }
              }
           }
        }
     }
}
```

Refer to the following image:

We used the `WSManConnectionInfo` class, which provides us with the connection information that is needed to connect to a remote runspace. Windows PowerShell uses a WinRM connection to connect to the computer on which the remote runspace is opened. Execute the following code:

```
WSManConnectionInfo connectioninfo = new WSManConnectionInfo(new
Uri("https://RemoteServer/OcsPowershell"), "http://schemas.microsoft.com/
powershell/Microsoft.PowerShell", credential);

"https://RemoteServer/OcsPowershell"
```

This is our remote Skype for Business server URL using which we can explore Skype for Business Web Front End Server (IIS). Using the preceding code, we can establish the connection and query information from the remote servers.

The same can be achieved using PowerShell. Execute the following code:

```
$cred = Get-Credential "Domain\SKBAdmin"

$session = New-PSSession -ConnectionURI "https://RemoteServer/
OcsPowershell" -Credential $cred

Import-PsSession $session

Error: Access denied due to incorrect credentials (401 status code)
```

The output of the code we just saw is shown in the following image:

For learning purpose, we can get the certificate information and add it to **Current User | Trusted Root Certification Authorities** and execute the PowerShell code – Yes! Connection establishes as expected.

To get the certificate information, you can go to the site, `https://RemoteServer/OCSPowerShell`. Take a look at the following image:

Click on the Lock button in your browser and get the information.

HTTP/HTTPS Listener

To configure the HTTP or HTTPS Listener, we need to ensure that the ports, 5985 and 5986, are opened. The transport happens through the respective ports. Using PowerShell, we can easily enable the HTTP listener. Run the following command:

```
Set-WSManQuickConfig
```

To avoid the access denied error, ensure that PowerShell is running as Administrator. This is applicable for Win 7 and 2008 server OS. The command works without elevated privileges if you run it under the local admin account. Take a look at the following image:

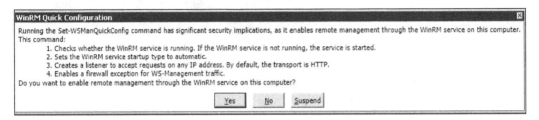

The output is as follows:

```
PS C:\Windows\system32> Winrm Enumerate Winrm/config/Listener
Listener
    Address = *
    Transport = HTTP
    Port = 5985
    Hostname
    Enabled = true
    URLPrefix = wsman
    CertificateThumbprint
    ListeningOn = <IPS>
```

By default, the HTTP listener will be created to enable HTTPS; we need to use the switch, -UseSSL.

Let's give it a try with the following command:

```
Set-WSManQuickConfig -UseSSL
```

The error is self-explanatory. This is the really cool stuff in Windows PowerShell. Take a look at the following image:

To overcome this, we can use the following code. You can check with your **certification authority (CA)** administrator for the certificate-related query:

```
$Cert = Get-ChildItem Cert:\LocalMachine\My | where {$_.Subject -match
$env:COMPUTERNAME}

"The installed SSL certificate: " + $Cert.Subject

$CertPrivKey = $Cert.PrivateKey

$KeyCertFile = Get-Item -path "$ENV:ProgramData\Microsoft\Crypto\RSA\
MachineKeys\*" | where {$_.Name -eq $CertPrivKey.CspKeyContainerInfo.
UniqueKeyContainerName}

$KeyAcl = (Get-Item -Path $KeyCertFile.FullName).
GetAccessControl("Access")

$perm = "NT AUTHORITY\NETWORK SERVICE","Read","Allow"

$accessRule = New-Object System.Security.AccessControl.
FileSystemAccessRule $perm

$KeyAcl.AddAccessRule($accessRule)

Set-Acl $KeyCertFile.FullName $KeyAcl
```

Now, the following code will work:

```
Set-WSManQuickConfig -UseSSL
```

The output is as shown in the following code:

```
Listener
    Address = *
    Transport = HTTPS
    Port = 5986
    Hostname
    Enabled = true
    URLPrefix = wsman
    CertificateThumbprint = D3438E6116227BA1459434943DB723C2C5D50C7C
    ListeningOn = <IPS>
```

In case this is a workgroup, we can add trusted hosts to accept the connections. This way, we can have more control in remoting. Your client accepts the connection only if it's listed in the trusted hosts.

Exploring CIM commands

We have covered a few basic examples of CIM and WMI in *Chapter 2, Unleashing Development Skills Using Windows PowerShell 5.0*; let's take a quick review here and proceed with a few more examples using PowerShell and C#.

You may wonder, why do we need CIM, and why not WMI? In this topic, we'll discover how CIM helps IT professionals.

- **Common Information Model (CIM)** is the DMTF standard [DSP0004] for describing the structure and behavior of managed resources such as storage, network, or software components
- **Windows Management Instrumentation (WMI)** is a CIM server that implements the CIM standard on Windows
- The **WS-Management (WSMan)** protocol is a SOAP-based, firewall-friendly protocol for management clients to communicate with CIM servers
- **Windows Remote Management (WinRM)** is the Microsoft implementation of the WSMan protocol on Windows.

CIM provides a rich experience in PowerShell and supports standard compliance—yes; CIM does work in Windows- and nonWindows-based machines.

CIM is introduced in Windows PowerShell 3.0 with the 2012 server by default, but this is limited; it supports down-level OS as well.

To know all the available CIM cmdlets, use the following code:

```
Get-Command -Module CimCmdlets | Select Name
```

Following is a list of available CIM cmdlets:

- Export-BinaryMiLog
- Get-CimAssociatedInstance
- Get-CimClass
- Get-CimInstance
- Get-CimSession
- Import-BinaryMiLog
- Invoke-CimMethod
- New-CimInstance
- New-CimSession
- New-CimSessionOption

- Register-CimIndicationEvent
- Remove-CimInstance
- Remove-CimSession
- Set-CimInstance

Take a look at the following image:

```
PS C:\> Get-Command -Module CimCmdlets

CommandType      Name                             Version     Source
-----------      ----                             -------     ------
Cmdlet           Export-BinaryMiLog               1.0.0.0     CimCmdlets
Cmdlet           Get-CimAssociatedInstance        1.0.0.0     CimCmdlets
Cmdlet           Get-CimClass                     1.0.0.0     CimCmdlets
Cmdlet           Get-CimInstance                  1.0.0.0     CimCmdlets
Cmdlet           Get-CimSession                   1.0.0.0     CimCmdlets
Cmdlet           Import-BinaryMiLog               1.0.0.0     CimCmdlets
Cmdlet           Invoke-CimMethod                 1.0.0.0     CimCmdlets
Cmdlet           New-CimInstance                  1.0.0.0     CimCmdlets
Cmdlet           New-CimSession                   1.0.0.0     CimCmdlets
Cmdlet           New-CimSessionOption             1.0.0.0     CimCmdlets
Cmdlet           Register-CimIndicationEvent      1.0.0.0     CimCmdlets
Cmdlet           Remove-CimInstance               1.0.0.0     CimCmdlets
Cmdlet           Remove-CimSession                1.0.0.0     CimCmdlets
Cmdlet           Set-CimInstance                  1.0.0.0     CimCmdlets
```

CIM cmdlets have auto tab completion, so it involves little typing and coding. Do remember that the default namespace is root/cimv2.

Now, let's take a look at the list of CIM classes:

```
using System;
using System.Collections.Generic;
using System.Linq;
using System.Text;
using System.Threading.Tasks;
using System.Management.Automation;
using System.Management.Automation.Host;
using System.Collections.ObjectModel;


namespace CIM_Exercise
{
    class Program
    {
        static void Main(string[] args)
        {
```

```
        using (PowerShell PowerShellInstance = PowerShell.Create())
        {
            PowerShellInstance.AddCommand("Get-CimClass");
            Collection<PSObject> result = PowerShellInstance.
Invoke();

            foreach (PSObject r in result)
            {
                Console.WriteLine(r);
                Console.ReadKey();
            }
        }
    }
}
```

Ensure that you call a property that exists. If we don't use an existing property, the following error will appear:

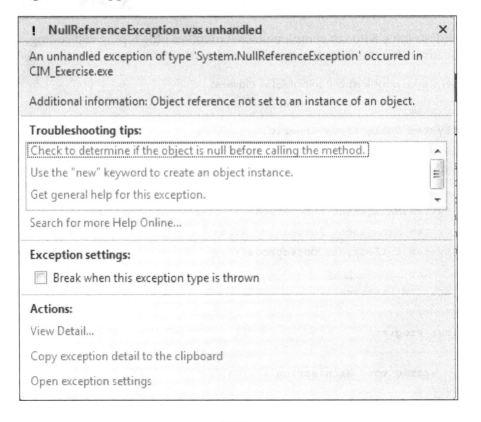

After a successful execution, we will obtain the list as shown in the following image:

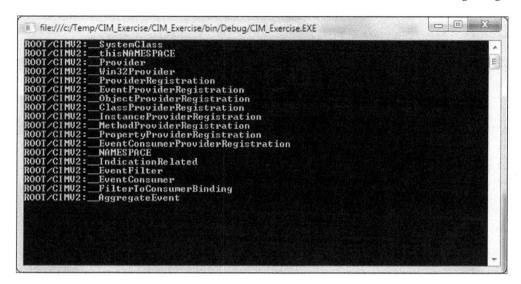

Using help commands, we can explore all the CIM commands.

Exploring CIM methods

Using the `Invoke-CimMethod` cmdlet, we can perform operations such as creating, terminating, restarting, and so on.

In this exercise, let's consider the basic example of opening a notepad. Yes! We can simply type the word `notepad` in PowerShell, and this will do it. But we will explore the CIM methods using the `Invoke-CimMethod` cmdlet and its parameters.

The following is a single line of code in PowerShell that uses the `Invoke-CimMethod` cmdlet:

```
Invoke-CimMethod -ClassName Win32_Process -MethodName "Create" -Arguments
@{Commandline = "notepad.exe"}
```

The following is a single line of code in PowerShell that uses the [WMICLASS] type accelerator:

```
([wmiclass]"root\cimv2:Win32_Process").Create('notepad.exe');
```

So, how do we find out the parameters of the methods? Run the following command and refer to the following image:

```
(Get-CimClass -ClassName Win32_Process).CimClassMethods
```

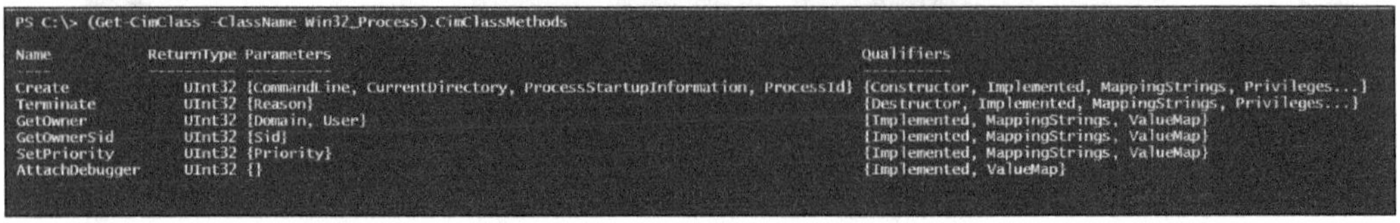

For each method name, we can see the parameters. It's easy to explore and use as required.

Now, let's create a small Windows form application and take note of the execution of CIM methods.

Following is the code used for this:

```csharp
using System;
using System.Collections.Generic;
using System.ComponentModel;
using System.Data;
using System.Drawing;
using System.Linq;
using System.Text;
using System.Threading.Tasks;
using System.Windows.Forms;
using System.Management.Automation;
using System.Management.Automation.Runspaces;
namespace CIM_Exercise
{
    public partial class Form1 : Form
    {
        public Form1()
        {
            InitializeComponent();
        }
        private void button1_Click(object sender, EventArgs e)
        {
```

```
    using(PowerShell PowerShellInstance = PowerShell.Create())
    {
        PowerShellInstance.AddScript("Invoke-CimMethod -ClassName
Win32_Process -MethodName Create -Arguments @{CommandLine = notepad.
exe}");
        PowerShellInstance.Invoke();
    }
}
private void button2_Click(object sender, EventArgs e)
{
    using (PowerShell PowerShellInstance = PowerShell.Create())
    {
        PowerShellInstance.AddScript("Invoke-CimMethod -ClassName
Win32_Process -MethodName Create -Arguments @{CommandLine = calc.exe}");
        PowerShellInstance.Invoke();
    }
}
}
}
```

To avoid overuse of Add parameters in the PowerShell instance, we used the type accelerator method. The Windows form provides the options of **Open Notepad**, which opens the **Notepad** application, and **Open Calc**, which opens the **Calculator** application, as shown in the following screenshot:

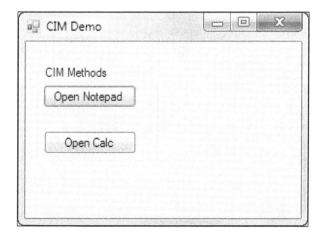

Querying the remote machines using CIM

As we have previously seen, CIM supports down-level OS. You may wonder, can we not use CIM commands in servers running Windows 2008 with PowerShell 2.0? Not really, but we can establish a remote session and execute the CIM commands.

Consider a scenario where we need to query the OS-installed date on remote machines. WMI will do it, but we need to add a snippet of code for creating the time format, which is as follows:

```
(Get-WmiObject -Class Win32_operatingSystem –ComputerName "Remote").
InstallDate
```

```
#20140326181309.000000+060
```

```
(Get-CimInstance -ClassName CIM_OperatingSystem –ComputerName "Remote").
InstallDate
```

```
#Wednesday, March 26, 2014 6:13:09 PM
```

Which one of these would our configuration management team prefer? Of course, they would prefer the one with the well-formatted date. Indeed, we can do this in WMI as well by adding a snippet of code as follows:

```
$os = (Get-WmiObject -Class Win32_operatingSystem)
```

```
[management.managementDateTimeConverter]::ToDateTime($os.InstallDate)
```

There are always multiple ways of doing things in PowerShell, and we can choose the one that best suits our requirement.

In this exercise, let's consider using the server remotely with PowerShell 2.0, and execute the CIM commands:

```
Test-WSMan -ComputerName RemoteServer

wsmid             : http://schemas.dmtf.org/wbem/wsman/identity/1/
wsmanidentity.xsd

ProtocolVersion : http://schemas.dmtf.org/wbem/wsman/1/wsman.xsd

ProductVendor   : Microsoft Corporation

ProductVersion  : OS: 0.0.0 SP: 0.0 Stack: 2.0
```

`OS: 0.0.0 SP: 0.0 Stack: 2.0` proves that the remote machine is PowerShell 2.0.

So now, let's establish a session using the following code and get the OS-installed date:

```
$Dcom = New-CimSessionOption -Protocol Dcom

$session = New-CimSession -ComputerName RemoteServer -SessionOption $Dcom

(Get-CimInstance -CimSession $session -ClassName Win32_OperatingSystem).
InstallDate
```

In this chapter, we explored the basics of Windows Remote Management; in the next chapter, we will discuss how to create DSC with MOF using class, deploying configuration, and the types of deployment modes.

Creating configuration scripts

In this topic, we will take a look at how to create a configuration using the `Configuration` and `Class` keywords. Configuration creates MOF, and this MOF needs to be pushed to or pulled by the target nodes. While using class, we will define the DSC resource and deploy the configurations.

Creating a configuration with MOF

We know that DSC is a declarative syntax, and this really helps developers and IT professionals to do more. In this section, we will see what developers can do with DSC.

We have discussed a few basic concepts of DSC and its stages; using this knowledge, let's build a web server. Most organizations face operational issues: the IT professional thinks that the infrastructure is good, and the code is at fault, but on the other hand, developers state that the code works fine in test but not in production. So, test and production are not identical. To fix this gap, we can use DSC and code our infrastructure.

Let's build a test web server using DSC. In this exercise, we will install IIS, as follows:

```
Configuration WebServer
{
    Node $env:COMPUTERNAME
    {
        WindowsFeature IIS
        {
            Name = 'Web-Server'
            Ensure = 'Present'
            IncludeAllSubFeature = $true
        }
    }
}
WebServer
```

While deploying this configuration, I did not note that my OS build version is 10074—Windows Server Technical Preview. This is a known issue, so the IIS installation failed as well, as shown in the following message:

Failed to start automatic updating for installed components. Error: 0x80040154

To fix this, we need to use `sconfig.cmd` and enter option 6—sounds weird! However, this is another bug in Technical Preview 2 Server OS, so let's download and install the updates.

This calls `Cscript.exe` to download and install updates; just give your system a reboot after this!

Now, we will fix the password issue and rerun the configuration script through the following code:

```
configuration WebServers
{
        Node $env:COMPUTERNAME
        {
            WindowsFeature WebServer
          {
            Name = 'Web-Server'
            Ensure = 'Present'
            IncludeAllSubFeature = $true
          }
        }
}
WebServers
Start-DSCOnfiguration .\WebServers -Wait -Verbose -Force
```

Yes, we can access localhost now, as shown in the following image:

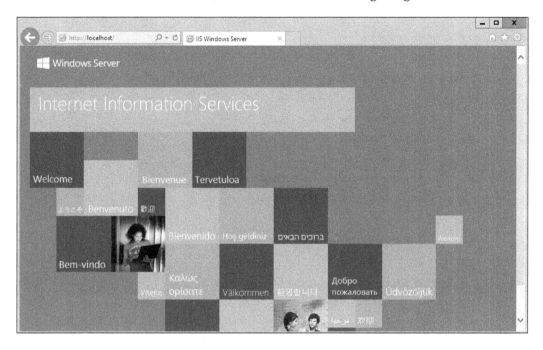

Now, let's remove IIS—do remember that this requires a reboot. So, it's good to check the LCM Meta Configuration. All we need is action to continue after the reboot and reboot if needed, set to true. Execute the following code:

```
[DscLocalConfigurationManager()]
Configuration LCM
{
    Node localhost
    {
        Settings
        {
            RebootNodeIfNeeded = $true
            ActionAfterReboot = "ContinueConfiguration"
        }
    }
}
LCM
Set-DscLocalConfigurationManager .\LCM
```

To uninstall the Windows feature, we will use the same code; however, we will change Present to Absent:

```
configuration WebServers
{
        Node $env:COMPUTERNAME
        {
                WindowsFeature WebServer
        {
            Name = 'Web-Server'
            Ensure = 'Absent'
            IncludeAllSubFeature = $true
        }
        }
}
```

The system reboots itself because we set the Meta. In the next topic, we will create a custom DSC resource using Class.

Creating a Class-defined DSC resource

To know more about Class, you can read the help document.

From version 5.0 onward, Windows PowerShell adds the language syntax to define classes and other user-defined types using formal syntax and semantics that are similar to other object-oriented programming languages.

You can refer to the release notes of WMF 5.0 for the class structure and more details.

Refer to the following link for the WMF 5.0 release notes on the skeleton class structure: https://www.microsoft.com/en-us/download/details.aspx?id=46889

Execute the following command:

```
enum Ensure
{
    Absent
    Present
}
[DscResource()]
class StringLiteral
{
```

```
[DscProperty(Key)]
[string] $Path


[DscProperty(Mandatory)]
[Ensure] $Ensure


[DscProperty(Mandatory)]
[string] $SourcePath
[DscProperty(NotConfigurable)]
[Nullable[datetime]] $CreationTime
[void] Set()
{
}
[bool] Test()
{
}


[StringLiteral] Get()
{
}
}
```

Now, using the `Class` keyword, let's define a DSC Resource. The significant benefits of this are as follows:

- There is no need for schema MOF anymore
- A `DSCResource` folder inside the module folder is not needed
- Multiple DSC resources can be packaged as a single module script file

In this exercise, we will follow a step-by-step procedure to create a Class-based DSC resource, which will simply create a file or directory.

1. Refer to the TechNet article for reference using the URL `https://technet.microsoft.com/en-us/library/dn948461.aspx`.

2. Create a folder structure. Run the following command:

```
$env: psmodulepath (folder)
    |- MyDscResources (folder)
        |- MyDscResource.psm1
           MyDscResource.psd1
```

3. Create a DSC resource using Class and save it as a PSM1 file.

4. Create a module manifest using the `New-ModuleManifest` cmdlet.

5. Test the configuration.

Let's create a DSC resource using the following code:

```
enum Ensure
{
    Absent
    Present
}
 [DscResource()]
class MyTestClassResource{
    [DscProperty(Key)]
    [string]$Path

    [DscProperty(Mandatory)]
    [Ensure] $Ensure
    [DscProperty(Mandatory)]
    [ValidateSet("Directory","File")]
    [string]$ItemType
    #Replaces Get-TargetResource
    [MyTestClassResource] Get()
    {
    $Item = Test-Path $This.Path
        If($Item -eq $True)
        {
            $This.Ensure = [Ensure]::Present
        }
        Else
        {
            $This.Ensure = [Ensure]::Absent
        }
        Return $This
    }
    #Replaces Test-TargetResource
    [bool] Test()
```

```
    {
$Item = Test-Path $This.Path
    If($This.Ensure -eq [Ensure]::Present)
    {
        Return $Item
    }
    Else
    {
        Return -not $Item
    }
}
#Replaces Set-TargetResource
[void] Set()
{
$Item = Test-Path $This.Path
    If($This.Ensure -eq [Ensure]::Present)
    {
        If(-not $Item)
        {
            Write-Verbose "Creating Folder"
            New-Item -ItemType Directory -Path $This.Path
        }
    }
    #If [Ensure]::Absent
    Else
    {
        If($Item)
        {
            Write-Verbose "File exists and should be absent.
Deleting file"
            Remove-Item -Path $This.Path
        }
    }
    }
}
```

Save the preceding code as a PSM1 file and create a module manifest. Save the files in C:\Program Files\WindowsPowerShell\Modules\ClassResourceDemo.

Save your class resource code as ClassResourceDemo.PSM1 in the folder that we created named ClassResourceDemo.

Now, create a module manifest using the New-ModuleManifest cmdlet, executing the following code:

```
New-ModuleManifest -Path 'C:\Windows\system32\WindowsPowerShell\v1.0\
Modules\Demo\DemoClass.psd1' `

-DscResourcesToExport 'MyTestClassResource' -PowerShellVersion 5.0
-Description 'Class based DSC resource' -ModuleVersion '1.0.0.0' -Guid
$([guid]::NewGuid()) -Author 'Chen' `

-RootModule '.\DemoClass.psm1' -CompanyName 'Something'
```

That's it! We are ready to test the resource using the following configuration code:

```
Configuration Test {
Import-DscResource -ModuleName ClassResourceDemo
Node Localhost {
 MyTestClassResource Testing
 {
    Ensure = 'Present'
    Path = 'C:\Test1'
    ItemType = 'Directory'
 }
}
}
Test
```

Use the Start-DscConfiguration cmdlet to deploy the configuration, as shown in the following image:

How does this work?

Take a look at the eight main steps in the following image:

```
enum Ensure       1
±{...}

  [DscResource()] 2       3
=class MyTestClassResource{|

        [DscProperty(Key)]  4
        [string]$Path

        [DscProperty(Mandatory)] 5
        [Ensure] $Ensure

        [DscProperty(Mandatory)]
        [ValidateSet("Directory","File")]
        [string]$ItemType

        #Replaces Get-TargetResource
        [MyTestClassResource] Get()  6
±       {...}

        #Replaces Test-TargetResource
        [bool] Test()  7
±       {...}

        #Replaces Set-TargetResource
        [void] Set()  8
±       {...}

  }
```

- **1**: Here, we used the `enum` keyword and named it `Ensure`
- **2**: Here, we used the `[DscResource()]` attribute to specify that the class is a DSC resource
- **3**: Here, we created a class named `MyTestClassResource`
- **4**: Here, we declared DSC properties — this value will be set before calling the instance
- **5**: The `Ensure` property is the enum type and is set to `Mandatory`
- **6**: The `Get()` method returns the instance of the class
- **7**: The `Test()` method returns a boolean value, `true` or `false`; this is called first, so check whether or not the resource is in the desired state
- **8**: The `Set()` method sets the resources to the desired state

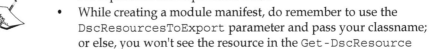

Here are a few key things to note:

- Inside enum, no numbers are allowed
- No separators are required in enum
- While creating a module manifest, do remember to use the DscResourcesToExport parameter and pass your classname; or else, you won't see the resource in the Get-DscResource output.
- You can create multiple class files and make use of the resources

Now that you have created your first Class-based DSC resource, it's easy and in a human, very readable format. To know more about Class and writing custom DSC resources, use the help document as follows:

```
help New-ModuleManifest -Detailed
help about_Classes -Detailed
help about_Modules -Detailed
```

Types of deployment modes

Windows PowerShell has two configuration modes: push and pull. In this topic, we will learn about implementing both push and pull modes. Before we start discussing the types of configuration modes, let's recap the high-level details of DSC.

Using Windows PowerShell, we will write a configuration. This contains the elements we need to configure on target nodes.

After the successful execution of the configuration script, we get a Managed Object Format file. The MOF files are then distributed to the target nodes.

Local Configuration Manager in the target node will parse the received configurations and ensure that the nodes are in the desired state.

Distributing the MOF files to the target node is very important. To carry this out, we need to follow either a push or pull method. Most organizations use the pull mode for the reasons of standard, security, and reliability.

The push mode

As the term implies, the push mode is unidirectional, and the action is immediate. The configurations are pushed to the target nodes and set to be in the desired state. Using the Start-DscConfiguration command, the configurations are applied to target nodes.

In this exercise, let's push the configuration to the remote nodes. Execute the following code:

```
Configuration PushDemo
{
    param([Parameter(Mandatory = $true)]$NodeName)
    Node $NodeName
    {
        Service Bits
        {
            Name = "Bits"
            Ensure = "Present"
            State = "Running"
        }
    }
}
PushDemo -NodeName WMF5Node02
Start-DscConfiguration .\PushDemo -ComputerName WMF5Node02 -Verbose -Wait
-Force
```

This is how the configurations are pushed to the target nodes. The output is illustrated in the following image:

The pull mode

In the DSC pull mode, a few additional steps are needed. As in the push mode, we can't easily carry out the steps, but we can configure the pull server with a few steps.

In the pull mode, the target nodes are the pull client and where we have the actual configurations is called the pull server. The basic process involves creating a Desired State Configuration for the target node and setting up a pull server and DSC on the target node.

In this topic, we will discuss building a pull server using the SMB share and HTTP/HTTPS protocols.

Creating a pull server using the SMB share

Perform the following steps:

1. Create a network share in your pull server.
2. Configure your pull client, which is the Local Configuration Manager (LCM) engine.
3. Create a configuration.
4. Use the pull client to pull the configuration from the pull server.

We will create the SMB share in the WMF5Node01 — domain controller. Execute the following code:

```
#Creates a Directory
New-Item C:\ -Name DSCShare -ItemType Directory -Verbose
#Creates a SMB Share and gives read access to everyone
New-SmbShare -Name SMBPullServer -Path C:\DSCShare -ReadAccess Everyone
-Description "PULL server SMB" -verbose
```

That's it! There's no more work in server for us. Let's log in to the client nodes, or connect to WMF5Node03, to configure LCM. Execute the following code:

```
Configuration SMBClient {
Node Localhost {
LocalConfigurationManager {
ConfigurationID = 'e86549dc-7a5f-45b6-9d66-560d980587a8'
RefreshMode = "Pull"
DownloadManagerName = "DscFileDownloadManager"
DownloadManagerCustomData = @{SourcePath = "\\WMF5Node01\DSCShare"}
ConfigurationModeFrequencyMins = 30
RefreshFrequencyMins = 20
}
}
}
SMBClient
Set-DscLocalConfigurationManager -Path .\SMBClient
```

What we should see after the execution of the preceding code is the output of the `Get-DscLocalConfigurationManager` cmdlet—observe the `RefreshMode`—changed to `Pull`. Take a look at the following image:

```
PS C:\> Get-DscLocalConfigurationManager

ActionAfterReboot                : ContinueConfiguration
AgentId                          : 4FA44C3A-3206-11E5-80C0-000D3A2135E3
AllowModuleOverwrite             : False
CertificateID                    :
ConfigurationDownloadManagers    : {}
ConfigurationID                  : c720b906-5e47-4ff1-b34c-24bed9905770
ConfigurationMode                : ApplyAndMonitor
ConfigurationModeFrequencyMins   : 50
Credential                       :
DebugMode                        : {NONE}
DownloadManagerCustomData        : {MSFT_KeyValuePair (key = "SourcePath")}
DownloadManagerName              : DscFileDownloadManager
LCMCompatibleVersions            : {1.0, 2.0}
LCMState                         : Idle
LCMStateDetail                   :
LCMVersion                       : 2.0
MaxPendingConfigRetryCount       :
StatusRetentionTimeInDays        : 10
PartialConfigurations            :
RebootNodeIfNeeded               : False
RefreshFrequencyMins             : 30
RefreshMode                      : Pull       Pull Mode
ReportManagers                   : {}
ResourceModuleManagers           : {}
PSComputerName                   :
```

Now, it's time for us to create the DSC resources and store them in the pull server. Execute the following code:

```
Configuration SMBDemoConfig {

Node 'c720b906-5e47-4ff1-b34c-24bed9905770' {

Service Bits {

Name = 'Bits'

State = 'Running'

}

}

}

SMBDemoConfig -OutputPath C:\DSCShare
```

After this, we will create a checksum file in the same shared location through the following code:

```
New-DscCheckSum -ConfigurationPath C:\DSCShare -OutPath C:\DSCShare
-Force
```

Now, at the `C:\DSCShare` location, we will see the following two files:

- The `c720b906-5e47-4ff1-b34c-24bed9905770.mof` file
- The `c720b906-5e47-4ff1-b34c-24bed9905770.mof.checksum` file

The reason we created the checksum file is that this is used to compute the configuration difference between the local configuration store and the one which is available in the actual pull server.

That's it! We are done. Now, either we can wait for the configuration to be applied or simply execute the following code:

```
Start-ScheduledTask -TaskName "Consistency" -TaskPath "\Microsoft\
Windows\Desired State Configuration\"
```

Creating the pull server using HTTP and HTTPS

Using HTTP and HTTPS is an optimal way for the IT infrastructure.

The pull server has two HTTP web services that manage the following:

- The configuration(s) hosted on that server
- DSC compliance

DSC compliance is used for a periodical checking of the configuration nodes synchronization.

These services each listen on a turned `off` TCP port. We will now configure 8080 (pull server) and 9080 (compliance). Execute the following code:

```
Configuration ConfigurePullServer
{
    param
    (
        [string[]]$ComputerName = "localhost"
    )
    Import-DSCResource -ModuleName xPSDesiredStateConfiguration
    Node $ComputerName
    {
        WindowsFeature DSCServiceFeature
        {
            Ensure = "Present"
            Name   = "DSC-Service"
```

```
    }
    xDscWebService PSDSCPullServer
    {
        Ensure                = "Present"
        EndpointName          = "PSDSCPullServer"
        Port                  = 8080
        PhysicalPath          = "$env:SystemDrive\inetpub\wwwroot\
PSDSCPullServer"
        CertificateThumbPrint = "AllowUnencryptedTraffic"
        ModulePath            = "$env:PROGRAMFILES\WindowsPowerShell\
DscService\Modules"
        ConfigurationPath     = "$env:PROGRAMFILES\WindowsPowerShell\
DscService\Configuration"
        State                 = "Started"
        DependsOn             = "[WindowsFeature]DSCServiceFeature"
    }
    xDscWebService PSDSCComplianceServer
    {
        Ensure                = "Present"
        EndpointName          = "PSDSCComplianceServer"
        Port                  = 9080
        PhysicalPath          = "$env:SystemDrive\inetpub\wwwroot\
PSDSCComplianceServer"
        CertificateThumbPrint = "AllowUnencryptedTraffic"
        State                 = "Started"
        IsComplianceServer    = $true
        DependsOn             = ("[WindowsFeature]DSCServiceFeature","[xD
SCWebService]PSDSCPullServer")
    }
  }
}
ConfigurePullServer -ComputerName localhost
```

The preceding code performs three simple tasks:

- It installs the DSC service on the localhost
- It generates a pull server web service — port 8080
- It generates a compliance server web service — port 9080

Note that we didn't install IIS and tools in the server. So, we won't explore it in this exercise.

We need to explore `C:\Install backup` folder, that contains the MOF file we need.

Carry out the same steps as you did with the SMB pull server configuration. Set up a pull client, as shown in the following code:

```
Configuration SetPullMode
{
    # param([string]$guid)
    Node WMF5Node03.DSCDemoLab.Com
    {
        LocalConfigurationManager
        {
            ConfigurationMode = "ApplyAndAutoCorrect"
            ConfigurationModeFrequencyMins = 15
            ConfigurationID = "479316c3-712a-4e5a-9b87-4fde1bf0433e"
            RefreshMode = 'Pull'
            DownloadManagerName = 'WebDownloadManager'
            DownloadManagerCustomData = @{
            ServerUrl = 'http://WMF5Node01.DSCDemoLab.Com:8080/
PSDSCPullServer.svc';
            AllowUnsecureConnection = 'true' }
        }
    }
}
SetPullMode
Set-DSCLocalConfigurationManager -Computer WMF5Node03.DSCDemoLab.Com
-Path "C:\SetPullMode" -Verbose
```

Then start creating a `Configuration`.

```
Configuration InstallBackup {

    param (
    [string[]]$ComputerName = "localhost"
    )



    Node $ComputerName {

        WindowsFeature Backup {
            Ensure = "Present"
            Name    = "Windows-Server-Backup"
        }
    }
}
InstallBackup -ComputerName WMF5Node03.DSCDemolab.com
```

It is important to enact the configuration we need to move the MOF and checksum MOF files to `C:\Program Files\WindowsPowerShell\DscService\Configuration`.

We only need to create a checksum file, and we are done!

HTTPS is a more secure way, so let's quickly take a look at the additional steps required to configure the HTTPS pull server:

1. Request and install a Web Server SSL certificate on the DSC pull server from a trusted certificate authority.

2. Get the certificate thumbprint. It will be needed for the pull server configuration. The best way to accomplish this task is to use PowerShell and the CERT: drive. So, execute the following code:

```
Get-ChildItem -Path cert: -Recurse |
Where { $_.FriendlyName –like "Web Server Ceritificate" } | select
Subject, FriendlyName, Thumbprint | Format-List
```

3. Now, in the `B04702_03_04.ps1` code file, change the line number 21 to the following along with the certificate thumbprint we generated and follow the same procedure as with the HTTP pull server configuration:

```
CertificateThumbPrint = "AllowUnencryptedTraffic"
```

Summary

In this chapter, we explored the basic concepts of Desired State Configuration, such as installing WMF 5.0 April 2015 Preview and imperative versus declarative programming and their significant features. If you think that built-in resources are limited, start building your own DSC resources and sharing them with the community. Using DSC, we can manage on-premises, and we can also manage the cloud environment using a declarative syntax. If you wish to learn about building Azure VM using DSC, refer to the following link:

```
http://blogs.msdn.com/b/powershell/archive/2014/08/07/introducing-
the-azure-powershell-dsc-desired-state-configuration-extension.aspx
```

In the next chapter, we will cover PowerShell and web technologies, in which we will have exercises based on JSON, REST API, PowerShell Web Access, Web services, OData extensions, and PowerShell Web Access. The examples in the next chapter will cover managing Office 365 environments using PowerShell and C#.

4
PowerShell and Web Technologies

IT professionals and developers require Windows PowerShell for various reasons, such as the following:

- To perform administration tasks
- For a continuous delivery
- To manage/automate deployments

The use of PowerShell is increasing day by day, which helps us to experience the growth and significant improvements of Windows PowerShell. IT professionals and developers can remotely operate servers from their mobiles and perform tasks on the fly.

In this chapter, we will cover the following:

- **PowerShell Web Access**
- **OData IIS Extension**
- Exploring web requests and web services
- Exploring the REST API and JSON

PowerShell Web Access

PowerShell Web Access (PSWA) was introduced in Windows Server 2012. In short, PSWA acts as a gateway to run the PowerShell cmdlets from a remote computer. The key benefit of this is that we don't need any remote management software on remote computers.

PSWA can be implemented using the following three steps:

1. Installing the PowerShell Web Access gateway
2. Configuring the gateway
3. Configuring authorization rule

Installing PowerShell Web Access

We can do a PSWA installation using GUI and PowerShell. Let's explore these methods one by one.

Installing Windows PowerShell Web Access using GUI is a straightforward approach. Yes! It's just click—click, and you're done. Perform the following steps:

1. Log in to the Windows 2012 server.
2. Click on Start icon.
3. Select **Control Panel**.
4. Alternatively, you can simply click on **Server manager** if you are familiar with Windows Server.
5. Now, we will see **Add Roles and Features Wizard**.
6. Windows PowerShell Web Access can be found under the **Features** tab; keep clicking on **Next** and you'll find it.
7. Select Windows PowerShell Web Access.
8. Click on Install.

After installation, the **Features** tab looks similar to the following image:

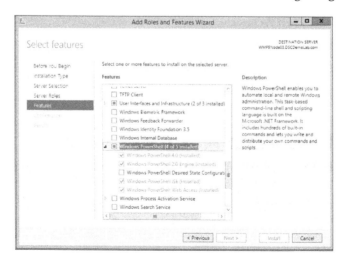

Using Windows PowerShell, we can install the Windows PowerShell Web Access feature through the following command:

```
Install-PswaWebApplication -UseTestCertificate -Verbose
```

Note that we haven't configured PowerShell Web Access yet; we have only installed it.

After the execution of the preceding PowerShell code, we can see PSWA on our server:

```
https://localhost/pswa
```

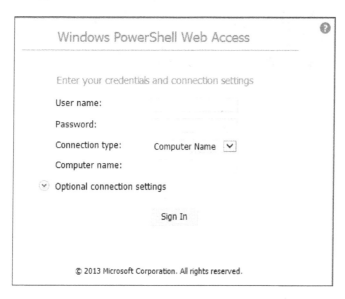

In the preceding example, we used the UseTestCertificate property. However, this is not recommended for the production environment, so you need to check with with the CA admin and get a valid certificate.

Now, let's take a look at the cmdlets available in the PowerShell Web Access module:

```
Get-Command -Module PowerShellWebAccess
```

```
PS C:\> Get-Command -Module PowerShellWebAccess

CommandType     Name                            Version    Source
-----------     ----                            -------    ------
Function        Install-PswaWebApplication      1.1.0.0    PowerShellWebAccess
Function        Uninstall-PswaWebApplication    1.1.0.0    PowerShellWebAccess
Cmdlet          Add-PswaAuthorizationRule       1.1.0.0    PowerShellWebAccess
Cmdlet          Get-PswaAuthorizationRule       1.1.0.0    PowerShellWebAccess
Cmdlet          Remove-PswaAuthorizationRule    1.1.0.0    PowerShellWebAccess
Cmdlet          Test-PswaAuthorizationRule      1.1.0.0    PowerShellWebAccess
```

Now let's take a look at the procedure to configure PowerShell Web Access with a few, custom settings. Let's uninstall PowerShell Web Access using the following PowerShell cmdlet:

```
Uninstall-PswaWebApplication -WebApplicationName pswa -Verbose
  -DeleteTestCertificate
```

The output is illustrated in the following image:

```
PS C:\> Uninstall-PswaWebApplication -WebApplicationName pswa -Verbose -DeleteTestCertificate
Removing web application pswa...

Removing application pool pswa_pool...

Removing self-signed certificate...
PS C:\>
```

This removes the following:

- The PSWA web application
- The pswa_pool application pool
- The self-signed certificate

This will retain the Windows PowerShell feature.

Let's configure PSWA using Desired State Configuration. Execute the following code:

```
Configuration PSWA
{
    WindowsFeature IIS {
        Name = 'Web-Server'
        Ensure = 'Present'
        IncludeAllSubFeature = $true
    }
    WindowsFeature PS {
        Name = "WindowsPowerShellWebAccess"
        Ensure = "Present"
        IncludeAllSubFeature = $true
    }
    Script PSWA {
        SetScript = {
            Install-PswaWebApplication
```

```
        }
        TestScript = {
            [bool](Get-WebApplication -Name pswa | where
              {$_.ApplicationPool -eq 'pswa_pool'}) -eq $true
        }
        GetScript = {
            $result = [bool](Get-WebApplication -Name pswa |
              where {$_.ApplicationPool -eq 'pswa_pool'})
            return @{Installed = $result}
        }
    }
}
PSWA
```

In the preceding code, we used the `Configuration` keyword and installed the Web Server feature and Windows PowerShell Web Access feature. Then, using the script resource, we installed PSWA.

In the script resource, the test script is executed first to test whether the Web application and pool exists for the default pswa and pswa_pool. The configuration happens dynamically.

Configuring PowerShell Web Access

Why do we need to do this? It's necessary to meet organization standards, naming conventions, and branding. Along with this, we need to use a valid certificate in the production environment. Remember that using a test certificate is not recommended practice for the production environment. However, as we will do this in a lab, we will use `-UseTestCertificate`.

Using the following steps, we can insert organization name in the login page:

1. Open IIS.
2. Explore the **Default Web Site**.
3. Right-click on **pswa** and select **Explore**.
4. The default location is `C:\Windows\Web\PowerShellWebAccess\wwwroot`.
5. Copy the `FormLayout.Master` file to the desired location and modify the code as required.

To change the organization name, just add the following piece of code:

```
this.document.title = "We are Testing this!" + L_FeatureName_Text;
```

Simply replace the document title text with your own text and load the page: `https://localhost/pswa`.

Applying authorization rules

We have installed and customized PSWA. Now, to use it, we need to apply authorization rules.

To do this, we will use the `Add-PswaAuthorizationRule` cmdlet, as follows:

```
help Add-PswaAuthorizationRule -Examples
```

Only for the purposes of the lab, we run the following command:

```
Add-PswaAuthorizationRule -UserName * -ComputerName *
  -ConfigurationName *
```

Remember that this is to turn off authorization rules and simply allow all the users to access all the endpoints in the computer. This is, however, not good for production. You can plan this for groups and delegate the access as required.

Using the following code, we will provide access to one admin ID:

```
$param = @{
UserName = 'DSCDEMOLAB\ChenV'
ComputerName = $env:COMPUTERNAME
ConfigurationName = 'Microsoft.PowerShell'
Force = $true
Verbose = $true
}
Add-PswaAuthorizationRule @param
```

We used the `Force` parameter to avoid the following prompt:

Once the preceding code is executed, we will get the following output:

Id	RuleName	User	Destination	ConfigurationName
0	Rule 0	DSCDEMOLAB\ChenV	WMF5Node03.DSCDemoLab.com	Microsoft.PowerShell

Now, we can use this application in our custom applications based on the scenario and requirements. All we need to ensure is security.

Management OData IIS Extensions

OData, which stands for **Open Data Protocol**, is a RESTful web protocol. OData is based on HTTP and JSON, and using this, we can perform operations such as querying and updating.

We will cover the ODataUtils class before starting with OData IIS Extensions.

OData allows us to create a client-side module based on the OData endpoints. This is based on CDXML. Just take a look at the Microsoft.PowerShell.ODataUtils module.

This module has a single command, Export-ODataEndpointProxy, but is very powerful for exploring management data.

Let's create a client-side module using the following code:

```
$Odata = @{
  Uri = 'http://services.odata.org/v3/(S(snyobsk1hhutkb2yulwldgf1))/
    odata/odata.svc'
  MetadataUri = 'http://services.odata.org/v3/
    (S(snyobsk1hhutkb2yulwldgf1))/odata/odata.svc/$metadata'
  OutputModule = 'C:\Temp\DemoModule'
  AllowUnSecureConnection = $true
}
Export-odataEndpointProxy @Odata
```

The output is illustrated in the following image:

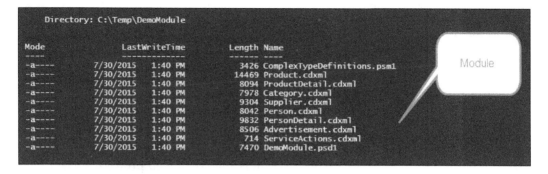

```
    Directory: C:\Temp\DemoModule


Mode                LastWriteTime         Length Name
----                -------------         ------ ----
-a----        7/30/2015     1:40 PM         3426 ComplexTypeDefinitions.psm1
-a----        7/30/2015     1:40 PM        14469 Product.cdxml
-a----        7/30/2015     1:40 PM         8094 ProductDetail.cdxml
-a----        7/30/2015     1:40 PM         7978 Category.cdxml
-a----        7/30/2015     1:40 PM         9304 Supplier.cdxml
-a----        7/30/2015     1:40 PM         8042 Person.cdxml
-a----        7/30/2015     1:40 PM         9832 PersonDetail.cdxml
-a----        7/30/2015     1:40 PM         8506 Advertisement.cdxml
-a----        7/30/2015     1:40 PM          714 ServiceActions.cdxml
-a----        7/30/2015     1:40 PM         7470 DemoModule.psd1
```

Module

In the preceding example, we have used the following parameters:

- The Uri parameter
- The MetadataUri parameter
- The OutputModule parameter
- The AllowUnsecureConnection parameter

Use the Import-Module cmdlet to use this module. Take a look at the following image:

```
PS C:\> Import-Module C:\Temp\DemoModule -Verbose
VERBOSE: Loading module from path 'C:\Temp\DemoModule\DemoModule.psd1'.
VERBOSE: Loading module from path 'C:\Temp\DemoModule\ComplexTypeDefinitions.psm1'.
VERBOSE: Loading module from path 'C:\Temp\DemoModule\ServiceActions.cdxml'.
VERBOSE: Loading module from path 'C:\Temp\DemoModule\Product.cdxml'.
VERBOSE: Importing function 'Get-Product'.
VERBOSE: Importing function 'New-Product'.
VERBOSE: Importing function 'Remove-Product'.
VERBOSE: Importing function 'Set-Product'.
VERBOSE: Loading module from path 'C:\Temp\DemoModule\ProductDetail.cdxml'.
VERBOSE: Importing function 'Get-ProductDetail'.
VERBOSE: Importing function 'New-ProductDetail'.
VERBOSE: Importing function 'Remove-ProductDetail'.
VERBOSE: Importing function 'Set-ProductDetail'.
VERBOSE: Loading module from path 'C:\Temp\DemoModule\Category.cdxml'.
VERBOSE: Importing function 'Get-Category'.
VERBOSE: Importing function 'New-Category'.
VERBOSE: Importing function 'Remove-Category'.
VERBOSE: Importing function 'Set-Category'.
VERBOSE: Loading module from path 'C:\Temp\DemoModule\Supplier.cdxml'.
VERBOSE: Importing function 'Get-Supplier'.
VERBOSE: Importing function 'New-Supplier'.
VERBOSE: Importing function 'Remove-Supplier'.
VERBOSE: Importing function 'Set-Supplier'.
VERBOSE: Loading module from path 'C:\Temp\DemoModule\Person.cdxml'.
VERBOSE: Importing function 'Get-Person'.
```

Import-Module - Result

To explore the available commands, we can use the following cmdlet:

```
Get-Command -Module DemoModule
```

```
PS C:\> Get-Command -Module DemoModule

CommandType     Name                        Version    Source
-----------     ----                        -------    ------
Function        Get-Advertisement           1.0        DemoModule
Function        Get-Category                1.0        DemoModule
Function        Get-Person                  1.0        DemoModule
Function        Get-PersonDetail            1.0        DemoModule
Function        Get-Product                 1.0        DemoModule
Function        Get-ProductDetail           1.0        DemoModule
Function        Get-Supplier                1.0        DemoModule
Function        New-Advertisement           1.0        DemoModule
Function        New-Category                1.0        DemoModule
Function        New-Person                  1.0        DemoModule
Function        New-PersonDetail            1.0        DemoModule
Function        New-Product                 1.0        DemoModule
Function        New-ProductDetail           1.0        DemoModule
Function        New-Supplier                1.0        DemoModule
Function        Remove-Advertisement        1.0        DemoModule
Function        Remove-Category             1.0        DemoModule
Function        Remove-Person               1.0        DemoModule
Function        Remove-PersonDetail         1.0        DemoModule
Function        Remove-Product              1.0        DemoModule
Function        Remove-ProductDetail        1.0        DemoModule
Function        Remove-Supplier             1.0        DemoModule
Function        Set-Advertisement           1.0        DemoModule
Function        Set-Category                1.0        DemoModule
Function        Set-Person                  1.0        DemoModule
Function        Set-PersonDetail            1.0        DemoModule
Function        Set-Product                 1.0        DemoModule
Function        Set-ProductDetail           1.0        DemoModule
Function        Set-Supplier                1.0        DemoModule
```

Available Commands

Now, we can use the following commands to get the management data information:

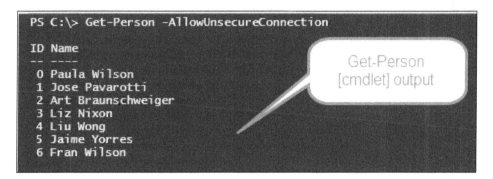

```
PS C:\> Get-Person -AllowUnsecureConnection

ID Name
-- ----
 0 Paula Wilson
 1 Jose Pavarotti
 2 Art Braunschweiger
 3 Liz Nixon
 4 Liu Wong
 5 Jaime Yorres
 6 Fran Wilson
```

Get-Person [cmdlet] output

We can also modify this module to suit our requirements. The OData endpoint we used is a read-only type, so we can't set the values for now.

You can open and explore CDXML. Don't break this because it's not easy to fix.

Creating the Management OData web service

The Management OData IIS extension is an infrastructure using which we can create an ASP.NET web service endpoint. This web service contains management data, which can be accessed using Windows PowerShell. In this exercise, let's create an OData web service; for this, we need the following:

- **OData Schema Designer**
- Features such as `IIS-WebServerRole`, `IIS-WebServer`, `IIS-HttpTracing`, and `IIS-Management` OData

Use the following link to download Management OData Schema Designer:

```
https://visualstudiogallery.msdn.microsoft.com/77bb35c1-7695-4f5e-
ba1a-9ffeb6fe0d14
```

There are handy codes available in gallery to create Management OData Web Service; they can be found at the following site:

```
https://code.msdn.microsoft.com/windowsdesktop/PswsRoleBasedPlugins-
9c79b75a
```

By following these steps, we can create Management OData Web Service.

Exploring web requests

Web requests help us request data from **Uniform Resource Identifier (URI)**. A developer performs many tasks using a web request, such as finding a response, downloading files, and reading files from the Internet.

In this topic, we will take a look at the cmdlets used for web requests and the `WebRequest` class.

Using the Windows PowerShell cmdlet, `Invoke-WebRequest`, we can perform a few tasks. Run the following command:

```
#Read the help document
help Invoke-WebRequest -Detailed
```

This gives the help content.

```
#Using the command
$site = Invoke-WebRequest http://www.Bing.com
$site | GM
```

This lists the members (Methods and Properties)

```
#Checking the Status Code
"The Site Status Code is `t" + $site.StatusCode
"Description`t" + $site.StatusDescription
```

The preceding command outputs the status code and description, as shown in the following image:

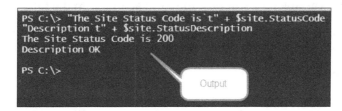

Now, run the following command:

```
Invoke-WebRequest -Uri http://www.Bing.com
```

The `Invoke-WebRequest` cmdlet sends http(s), FTP, and file requests and returns the collections of forms, links, images, and related HTML, as shown in the following image:

```
StatusCode        : 200
StatusDescription : OK
Content           : <!DOCTYPE html PUBLIC "-//W3C//DTD XHTML 1.0 Transitional//EN"
                    "http://www.w3.org/TR/xhtml1/DTD/xhtml1-transitional.dtd"><html lang="nl"
                    xml:lang="nl" xmlns="http://www.w3.org/1999/xhtml"><script type...
RawContent        : HTTP/1.1 200 OK
                    Vary: Accept-Encoding
                    Content-Length: 59399
                    Cache-Control: private, max-age=0
                    Content-Type: text/html; charset=utf-8
                    P3P: CP="NON UNI COM NAV STA LOC CURa DEVa PSAa PSDa OUR IND"...
Forms             : {sb_form}
Headers           : {[Vary, Accept-Encoding], [Content-Length, 59399], [Cache-Control, private,
                    max-age=0], [Content-Type, text/html; charset=utf-8]...}
Images            : {@{innerHTML=; innerText=; outerHTML=<IMG id=id_p class="b_icon id_avatar"
                    style="DISPLAY: none" src="data:image/gif;base64,R0lGODlhAQABAIAAAAAAAP///yH5BAEAA
                    AEALAAAAAABAAEAAAIBTAA7">; outerText=; tagName=IMG; id=id_p; class=b_icon
                    id_avatar; style=DISPLAY: none; src=data:image/gif;base64,R0lGODlhAQABAIAAAAAAAP//
                    /yH5BAEAAAEALAAAAAABAAEAAAIBTAA7}}
InputFields       : {@{innerHTML=; innerText=; outerHTML=<INPUT spellcheck=false id=sb_form_q
                    title="Voer de zoekterm in" class=b_searchbox maxLength=1000 name=q
                    autocomplete="off" autocorrect="off" autocapitalize="off">; outerText=;
                    tagName=INPUT; spellcheck=false; id=sb_form_q; title=Voer de zoekterm in;
                    class=b_searchbox; maxLength=1000; name=q; autocomplete=off; autocorrect=off;
                    autocapitalize=off}, @{innerHTML=; innerText=; outerHTML=<INPUT tabIndex=0
                    id=sb_form_go title=Zoeken class=b_searchboxSubmit type=submit value="Submit
                    Query" name=go>; outerText=; tagName=INPUT; tabIndex=0; id=sb_form_go;
```

Let's try to log in to Facebook using the `Invoke-WebRequest` cmdlet:

```
$request = Invoke-WebRequest 'https://www.facebook.com/login.php'
  -SessionVariable lgn
$Forms = $request.Forms[0]
$Forms.Fields
```

This returns the internal field names. We can do the same using the **View Source** option in the browser. Run the following command:

```
$Forms.Fields['email'] = 'UserID'
$Forms.Fields['Password'] = 'Password'
```

Using the preceding code, we can pass the username and password credentials.

Using the session variable, we will post the form action. Run the following command:

```
$login =Invoke-WebRequest -Uri ("https://www.facebook.com" +
  $form.Action) -WebSession $lgn -Method POST -Body $Forms.Fields
```

The output of the session variable `$lgn` is shown in the following image:

```
Headers               : {}
Cookies               : System.Net.CookieContainer
UseDefaultCredentials : False
Credentials           :
Certificates          :
UserAgent             : Mozilla/5.0 (Windows NT; Windows NT 6.1; en-US) WindowsPowerShell/5.0.10100.0
Proxy                 :
MaximumRedirection    : -1
```

Now, let's take a look at the POST action's output:

```
$login =Invoke-WebRequest -Uri ("https://www.facebook.com" +
  $form.Action) -WebSession $lgn -Method POST -Body $Forms.Fields
$fb = $login.Forms[0]
$fb
```

The output is illustrated in the following image:

```
PS C:\> $login =Invoke-WebRequest -Uri ("https://www.facebook.com" + $form.Action) -WebSession $lgn -Method POST -Body $Forms.Fields
$fb = $login.Forms[0]
PS C:\> $fb
                                             Action
Id          Method Action                                        Fields
--          ------ ------                                        ------
login_form post   https://www.facebook.com/login.php?login_attempt=1 {[lsd, AVolEewt], [email, ], [pass, ], [u_0_v, Aanmelden]...}
```

Executing the following command returns the e-mail ID:

```
$Forms.Fields
```

However, the password will not be shown here. So, you can run the following command, which will show you the information:

```
$login.RawContent
```

In order to play with **Representation State Transfer** (**REST**), PowerShell has the `Invoke-RestMethod` cmdlet:

```
help Invoke-RestMethod -Detailed
```

The cool feature of Windows PowerShell is that it will format the return type based on the output response. If the output response is in RSS or ATOM, the XML nodes will be in those formats; however, for JSON and XML, they will be deserialized as objects.

In contrast to `Invoke-WebRequest`, we use `Invoke-RestMethod` because we obtain the contents, and it excludes the headers.

The following code returns the contents; this is not a friendly output:

```
Invoke-RestMethod -Uri http://blogs.technet.com/b/wikininjas/rss.aspx
```

So, we can play with this to get the information required, as follows:

```
Invoke-RestMethod -Uri http://blogs.technet.com/b/wikininjas/rss.aspx |
Select Creator , link
```

We can explore the methods and properties and get the output, as follows:

```
Invoke-RestMethod -Uri http://blogs.technet.com/b/wikininjas/rss.aspx |
Select Creator , PubDate
```

Downloading files from the Internet

Using PowerShell, we can download files from the Internet. Let's consider that you need to download a bunch of files from various portals and process them for reporting. Windows PowerShell is an easy way to achieve this. Run the following command:

```
$param = @{
  URI = 'http://powershell.com/Mastering-PowerShell.pdf'
  Outfile = 'C:\Temp\Mastering-PowerShell.pdf'
}
Invoke-RestMethod @param
```

Now, we will find the `Mastering-PowerShell.pdf` file in our `C:\Temp` folder.

Alternatively, we can use `System.Net.WebClient` as well. Run the following command:

```
$wc = New-Object System.Net.WebClient

$wc.DownloadFile('http://powershell.com/Mastering-PowerShell.pdf' ,
  'C:\Temp\Mastering-PowerShell.pdf')
```

As we will use this for multiple downloads, naming each file is not a good option. So, we will tweak it a little more and save the file with the default name. Run the following command:

```
$Images = 'Url1/image1.jpg , url1/image2.jpg'

$Dir = 'C:\Temp\'

$wc = New-Object System.Net.WebClient

foreach ($sourceFile in $Images){

  $sourceFileName =
    $sourceFile.SubString($sourceFile.LastIndexOf('/')+1)

  $targetFileName = $targetDirectory + $sourceFileName

  $wc.DownloadFile($sourceFile, 'C:\Temp')

}
```

Reading a file from the Internet

Reading files from the Internet using PowerShell is a good option, but we don't want to open the browser all the time. We can read RSS and obtain information related to it. We did this using the `Invoke-WebRequest` cmdlet in the previous topic. Now, we will use the `WebClient` class. Run the following command:

```
$url = "http://blogs.technet.com/b/wikininjas/rss.aspx"
```

The URL we have picked up is TechNet Wiki Ninjas RSS.

In the following code, we will typecast it with XML:

```
[xml]$xml = (New-object System.Net.WebClient).DownloadString($url)
```

Let's consider the output of XML; take a look at the following command and the subsequent image:

```
$url = "http://blogs.technet.com/b/wikininjas/rss.aspx"

[xml]$xml = (New-object System.Net.WebClient).DownloadString($url)

$xml
```

```
PS C:\> $url = "http://blogs.technet.com/b/wikininjas/rss.aspx"
[xml]$xml = (New-object System.Net.WebClient).DownloadString($url)
$xml                                                                          RSS - Easy to
                                                                              play now!
xml                              xml-stylesheet                                        rss
---                              --------------                                        ---
version="1.0" encoding="UTF-8" type="text/xsl" href="http://blogs.technet.com/utility/feedstylesheets/rss.xsl" media="screen" rss
```

To read the description of the given RSS feed, we will execute the following code:

```
$xml.rss.channel.description
```

This returns the following:

```
Wiki Ninjas is a group of authors who celebrate and evangelize the
community catalyst and social-authoring excellence that is called TechNet
Wiki.
```

To read the creators, we will execute the following code:

```
$url = "http://blogs.technet.com/b/wikininjas/rss.aspx"

[xml]$xml = (New-object System.Net.WebClient).DownloadString($url)

$xml.rss.channel | %{$_.item} | ? {[DateTime]$_.pubDate -gt
   (Get-Date).AddMonths(-3)} | FT creator
```

You can add `link`, `pubdate`, and perform many other tasks. To see a post that was published one week earlier, run the following command:

```
$url = "http://blogs.technet.com/b/wikininjas/rss.aspx"

[xml]$xml = (New-object System.Net.WebClient).DownloadString($url)

$xml.rss.channel | %{$_.item} | ? {[DateTime]$_.pubDate -gt
   (Get-Date).AddDays(-7)} | FT creator , pubdate -AutoSize
```

Take a look at the following image:

```
PS C:\> $url = "http://blogs.technet.com/b/wikininjas/rss.aspx"
[xml]$xml = (New-object System.Net.WebClient).DownloadString($url)
$xml.rss.channel | %{$_.item} | ? {[DateTime]$_.pubDate -gt (Get-Date).AddDays(-7)} | FT creator , pubdate -AutoSize

creator           pubDate
-------           -------
Durval Ramos      Fri, 31 Jul 2015 02:03:08 GMT
Ed Price - MSFT   Tue, 28 Jul 2015 07:00:00 GMT
Ed Price - MSFT   Sun, 26 Jul 2015 17:10:00 GMT
XAML guy          Sat, 25 Jul 2015 23:07:23 GMT
Ed Price - MSFT   Sat, 25 Jul 2015 00:35:00 GMT
```

Exploring web services

A web service is generally an XML-based program. Using this, we can exchange data over a network. A web service is nothing but an application component, which works on an open protocol, can be used by other applications, and is reusable.

Web services allow interaction between applications and use standardized XML. Simply put, it's a combination of XML and HTTP. The following components work for all web services:

- **Simple Object Access Protocol (SOAP)**
- **Universal Description, Discovery, and Integration (UDDI)**
- **Web Services Description Language (WSDL)**

In this topic, we will demonstrate the use of web services and complex web services using Windows PowerShell.

Using web services

`New-WebServiceProxy` is a cmdlet that allows us to create a proxy object of any given valid web service.

For our example, we will use the following web service:

```
http://www.webservicex.net/CurrencyConvertor.asmx?WSDL
```

Run the following command:

```
$var = New-WebServiceProxy -Uri
  http://www.webservicex.net/CurrencyConvertor.asmx?WSDL
```

```
$var.ConversionRate
```

This returns the overload definitions of the conversion rate method, as shown in the following image:

Points marked in the image we just saw are explained as follows:

- **1**: The first argument should be `FromCurrency`
- **2**: The second argument should be `ToCurrency`

Here is a simple example of this:

```
$var = New-WebServiceProxy -Uri
  http://www.webservicex.net/CurrencyConvertor.asmx?WSDL
$var.ConversionRate('Eur','US')
```

This returns the output as `1.0979` — the current conversion value.

How do we know the currency codes? Just open the following URL in a browser:

```
http://www.webservicex.net/CurrencyConvertor.asmx?WSDL
```

This shows the output as illustrated in the following image:

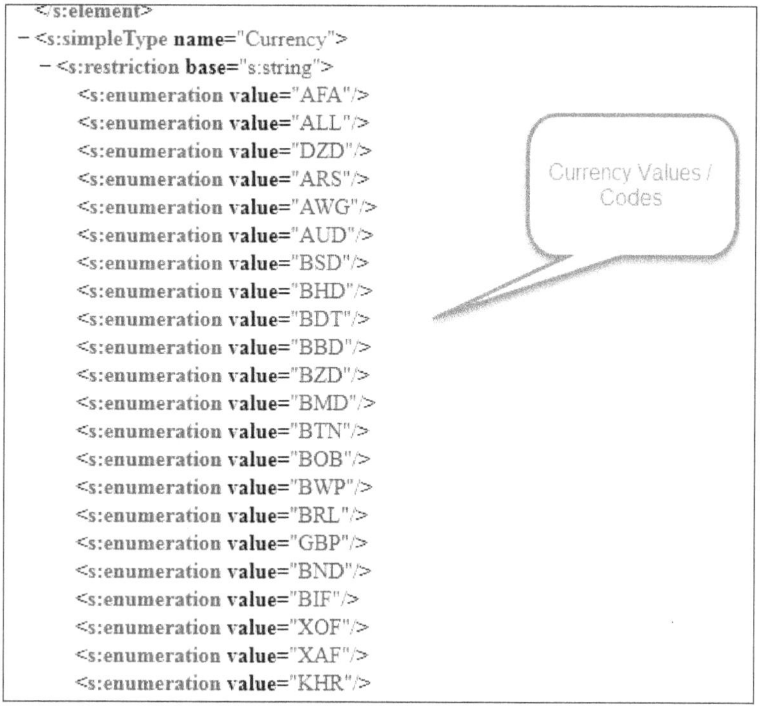

Similarly, we can use the **GlobalWeather** web service to retrieve information:

```
http://www.webservicex.net/globalweather.asmx?wsdl
```

Run the following command:

```
$weather = New-WebServiceProxy -uri
  http://www.webservicex.com/globalweather.asmx?WSDL
([XML]$weather.GetWeather('Amsterdam','Netherlands')).CurrentWeather
```

The output is illustrated in the following image:

Web services are usually limited to XML and SOAP, but they may be in the JSON format as well. So, it's worth considering an example that returns results in the JSON format.

Let's use an Apple iTunes URL, which returns an output in the JSON format:

```
http://itunes.apple.com/search?term=metallica
```

If we open this URL in the browser, we will see the output as shown in the following image:

Here, we will not use the `Invoke-RestMethod` cmdlet because it formats the data by default. Instead, we will use the `Invoke-WebRequest` cmdlet for the `ConvertFrom-Json` cmdlet:

```
$Json = Invoke-WebRequest -Uri
  "http://itunes.apple.com/search?term=metallica"

$Json
```

Take a look at the following image:

```
StatusCode        : 200
StatusDescription : OK
Content           :

                           {
                            "resultCount":50,
                            "results": [
                            {"wrapperType":"track", "kind":"song", "artistId":3996865, "collectionId":579372950, "trackId":579373079, "artistName":"Metallica",
                            "collectionName":"Metallica", ...
RawContent        : HTTP/1.1 200 OK
                    x-apple-jingle-correlation-key: IIGLVAHYXJEPAMBMJGYB2LTHAE
                    x-apple-translated-wo-url: /WebObjects/MZStoreServices.woa/ws/wsSearch?term=metallica&urlDesc=
                    x-apple-orig-url: http://it...
Forms             : {}
Headers           : {[x-apple-jingle-correlation-key, IIGLVAHYXJEPAMBMJGYB2LTHAE], [x-apple-translated-wo-url,
                    /WebObjects/MZStoreServices.woa/ws/wsSearch?term=metallica&urlDesc=], [x-apple-orig-url,
                    http://itunes.apple.com/search?term=metallica], [x-apple-application-site, ST11]...}
Images            : {}
InputFields       : {}
Links             : {}
ParsedHtml        : mshtml.HTMLDocumentClass
RawContentLength  : 76958
```

JSON in PowerShell as Content

Now, we will play with the PowerShell code to convert this content into a readable format:

```
$Json = Invoke-WebRequest -Uri
    "http://itunes.apple.com/search?term=metallica"
```

```
($Json | ConvertFrom-Json).Results | Select WrapperType, trackName |
    Select -First 25
```

Now, consider the following image:

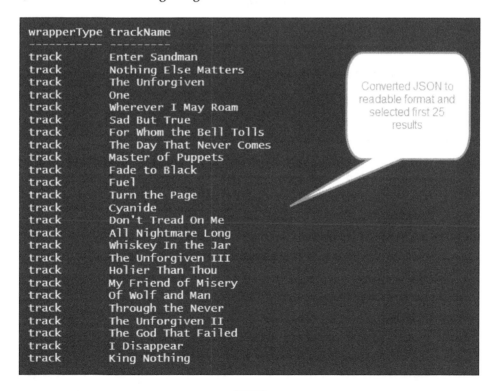

```
wrapperType trackName
----------- ---------
track       Enter Sandman
track       Nothing Else Matters
track       The Unforgiven
track       One
track       Wherever I May Roam
track       Sad But True
track       For Whom the Bell Tolls
track       The Day That Never Comes
track       Master of Puppets
track       Fade to Black
track       Fuel
track       Turn the Page
track       Cyanide
track       Don't Tread On Me
track       All Nightmare Long
track       Whiskey In the Jar
track       The Unforgiven III
track       Holier Than Thou
track       My Friend of Misery
track       Of Wolf and Man
track       Through the Never
track       The Unforgiven II
track       The God That Failed
track       I Disappear
track       King Nothing
```

Converted JSON to readable format and selected first 25 results

Alternatively, we can use the `Invoke-RestMethod` cmdlet and do the same:

```
$Json = Invoke-RestMethod -Uri
  "http://itunes.apple.com/search?term=metallica"
$Json.results | Select WrapperType , trackName | Select -First 25
```

Building web services

In this exercise, we will take a look at the steps required to build web services. For this, we will use the following environments:

- Windows Server 2012
- Visual Studio 2013
- The installed IIS server

We configured IIS in WMF5Node03 to demonstrate PowerShell web access; now, let's connect to the same box and build a small web service. Perform the following steps:

1. Open **Visual Studio**.
2. Select **.NET framework 3.5**.
3. Then, select **ASP.NET Web Service**.
4. Select **HTTP** and name your site.
5. In our scenario, we will name it `http://localhost/website`.

Visual Studio builds the basic web service. You can run the following command:

```
Imports System.Web
Imports System.Web.Services
Imports System.Web.Services.Protocols
' To allow this Web Service to be called from script, using ASP.NET AJAX,
uncomment the following line.
' <System.Web.Script.Services.ScriptService()> _
<WebService(Namespace:="http://tempuri.org/")> _
<WebServiceBinding(ConformsTo:=WsiProfiles.BasicProfile1_1)> _
<Global.Microsoft.VisualBasic.CompilerServices.DesignerGenerated()> _
Public Class Service
    Inherits System.Web.Services.WebService
    <WebMethod()> _
    Public Function HelloWorld() As String
```

```
        Return "This is a Basic and Default Web Service!"
    End Function
End Class
```

Take a look at the following image:

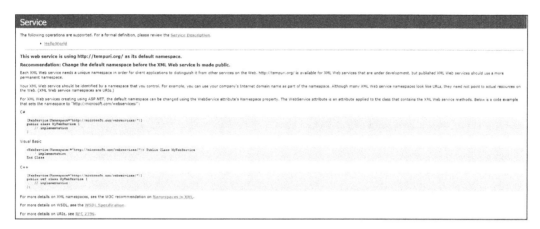

So, now we have the URL; we simply changed the `Hello World` text to something else, as follows:

`http://localhost/website/Service.asmx`

Okay, spin up PowerShell now!

Points marked in the figure are explained as follows:

- **1**: At the end of the URL, append `?wsdl`
- **2**: Assign it to the variable named `$local`
- **3**: Invoke the function `HelloWorld()`
- **4**: It returns the default output

Invoke after doing text changes in the code which return your newly updated text

Now, in `Service.vb`, add the following code:

```
<WebMethod()> _
Public Function Add(a, b) As Int32
    Return a + b
End Function
```

We can add two values in Windows PowerShell:

```
$local.Add(2,3)
```

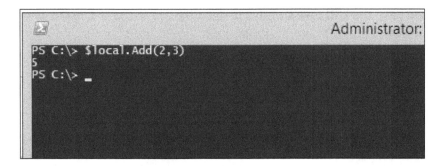

Create your own web service and consume Windows PowerShell to use it.

Exploring the REST API

REST is the abbreviated form of Representational State Transfers. Using this, we can connect to the server from a client over HTTP and manipulate resources. In short, REST is a software architectural model commonly used on the World Wide Web.

Take a look at the help document of the `Invoke-RestMethod` method which sends an HTTP or HTTPS request to a RESTful web service.

Using the Azure REST API in PowerShell

Managing **Azure** is easy using the REST API and PowerShell. No need for employees clicking Azure machines to retrieve information from the Azure portal. Many IT professionals use the Azure module to automate tasks in Azure, such as building, restarting, and removing the server, and many more. Before we start using the REST API, let's explore a few Azure cmdlets.

As with any other module, we need to import the Azure module as well. A few errors in the Azure module might be misleading, but we can safely ignore these for now.

The first step is to get the Azure publish settings file. Run the following command:

```
Import-Module Azure -verbose
Get-AzurePublishSettingsFile
```

The preceding command opens up your default browser and downloads the file. The next step is to import the Azure file. Run the following command:

```
Import-AzurePublishSettingsFile -PublishSettingsFile C:\Temp\File
```

That's it! Now, we can play with the Azure cmdlets.

Approximately 737 cmdlets are available in the Azure module. Explore the help and automate your tasks. As this topic is about the Azure REST API, let's create a website for us to walk through. Run the following command:

```
New-AzureWebsite -Name "MyAzureSiteDemo" -Verbose
```

Well! We've now created an Azure website. Very much in a human readable style which is PowerShell Verb-Noun with parameters. You may wonder, what does the preceding command do? It simply creates a new Azure website. Indeed, you can create multiple sites; for this, we need to consider the Name property. Run the following command:

```
help New-AzureWebsite -Parameter Name
```

Now, take a look at the following image:

```
PS C:\> help New-AzureWebsite -Parameter Name

-Name <String>
    The name of the website

    Required?                       false
    Position?                       1
    Default value
    Accept pipeline input?          true (ByPropertyName)
    Accept wildcard characters?     false
```

This accepts pipeline inputs. The following code shows the method to process multiple sites.

```
"Site1" , "Site2" | %{

  New-AzureWebsite -Name $_ -Verbose

}
```

Now, let us see the **Kudu** project from Git—It's huge, so you need to go through the details using the following link:

```
https://github.com/projectkudu/kudu
```

With reference to this link, we will try to fetch the version with the site's last modified time stamp, as follows:

```
$site = Get-AzureWebsite -Name MyAzureSiteDemo

$username = $site.PublishingUsername

$password = $site.PublishingPassword

$base64AuthInfo = [Convert]::ToBase64String([Text.Encoding]
  ::ASCII.GetBytes(("{0}:{1}" -f $username,$password)))

$api = "https://$($site.Name).scm.azurewebsites.net/api"

$kudu = Invoke-RestMethod -Uri "$api/environment" -Headers
  @{Authorization=("Basic {0}" -f $base64AuthInfo)} -Method GET

$kudu
```

Output of the command is shown in the following figure:

```
PS C:\> $site = Get-AzureWebSite -Name MyAzureSiteDemo  ①
$username = $site.PublishingUsername  ②
$password = $site.PublishingPassword
$base64AuthInfo = [Convert]::ToBase64String([Text.Encoding]::ASCII.GetBytes(("{0}:{1}" -f $username,$password)))  ③
$api = "https://$($site.Name).scm.azurewebsites.net/api"  ④
$kudu = Invoke-RestMethod -Uri "$api/environment" -Headers @{Authorization=("Basic {0}" -f $base64AuthInfo)} -Method GET
$kudu  ⑤                        ⑥                        ⑦

version        siteLastModified
-------        ----------------       ⑧
47.40727.1709.0 2015-07-31T16:42:45.7700000Z
```

The code performs eight actions to fetch the information we need:

- **1**: First, it obtains the azure website information as Object.

- **2**: Then, it gets the username and password of the site (This is a property of the `Get-AzureWebSite` cmdlet).

- **3**: By typecasting the code, it will convert the authentication to base64 encoding.

- **4**: Here, we used the API URL—this is REST (Note that the site we created doesn't have the GIT resource mapped—it's just a dummy site).

- **5**: Now, the power of the `Invoke-WebRequest` cmdlet comes into the picture—we have come across this cmdlet and its features in the previous topic.

- **6**: In the preceding code, we used an environment in the URL. If you are interested in exploring and doing more, refer to the following link and proceed further: `https://github.com/projectkudu/kudu/wiki/REST-API`

- **7**: In this step, we used the `Authorization` headers. This parameter is of the `<IDictionary>` type and can't be used for the user agent or cookie. Just specify the header like shown in the code. Here we are passing the authorization value as `Basic` and `{0}` represents the place holder. The value of the `$base64AuthInfo` variable will be passed like `Basic <$base64AuthInfo>`.

- **8**: Finally, we retrieved the output, as you saw in the figure.

However, this is not enough for the infrastructure, so we need to do more! We need to jump-start **Azure Resource Manager (ARM)**. We do have a module for this where we can manage the Azure environment—behind the scenes, it invokes the REST API.

If you are a DevOps looking for an ARM and **Application Lifecycle Management (ALM)** integration, use the following link:

```
https://www.microsoftvirtualacademy.com/en-us/training-courses/azure-
resource-manager-devops-jump-start-8413
```

As the following modules are separated:

- `AzureResourceManager`
- `AzureServiceManagement`

To explore resource manager, we should first run the following command:

```
Switch-AzureMode -Name AzureResourceManager
#or
Switch-AzureMode -Name AzureServiceManagement
```

Read the help document, explore Azure, and use the REST API.

Exploring JSON

JavaScript Object Notation (JSON) is a lightweight, text-based, open standard that is designed for data interchange. It is language-independent, with parsers available for Windows PowerShell.

The JSON format is often used to serialize and transmit structured data over a network connection. It is used primarily to transmit data between a server and a web application, as an alternative to XML.

You can use the following link to validate the JSON format:

`http://jsonformatter.curiousconcept.com/`

Here is a simple example of the JSON Format:

```
{
    "Title":   "Mr.",
    "Name":   "Scripting"
}
```

Windows PowerShell has two cmdlets: `ConvertFrom-Json` and `ConvertTo-Json`. Take a look at the following image:

```
PS C:\> Get-Command -Name *JSON*

CommandType     Name                Version     Source
-----------     ----                -------     ------
Cmdlet          ConvertFrom-Json    3.1.0.0     Microsoft.PowerShell.Utility
Cmdlet          ConvertTo-Json      3.1.0.0     Microsoft.PowerShell.Utility
```

As the name reads, it converts to and from. Let's take a look at how the following code works:

```
$json = @"
{
    "Title":  "Mr.",
    "Name":  "Scripting"
}
"@
$json | ConvertFrom-Json
```

Now, consider the following image:

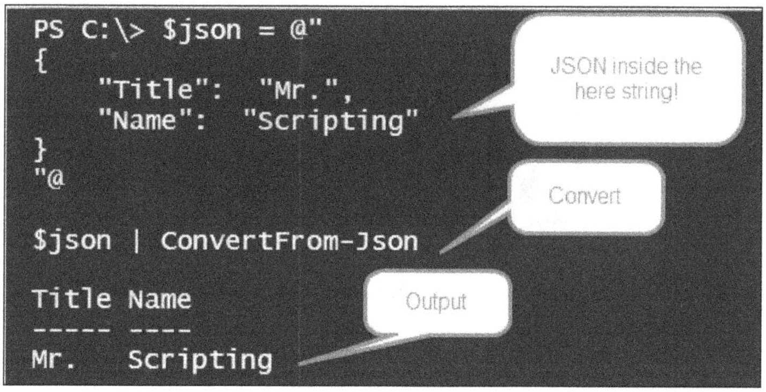

The steps performed in the figure we just saw is explained as follows:

- We have passed the JSON formatted code inside the here-string
- Using pipeline we are converting the JSON to a PSCustomObject
- Where Title and Name will be a NoteProperty with the values

Take a look at the following image:

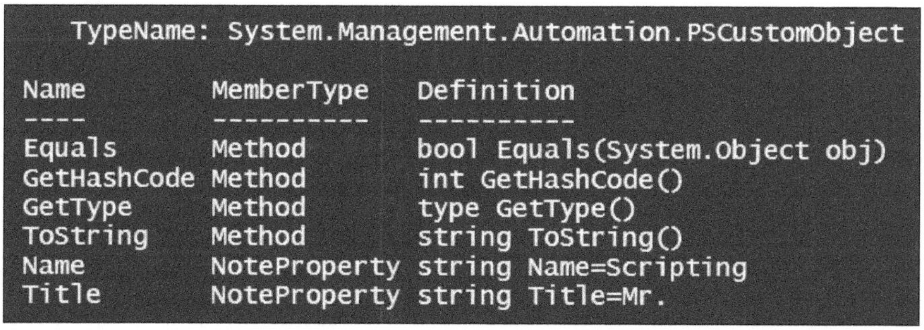

Using JSON cmdlets, we can manipulate the contents as required:

```
$json = @"
{
    "User1": {"Name": "Chen", "Role": "SharePoint IT Pro"},
      "User2": {"Name":"Keanu"}
}
"@
$data = $json | ConvertFrom-Json
$data.User1
$data.User2
```

Now, consider the following image:

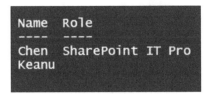

It's easy to read a JSON file in PowerShell. Let's consider that we have a JSON file, as follows:

```
{
"1": "One",
"2": "Two",
"3": "Three"
}
$data = Get-Content C:\Temp\JSON.json -Raw | ConvertFrom-Json
$data.psobject.Properties.Name
```

The preceding code will provide the output as 1, 2, and 3.

Summary

In this chapter, we explored a few, good features of Windows PowerShell, especially the ones related to web technologies. Using this, we can automate tasks such as installing or uninstalling PowerShell Web Access and configuring it, tasks related to web requests, and consuming web services to perform some tasks. As JSON is considered to be an alternative to XML, and is language–independent, we can use it in Windows PowerShell and perform our web-based queries or other tasks easily and effectively.

In the next chapter, we will discuss the usage of **Application Programming Interfaces (API)** in Windows PowerShell.

5
Exploring Application Programming Interface

Application Programming Interface (**API**) is a set of protocols, routines, and tools used to build software applications. The main purpose of API is data exchange and integration, whereas **Software Development Kit** (**SDK**) is customization. The type of API varies based on the data exchange and transport mechanism. The transport mechanism may be web-based, source code, or binary function.

Following are the most common types of API:

- Web Services API
  - ° This is an API that is highly useful in up and coming technologies. It is hypertext-based and the standards used are REST, SOAP, XML-RPC, and JSON-RPC.
  - ° It is commonly used in web applications and **service-oriented architecture** (**SOA**).

- Source code API
  - ° This offers libraries of objects, classes, and so on
  - ° It is commonly used in development projects
  - ° The standards used vary based on the platform, such as .NET or J2EE

In this chapter, we will cover the following topics:

- Exploring API using PowerShell
- The **Exchange Web Services** (**EWS**) API for managing online exchange, along with a demo involving purging items in mailbox folders and deleting items

- The Lync 2013 / Skype for Business client-side API—installing the Lync API, exploring the client settings, automating test calls, and holding an IM conversation with contacts
- Client server object model for managing **SharePoint Online**—installing client-side SDK
- Exploring **client-side object model (CSOM)**
- Manipulating SharePoint lists using CSOM in PowerShell

Developers use APIs to accomplish many tasks; using PowerShell, we can only achieve our tasks to some extent. For example, let's consider a scenario where we need to interact with a Windows API; to achieve this, we can use the Windows API. Most IT professionals don't use API considering the fact that it's meant for development. However, we can leverage APIs in Windows PowerShell to perform administration as well as development tasks.

In the following example, we will try to use the Windows API in PowerShell as a jump start. Let's take a look at the PowerShell way of playing with the `User32.dll` file.

 You can also refer to `https://msdn.microsoft.com/en-us/` `library/windows/desktop/ms633548%28v=vs.85%29.aspx`

The C++ code used is as follows:

```
BOOL WINAPI ShowWindow(
  _In_  HWND hWnd,
  _In_  int nCmdShow
);
```

In Windows PowerShell, we will use the `Add-type` command for this exercise. This is not a big deal! It's a pretty old concept. However, to begin, we need to know how PowerShell loads the standard assembly. Later in this topic, we will examine the managed assemblies as well. Run the following command:

```
Help Add-Type -Detailed
```

Yes, as like all other cmdlets, we need to first read the help document before we proceed further. Using the preceding result, we can explore the parameters and related information. Now, we will build a PowerShell script that performs a few actions on Windows, which is as follows:

```
Function Set-Window {
  Param(
    [Parameter(Mandatory = $true)]
```

```
    $ID
)
$code = @"
[DllImport("user32.dll")]
public static extern bool ShowWindowAsync(IntPtr hWnd, int
    nCmdShow);
"@
$demo = Add-Type -MemberDefinition $code -Name "Demo" -Namespace
    Win32Functions -PassThru
$demo::ShowWindowAsync((Get-Process -id $ID).MainWindowHandle , 2)
}
Set-Window -ID $pid
```

How does this work? We created a PowerShell function named Set-Window, which accepts a parameter called ID. Run the following command:

```
$code = @"
[DllImport("user32.dll")]
public static extern bool ShowWindowAsync(IntPtr hWnd, int nCmdShow);
"@
```

Using the previous snippet of code inside the here-string, we will import the user32.dll file and consume the ShowWinodAsync function. This accepts the following two overloads:

- hWnd: An example of this is process information
- nCmdShow: This is a set of valid parameters listed in the following table:

Value	Meaning
SW_FORCEMINIMIZE 11	This minimizes a window even if the thread that owns the window is not responding. This flag should only be used while minimizing windows from a different thread.
SW_HIDE 0	This hides the window and activates another window.
SW_MAXIMIZE 3	This maximizes the specified window.
SW_MINIMIZE 6	This minimizes the specified window and activates the next top-level window in the Z order.

Value	Meaning
SW_RESTORE 9	This activates and displays the window. If the window is minimized or maximized, the system restores it to its original size and position. An application should specify this flag while restoring a minimized window.
SW_SHOW 5	This activates the window and displays it in its current size and position.
SW_SHOWDEFAULT 10	This sets the show state based on the *SW_* value specified in the STARTUPINFO (https://msdn.microsoft.com/en-us/library/windows/desktop/ms686331(v=vs.85).aspx) structure passed to the CreateProcess (https://msdn.microsoft.com/en-us/library/windows/desktop/ms682425(v=vs.85).aspx) function by the program that started the application.
SW_SHOWMAXIMIZED 3	This activates the window and displays it as a maximized window.
SW_SHOWMINIMIZED 2	This activates the window and displays it as a minimized window.
SW_ SHOWMINNOACTIVE 7	This displays the window as a minimized window. This value is similar to SW_SHOWMINIMIZED, except that the window is not activated.
SW_SHOWNA 8	This displays the window in its current size and position. This value is similar to SW_SHOW, except that the window is not activated.
SW_ SHOWNOACTIVATE 4	This displays a window in its most recent size and position. This value is similar to SW_SHOWNORMAL, except that the window is not activated.
SW_SHOWNORMAL 1	This activates and displays a window. If the window is minimized or maximized, the system restores it to its original size and position. An application should specify this flag while displaying the window for the first time.

To instantiate the ShowWindowAsnc function, we will use the Add-Type cmdlet and assign it to the $demo variable, as shown in the following command line:

```
$demo = Add-Type -MemberDefinition $code -Name "Demo" -Namespace
   Win32Functions -PassThru
$demo::ShowWindowAsync((Get-Process -id $ID).MainWindowHandle , 2)
Set-Window -ID $pid
```

As we used $pid while executing the function, the code will affect the current PowerShell console and minimize it. We can perform the advanced functions as required and build a PowerShell code with reference to the User32.dll file.

In this chapter, we will cover PowerShell and API use for Microsoft technologies such as SharePoint, Exchange, and Lync; so, for another short example of .NET, let's take a look at the speech API.

 Refer to the following URL for the System.Speech API:
https://msdn.microsoft.com/en-us/library/
gg145021%28v=vs.110%29.aspx

Run the following command:

```
Add-Type -AssemblyName System.Speech
$speak = New-Object System.Speech.Synthesis.SpeechSynthesizer
$speak.Rate = 1
$speak.Speak("Welcome to PowerShell 5.0")
```

The preceding code will speak out the text in the last line:

"Welcome to PowerShell 5.0"

This command will perform the following functions:

- It will load the System.Speech assembly
- It will create a $speak object
- It will control the speaking rate at 1
- It will speak out the text

Exploring API using PowerShell

We considered a basic example of using the Windows API. There are different ways to use APIs in PowerShell based on the requirements. Windows PowerShell has the feature of interacting with .NET DLL files as well. Let's consider that you have a code that simply performs addition operations that we can load in PowerShell and then explores the methods. But why are we discussing DLL now? Here is a comparison of API and DLL:

API	DLL
Abstract	Concrete
In this, the interface is implemented by the software program	This is a method of providing APIs
An API is an interface to the library of code	DLL is nothing but a library of code

In short, DLL is a file format and a way to use API.

Let's take a look at a demo where we will use a custom DLL file in Windows PowerShell. For this, we will choose a class library in Visual C# and build a code that will simply add two given integers.

The C# code is as follows:

```
using System;
using System.Collections.Generic;
using System.Linq;
using System.Text;
using System.Threading.Tasks;
namespace ClassLibrary2
{
    public class Class1
    {
        public static int sum(int a,int b)
        {
            return a + b;
        }
    }
}
```

Note that you can rename namespace and class, which helps others understand them. Here, we have selected the default options for demonstration purposes.

We can directly use this with the here-string, and with the help of the Add-Type cmdlet, we can call the sum function and add two integer values. Run the following command:

```
$code = @"
using System;
using System.Collections.Generic;
using System.Linq;
using System.Text;
using System.Threading.Tasks;
namespace ClassLibrary2
{
    public class Class1
    {
        public static int sum(int a,int b)
        {
            return a + b;
        }
    }
}
"@
Add-Type -TypeDefinition $code
[ClassLibrary2.Class1]::sum(34,45)
```

The output is illustrated in the following image:

```
PS C:\> $code = @"  (1)
using System;
using System.Collections.Generic;
using System.Linq;
using System.Text;
using System.Threading.Tasks;

namespace ClassLibrary2
{
    public class Class1
    {
        public static int sum(int a,int b)
        {
            return a + b;
        }
    }
}
"@  (2)           (3)              (4)
Add-Type -TypeDefinition $code
[ClassLibrary2.Class1]::sum(34,45)  (5)
79  (6)
```

Points marked in the figure can be explained as follows:

- **1**: Everything between @" and "@ is the here-string
- **2**: Here, we use the Add-Type cmdlet
- **3**: Using the TypeDefinition parameter, we specify the source code
- **4**: In the $code variable, we have our source code in the here-string format
- **5**: Here, we make use of the namespace, the class, and the sum method
- **6**: Here, it returns the output value

Now, in Visual Studio, compile the code and find the DLL file; in our case, we have the DLL file in the Temp folder, so we can use the following snippet of code in PowerShell:

```
Import-Module
  C:\Temp\ClassLibrary2\ClassLibrary2\bin\Debug\ClassLibrary2.dll

[ClassLibrary2.Class1]::sum(45,56)
```

Take a look at the following image:

```
PS C:\> Import-Module C:\Temp\ClassLibrary2\ClassLibrary2\bin\Debug\ClassLibrary2.dll
PS C:\> [ClassLibrary2.Class1]::sum(45,56)
101
PS C:\> |
```

Note that we have a `Class` keyword in WMF 5.0; we could use that. However, in PowerShell, we have a few constraints—refer to the WMF 5.0 release notes.

In the next topic, we will explore the EWS API for managing **Exchange Online**.

The EWS API for managing Exchange Online

The **Exchange Web Services** (**EWS**) Managed API provides a managed interface for developing .NET client applications that use EWS. Using the EWS Managed API, we can access most of the information stored in Office 365, Exchange Online, or the Exchange Server mailbox.

The EWS Managed API is now available as an open source project on GitHub. You can share your contributions and bug report bugs in GitHub.

For the contributions, refer to the following link:
https://github.com/OfficeDev/ews-managed-api/blob/master/CONTRIBUTING.md
To report issues, refer to the following link:
https://github.com/OfficeDev/ews-managed-api/issues
For the MSDN documentation, refer to the following link:
https://msdn.microsoft.com/en-us/library/office/dd633710%28v=exchg.80%29.aspx
To download the EWS Managed API 2.2, refer to the following link:
http://www.microsoft.com/en-us/download/details.aspx?id=42951

The installation of the EWS Managed API is as simple as a click—click and it's done! For an easy reference and quick demo, we moved the DLL file to the `C:\Temp\EWS` folder.

One of the easiest methods to explore the items in the mailbox folder is using the `MSOnline` module.

To connect to Exchange Online, we will use the following snippet of code:

```
Import-Module MSOnline

$O365Cred = Get-Credential

$O365Session = New-PSSession -ConfigurationName Microsoft.Exchange
  -ConnectionUri https://outlook.office365.com/powershell-liveid/?
  proxymethod=rps -Credential $O365Cred -Authentication Basic
  -AllowRedirection

Import-PSSession $O365Session

Connect-MsolService -Credential $O365Cred
```

Here is the PowerShell code:

```
Get-MailboxFolderStatistics -Identity "TargetMailBoxID" |
  Select FolderType , Name , ItemsinFolder
```

Refer to the following image:

```
FolderType                        Name                                              ItemsInFolder
----------                        ----                                              -------------
Root                              Top of Information Store                                     96
Calendar                          Calendar                                                    347
Contacts                          Contacts                                                     24
ImContactList                     {A9E2BC46-B3A0-4243-B315-60D991004455}                        0
GalContacts                       GAL Contacts                                                  0
OrganizationalContacts            Organizational Contacts                                       0
PeopleCentricConversationBuddies  PeopleCentricConversation Buddies                             0
RecipientCache                    Recipient Cache                                             116
QuickContacts                     Skype for Business Contacts                                   0
ConversationActions               Conversation Action Settings                                  0
DeletedItems                      Deleted Items                                                 2
User Created                      Backup                                                       56
Drafts                            Drafts                                                        0
Inbox                             Inbox                                                      7127
Journal                           Journal                                                       1
JunkEmail                         Junk E-mail                                                   5
User Created                      News Feed                                                     0
```

We installed the EWS API 2.2 and moved the DLL file to the desired location. On the EWS managed API, we can do this using the following code:

```
#Target MailboxID's

$MailboxNames =  "TargetMailID"

#Any Exchange Admin ID with appropriate permissions

$AdminID = "AdminID"

#Fetch password as secure string

$AdminPwd = Read-Host "Enter Password" -AsSecureString
```

```
#Load the Exchange Web Service DLL
$dllpath = "C:\Temp\Microsoft.Exchange.WebServices.dll"
[Reflection.Assembly]::LoadFile($dllpath)
#Create a Exchange Web Service
$Service = New-Object Microsoft.Exchange.WebServices.Data.
  ExchangeService([Microsoft.Exchange.WebServices.Data.
  ExchangeVersion]::Exchange2013_SP1)
#Credentials to impersonate the mail box
$Service.Credentials = New-Object
  System.Net.NetworkCredential($AdminID , $AdminPwd)
foreach($MailboxName in $MailboxNames)
{
#Impersonate using Exchange WebService Class
$Service.ImpersonatedUserId = New-Object
  Microsoft.Exchange.WebServices.Data.ImpersonatedUserId(
  [Microsoft.Exchange.WebServices.Data.ConnectingIdType]::
  SmtpAddress, $MailboxName)
$Service.AutodiscoverUrl($MailboxName,{$true})
#Assing EWS URL
$service.Url = 'https://outlook.office365.com/EWS/Exchange.asmx'
Write-Host "Processing Mailbox: $MailboxName" -ForegroundColor Green
#Fetch Root Folder ID
$RootFolderID = New-object Microsoft.Exchange.WebServices.Data.
  FolderId([Microsoft.Exchange.WebServices.Data.WellKnownFolderName]
  ::Root, $MailboxName)
$RootFolder = [Microsoft.Exchange.WebServices.Data.Folder]::Bind(
  $Service,$RootFolderID)
#Create a Folder View
$FolderView = New-Object Microsoft.Exchange.WebServices.Data.
FolderView(1000)
$FolderView.Traversal = [Microsoft.Exchange.WebServices.Data.
  FolderTraversal]::Deep
#Retrive the Information
$response = $RootFolder.FindFolders($FolderView)
$response | Select DisplayName , TotalCount , FolderClass
}
```

This returns the same output as shown in the following image, but provides in-depth information:

```
DisplayName                              TotalCount FolderClass
-----------                              ---------- -----------
AllContacts                                     267 IPF.Note
AllItems                                      15767 IPF
BlackBerryHandheldInfo                            2
BrokerSubscriptions                               0
Calendar Version Store                         1031 IPF.Note
CalendarItemSnapshots                             0
Common Views                                      0
Deferred Action                                   0
Document Centric Conversations                    0 IPF.Note
ExchangeSyncData                                  0
```

You can spin up PowerShell and customize the scripting according to your needs.

At times, we may consider building a unique interface to collect and audit organization information such as AD, Mailbox, SharePoint, Lync, and so on. Let's accommodate PowerShell in C# to call the Exchange Online cmdlets; the reason for this is the unique and clean interface, which helps us query multiple sources. In the following example, we will obtain information from Exchange Online.

Here is a demo code that will print your Exchange Online user's display name and SMTP address:

```csharp
using System;
using System.Collections.Generic;
using System.Linq;
using System.Management.Automation;
using System.Management.Automation.Remoting;
using System.Management.Automation.Runspaces;
using System.Security;
using System.Collections.ObjectModel;
using System.Text;
namespace Office365
{
    class Program
    {
        static void Main(string[] args)
        {
            string username = "ExchangeAdminID";
```

```csharp
string password = "Password";
System.Security.SecureString securepassword = new
  System.Security.SecureString();
foreach (char c in password)
{
    securepassword.AppendChar(c);
}
PSCredential credential = new PSCredential(username,
  securepassword);
WSManConnectionInfo connectioninfo = new
  WSManConnectionInfo(new Uri(
  "https://ps.outlook.com/powershell"),
  "http://schemas.microsoft.com/powershell/Microsoft.
Exchange",
  credential);
connectioninfo.AuthenticationMechanism =
  AuthenticationMechanism.Basic;
//connectioninfo.AuthenticationMechanism =
  AuthenticationMechanism.Basic;
connectioninfo.MaximumConnectionRedirectionCount = 2;
//connectioninfo.MaximumConnectionRedirectionCount = 2;
using (Runspace runspace =
  RunspaceFactory.CreateRunspace(connectioninfo))
{
    runspace.Open();
    using (PowerShell powershell = PowerShell.Create())
    {
        powershell.Runspace = runspace;
        //Create the command and add a parameter
        powershell.AddCommand("Get-Mailbox");
        powershell.AddParameter("RecipientTypeDetails",
          "UserMailbox");
        //powershell.
        //Invoke the command and store the results in a
          PSObject collection
        Collection<PSObject> results =
          powershell.Invoke();
        foreach (PSObject result in results)
        {
```

```
                            string createText = string.Format("Name: {0}
                                Alias: {1} Mail: {2}", result.Properties[
                                "DisplayName"].Value.ToString(), result.
                                Properties["Alias"].Value.ToString(),
                                result.Properties["PrimarySMTPAddress"].
                                Value.ToString());

                            System.IO.File.WriteAllText("C:\\User.txt",
                                createText);
                        }
                    }
                }
            }
        }
    }
```

The output is illustrated in the following image:

Purging items in the mailbox folder

Most organizations are moving to cloud-based storage, and as we know, all Microsoft products have a PowerShell interface. This eventually helps both developers and administrators to perform tasks without using a GUI. Not only automating tasks, using PowerShell we troubleshoot issues, identify the root cause, and so on.

Let's consider an operational requirement to purge Lync contact entries. Ignore the technical background and requirements or designs such as unified contact stores and so on; all we need to know is how to consume the EWS API and explore objects. Perform the following steps:

1. Get the target mailbox for which the items need to be purged.

2. You will need the appropriate permission to perform this task. Connect with your exchange admin account and plan the authentication and security process based on your organization's rules.

3. Pass the admin ID credentials.

4. Load the Exchange Web Service DLL file. Run the following command:

```
#Target MailboxID's
$MailboxNames =  "TargetMailBoxID1" , "TargetMailBoxID1"
#Any Exchange Admin ID with appropriate permissions
$AdminID = "AdminID"
#Fetch password as secure string
$AdminPwd = Read-Host "Enter Password" -AsSecureString
#Load the Exchange Web Service DLL
$dllpath = "C:\Temp\Microsoft.Exchange.WebServices.dll"
[Reflection.Assembly]::LoadFile($dllpath)
```

Now, perform the following steps:

1. Create an Exchange Web service.

2. Using the admin credentials, impersonate the target mailbox. Run the following command:

```
#Create a Exchange Web Service
$Service = New-Object
  Microsoft.Exchange.WebServices.Data.ExchangeService(
  [Microsoft.Exchange.WebServices.Data.ExchangeVersion]
  ::Exchange2013_SP1)
#Credentials to impersonate the mail box
$Service.Credentials = New-Object
  System.Net.NetworkCredential($AdminID , $AdminPwd)
```

After this, perform the following steps:

1. Impersonate each target mailbox using EWS.

2. Assign the EWS URL.

3. Retrieve the root folder ID.

4. Traverse and get the folder view. Here, we will use 1000 items taking the possibility of throttling into consideration.

5. Retrieve the folders from the view.

6. Query the folder name with its class.

7. Purge the items using soft delete; do not use hard delete as it makes it impossible to restore the items from the dumpster.

8. Call the `Load` method. Run the following command:

```
foreach($MailboxName in $MailboxNames)
{
#Impersonate using Exchange WebService Class
$Service.ImpersonatedUserId = New-Object
  Microsoft.Exchange.WebServices.Data.ImpersonatedUserId(
  [Microsoft.Exchange.WebServices.Data.ConnectingIdType]
  ::SmtpAddress, $MailboxName)

$Service.AutodiscoverUrl($MailboxName,{$true})

#Assing EWS URL
$service.Url =
  'https://outlook.office365.com/EWS/Exchange.asmx'

Write-Host "Processing Mailbox: $MailboxName" -ForegroundColor
  Green

#Fetch Root Folder ID
$RootFolderID = New-object Microsoft.Exchange.WebServices.
  Data.FolderId([Microsoft.Exchange.WebServices.Data.
  WellKnownFolderName]::Root, $MailboxName)

$RootFolder = [Microsoft.Exchange.WebServices.Data.Folder]
  ::Bind($Service,$RootFolderID)

#Create a Folder View
$FolderView = New-Object
  Microsoft.Exchange.WebServices.Data.FolderView(1000)

$FolderView.Traversal =
  [Microsoft.Exchange.WebServices.Data.FolderTraversal]::Deep

#Retrieve Folders from view
$response = $RootFolder.FindFolders($FolderView)

#Query Folder which has display name like Lync Contacts
$Folder =  $response | ? {$_.FolderClass -eq
  'IPF.Contact.MOC.QuickContacts'}

$Folder | Select DisplayName , TotalCount

#Purge the items
$Folder.Empty([Microsoft.Exchange.WebServices.Data.DeleteMode]
  ::SoftDelete, $false)

$Folder.Load()
}
```

Deleting items from the mailbox folder

Deleting items from the mailbox folder is almost similar to purging. We can delete items using the following lines of code:

```
$Folder.Delete([Microsoft.Exchange.WebServices.Data.DeleteMode]
  ::SoftDelete)
```

```
$Folder.Load()
```

We cannot remove the Lync contacts entries in Outlook by simply right–clicking and deleting. We need to purge the items and then delete the entries in the contact folders. However, we can't communicate to the users to perform the delete operations themselves after performing purge, so simply executing the preceding code will complete the task. Using the previously mentioned methods we can perform administration tasks remotely without the user's intervention.

The Lync 2013 client-side API

For most of its products, Microsoft releases an SDK, using which we can automate a few things on the client side. The Microsoft Lync 2013 SDK is designed for software developers who build custom Microsoft Lync 2013 applications. It is also useful to those developers who embed the collaboration functionality in **line-of-business** (**LOB**) applications, which interoperate with other custom Lync SDK clients or with Lync 2013 and Microsoft Lync Server 2013.

However, this is not limited only to developers; IT professionals can also perform tasks using Windows PowerShell. In this topic, we will cover both:

- You can learn PowerShell scripting Lync 2010 SDK using the Lync Model API at https://msdn.microsoft.com/en-us/library/office/hh243705%28v=office.14%29.aspx

- You can learn PowerShell Scripting Lync 2010 SDK using Lync Extensibility API at https://msdn.microsoft.com/en-us/library/gg581082.aspx

Installation of LYNC SDK

To download the LYNC client SDK refer to the following link – Read the installation documents and choose the 32 bit or 64 bit based on your LYNC client.

https://www.microsoft.com/en-us/download/details.aspx?id=36824

The LYNC 2013 SDK installation is just two steps as shown in the following image.

1. The first step is:

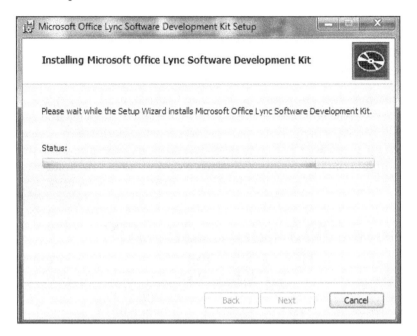

2. The second step is:

That's it, we are done with SDK Installation, now we can browse to the default location C:\Program Files (x86)\Microsoft Office\Office15\LyncSDK\ Assemblies\Desktop\Microsoft.Lync.Model.dll

So, using the Import-Module cmdlet, let us load the DLL, as follows:

```
Import-Module -Name 'C:\Program Files (x86)\Microsoft Office\
  Office15\LyncSDK\Assemblies\Desktop\Microsoft.Lync.Model.dll'
```

Now, we will explore the LYNC client SDK in PowerShell:

```
$client = [Microsoft.Lync.Model.LyncClient]::GetClient()
$client | GM -Force
```

The following figure is the output of the command $client | GM | Out-GridView:

CapabilitiesChanged	Event	System.EventHandler`1[Microsoft.Lync.Model.PreferredCapabilitiesChangedEventArgs] CapabilitiesChanged(System.Object, Microsoft.Lync.Model.PreferredCapabilitiesChangedEventArgs)
ClientDisconnected	Event	System.EventHandler ClientDisconnected(System.Object, System.EventArgs)
CredentialRequested	Event	System.EventHandler`1[Microsoft.Lync.Model.CredentialRequestedEventArgs] CredentialRequested(System.Object, Microsoft.Lync.Model.CredentialRequestedEventArgs)
DelegatorClientAdded	Event	System.EventHandler`1[Microsoft.Lync.Model.DelegatorClientCollectionEventArgs] DelegatorClientAdded(System.Object, Microsoft.Lync.Model.DelegatorClientCollectionEventArgs)
DelegatorClientRemoved	Event	System.EventHandler`1[Microsoft.Lync.Model.DelegatorClientCollectionEventArgs] DelegatorClientRemoved(System.Object, Microsoft.Lync.Model.DelegatorClientCollectionEventArgs)
SignInDelayed	Event	System.EventHandler`1[Microsoft.Lync.Model.SignInDelayedEventArgs] SignInDelayed(System.Object, Microsoft.Lync.Model.SignInDelayedEventArgs)
StateChanged	Event	System.EventHandler`1[Microsoft.Lync.Model.ClientStateChangedEventArgs] StateChanged(System.Object, Microsoft.Lync.Model.ClientStateChangedEventArgs)
BeginInitialize	Method	System.IAsyncResult BeginInitialize(System.AsyncCallback callback, System.Object state)
BeginShutdown	Method	System.IAsyncResult BeginShutdown(System.AsyncCallback communicatorClientCallback, System.Object state)
BeginSignIn	Method	System.IAsyncResult BeginSignIn(string userUri, string domainAndUsername, string password, System.AsyncCallback communicatorClientCallback, System.Object state)
BeginSignOut	Method	System.IAsyncResult BeginSignOut(System.AsyncCallback communicatorClientCallback, System.Object state)
CreateApplicationRegistration	Method	Microsoft.Lync.Model.Extensibility.ApplicationRegistration CreateApplicationRegistration(string appGuid, string appName)
CreateObjRef	Method	System.Runtime.Remoting.ObjRef CreateObjRef(type requestedType)
EndInitialize	Method	void EndInitialize(System.IAsyncResult asyncResult)
EndShutdown	Method	void EndShutdown(System.IAsyncResult asyncResult)
EndSignIn	Method	void EndSignIn(System.IAsyncResult asyncResult)
EndSignOut	Method	void EndSignOut(System.IAsyncResult asyncResult)
Equals	Method	bool Equals(System.Object obj)
GetHashCode	Method	int GetHashCode()
GetLifetimeService	Method	System.Object GetLifetimeService()
GetType	Method	type GetType()
InitializeLifetimeService	Method	System.Object InitializeLifetimeService()
ToString	Method	string ToString()
Capabilities	Property	Microsoft.Lync.Model.LyncClientCapabilityTypes Capabilities {get;}
ContactManager	Property	Microsoft.Lync.Model.ContactManager ContactManager {get;}
ConversationManager	Property	Microsoft.Lync.Model.Conversation.ConversationManager ConversationManager {get;}
DelegatorClients	Property	System.Collections.Generic.IList[Microsoft.Lync.Model.DelegatorClient] DelegatorClients {get;}

We will see a series of examples to explore the LYNC/S4B (Skype for Business) client.

 This works for Skype for Business clients as well. So, we will examine the functionality. If you read IM client in this topic it refers to LYNC or Skype for Business client.

Retrieve the groups created using the following command:

```
$client = [Microsoft.Lync.Model.LyncClient]::GetClient()
$client.ContactManager.Groups.InnerObject.Name
```

The output of this command is illustrated in the following image:

```
PS C:\windows\system32> $client = [Microsoft.Lync.Model.LyncClient]::GetClient()
$client.ContactManager.Groups.InnerObject.Name
Other Contacts
Pinned Contacts
SharePoint Portal Team
Project Management
End User Computing



SharePoint Development
```

Execute the following command:

```
$client = [Microsoft.Lync.Model.LyncClient]::GetClient()
$client.ContactManager | GM
```

This command returns the members of the ContactManager which is Microsoft.Lync.Model.ContactManager that has the BeginAddGroup method accepting three overloads.

```
$client = [Microsoft.Lync.Model.LyncClient]::GetClient()
$client.ContactManager.BeginAddGroup
```

The output of this command is illustrated in the following image:

```
PS C:\windows\system32> $client = [Microsoft.Lync.Model.LyncClient]::GetClient()
$client.ContactManager.BeginAddGroup

OverloadDefinitions
-------------------
System.IAsyncResult BeginAddGroup(string customGroupName, System.AsyncCallback contactsAndGroupsCallback, System.Object state)
System.IAsyncResult BeginAddGroup(Microsoft.Lync.Model.Group.DistributionGroup distributionGroup, System.AsyncCallback
contactsAndGroupsCallback, System.Object state)
```

Execute the following command:

```
$client = [Microsoft.Lync.Model.LyncClient]::GetClient()
$client.ContactManager.BeginAddGroup($GroupName, $null, $null)
```

For now, we will use the $GroupName parameter and the $null parameter for the other two overloads.

```
Function Create-LyncClientGroup{
  param([Parameter(Mandatory = $true,ValueFromPipeline = $true)]
    [String[]]$GroupName
```

```
    )
    $client = [Microsoft.Lync.Model.LyncClient]::GetClient()
    $client.ContactManager.BeginAddGroup($GroupName, $null,$null)
}
"Test1" | Create-LyncClientGroup
```

The above code creates a new group in the client called Test1 as shown in the following figure with no contacts:

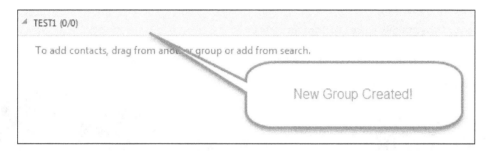

Exploring client settings

We haven't started the extensibility API yet, so before that let us see few more client settings options. The below code shows more properties which can be viewed, as well as methods to invoke and perform tasks as shown below, even without a single click!

- Active audio devices
- SIP ID information
- Sign in configuration
- Photo information

Execute the following command to check the active audio device:

```
#To check the Active Audio Device
$client.DeviceManager.ActiveAudioDevice
```

The output of this command is illustrated in the following image:

```
IsCertified : False
Priority    : 4194304
Type        : Custom
IsActive    : True
Name        : Speakers (Realtek High Definition Audio)/Microphone (Realtek High Definition Audio)
InnerObject : Microsoft.Office.Uc.AudioDeviceClass
```

Execute the following command to check self URI:

```
#To Check Self URI
$client.InnerObject.Self.Contact.Uri
```

The output of this command is illustrated in the following image:

```
PS C:\windows\system32> $client =              nc.Model.LyncClient]::GetClient()
$client.InnerObject.Self.Contact.
sip:chendrayan.venkatesan@                SIP ID of IM

PS C:\windows\system32> |
```

Execute the following command to check sign-in configuration:

```
#To Check SigninConfiguration
$client.SignInConfiguration
```

The output of this command is illustrated in the following image:

```
PS C:\windows\system32> $client = [Microsoft.Lync.Model.LyncClient]::GetClient()
$client.SignInConfiguration


ExternalServerUrl    : sipdir.online.lync.com:443        Sign in Configuration!
InternalServerUrl    : sipdir.online.lync.com:443
IsPasswordSaved      : False
Mode                 : Auto
SignedInFromIntranet : True
SignInAsAvailability : None
SignInAutoRetry      : False
TransportMode        : TcpTransport
UserName             : Chendrayan.Venkatesan@
InnerObject          : Microsoft.Office.Uc.SignInConfigurationClass
```

Execute the following command to check photo display settings:

```
#To Check if Photo Display Settings
$client.Self.PhotoDisplayed
```

This command returns True or False.

Following is the demo code to change the IM Client status:

```
Import-Module -Name 'C:\Program Files (x86)\Microsoft Office\
  Office15\LyncSDK\Assemblies\Desktop\Microsoft.Lync.Model.dll'
$Client = [Microsoft.Lync.Model.LyncClient]::GetClient()
$self = $Client.Self
$contactInfo = New-object 'System.Collections.Generic.Dictionary[
  Microsoft.Lync.Model.PublishableContactInformationType, object]'
$contactInfo.Add([Microsoft.Lync.Model.
  PublishableContactInformationType]::Availability,6500)
$ar = $self.BeginPublishContactInformation($contactInfo,
  $null, $null)
$self.EndPublishContactInformation($ar)
```

This code will change your IM client status to BUSY. 6500 is the value of BUSY. Let us make another piece of code to retrieve the values of IM client statuses—So that we can build a custom function for a quick status change without a click!

```
[Microsoft.Lync.Model.ContactAvailability]::Away.value
```

This command returns 15500.

To retrieve all values, use the following code:

```
[enum]::GetValues([System.Globalization.NumberStyles]) |
  %{ "{0,3} {1}" -f $([int]$_),$_ }
```

```
PS C:\> [enum]::GetValues([Microsoft.Lync.Model.ContactAvailability])
None
Free
FreeIdle
Busy                          Status
BusyIdle
DoNotDisturb
TemporarilyAway
Away
Offline
Invalid

PS C:\> [enum]::GetValues([Microsoft.Lync.Model.ContactAvailability]) | %{ "{0,3} {1}" -f $([int]$_),$_ }
   0 None
3500 Free
5000 FreeIdle             Status with
6500 Busy                   values
7500 BusyIdle
9500 DoNotDisturb
12500 TemporarilyAway
15500 Away
18500 Offline
  -1 Invalid
```

We know that PowerShell is built on .NET framework and we can consume the cmdlets in C#. We have seen a demo in the previous chapter, by applying the same concepts, let us build a module which will have just one cmdlet Get-LyncStatus.

In PowerShell the code is as follows:

```
$client.SigninConfiguration.SigninIntranet
```

This command returns `True` or `False` — Boolean value. In C# we will build a binary module using LYNC SDK and PowerShell.

C# code is as follows:

```csharp
using System;
using System.Collections.Generic;
using System.Linq;
using System.Text;
using System.Threading.Tasks;
using System.Management.Automation;
using System.Management.Automation.Runspaces;
using Microsoft.Lync.Model;
namespace LyncAPIDemo
{
    [Cmdlet(VerbsCommon.Get, "LyncStatus")]
    public class LyncAPIDemo : PSCmdlet
    {
        protected override void ProcessRecord()
        {
            var client = LyncClient.GetClient();
            bool status =
              client.SignInConfiguration.SignedInFromIntranet;
            if(status == true)
            {
                Console.WriteLine("You are signed in!");
            }
            else
            {
                Console.WriteLine("Singed Off!");
            }
        }
    }
}
```

The above code will not check for existence of the LYNC client — the code assumes LYNC client/Skype for business exists.

Once you have compiled the code in class library, import the module in PowerShell and make use of the cmdlet using the following command:

```
Import-Module 'c:\Temp\LyncAPIDemo\LyncAPIDemo\bin\Debug\
  LyncAPIDemo.dll'
```

```
Get-LyncStatus
```

The output of this command is illustrated in the following figure:

```
PS C:\windows\system32> Import-Module 'c:\Temp\LyncAPIDemo\LyncAPIDemo\bin\Debug\LyncAPIDemo.dll' ❶
Get-LyncStatus ❷
You are signed in! ❸

PS C:\windows\system32> |
```

Points marked in the figure are explained as follows:

- Here, we import the module
- Here, we execute the cmdlet
- Here, the details are printed — the status is true, so we got the text `You are signed in!`

Automating test calls

Very often we may do test audio calls in Lync/Skype for Business. How about automating this? Not only to avoid clicks, but also start audio conversations with others.

The following code is very basic and just makes a test call:

```
Import-Module 'C:\Program Files (x86)\Microsoft Office\
  Office15\LyncSDK\Assemblies\Desktop\Microsoft.Lync.Model.dll'

$LyncClient = [Microsoft.Lync.Model.LyncClient]::Getclient()

$Conversation = $LyncClient.ConversationManager.AddConversation()

[Void]$Conversation.AddParticipant($LyncClient.Self.TestCallEndpoint)

[Void]$Conversation.Modalities['AudioVideo'].BeginConnect({},0)
```

Following is the screenshot of the test call:

After the execution of this code, the audio test service begins and we need to manually disconnect. To completely automate this, the following code will help:

```
#region
Import-Module 'C:\Program Files (x86)\Microsoft Office\
  Office15\LyncSDK\Assemblies\Desktop\Microsoft.Lync.Model.dll'
$Client = [Microsoft.Lync.Model.LyncClient]::GetClient()
$TestCall = {
    $Conversation = $this.ConversationManager.AddConversation();
    [void]$Conversation.AddParticipant($this.Self.TestCallEndpoint);
    [void]$Conversation.Modalities['AudioVideo'].BeginConnect({}, 0);
    Add-Member -InputObject $Conversation -MemberType ScriptMethod
      -Name EndCall -Value {
        [void]$this.Modalities['AudioVideo'].BeginDisconnect(
          [Microsoft.Lync.Model.Conversation.
            ModalityDisconnectReason]::None, {}, 0);
      } -PassThru
    }
Add-Member -InputObject $Client -MemberType ScriptMethod
  -Name TestCall -Value $TestCall -Force;
#endregion
#region
$Conversation = $Client.TestCall()
Start-Sleep 15
$Conversation.EndCall()
#endregion
```

The call will disconnect after 15 seconds—during the audio test service, the IM service will not work, as shown in the following image:

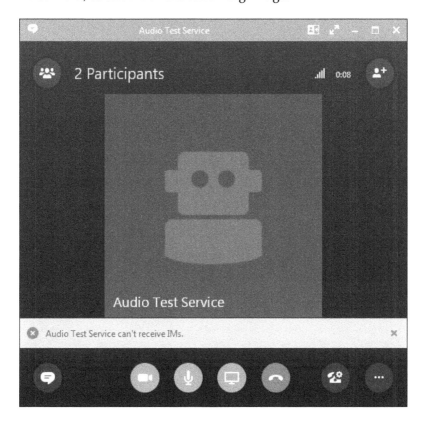

IM with contacts

We can start IM conversation using LYNC SDK and PowerShell. Why? Why not use the IM client? Imagine a scenario where you need to ping a few users for testing purposes, or greet them! There are no concrete reasons for automating IM conversations, but it's good to know the flavors of .NET.

So, to do this we can use the following PowerShell code:

```
Function Send-SelfIM{
    $LyncClient = [Microsoft.Lync.Model.LyncClient]::GetClient()
    $ConversationManager = $LyncClient.ConversationManager;
    $Conversation = $ConversationManager.AddConversation();
```

```
    [void]$Conversation.AddParticipant($LyncClient.Self.Contact)

    $Conversation.Modalities['InstantMessage'].BeginSendMessage(
      "Okay! This Works",$null,$null);
}
Send-SelfIM
```

Well! You can parameterize the text link shown as follows:

```
Function Send-SelfIM{
    Param([Parameter(Mandatory = $true)]
        [String[]]$Greet
    )
    $LyncClient = [Microsoft.Lync.Model.LyncClient]::GetClient()
    $ConversationManager = $LyncClient.ConversationManager;
    $Conversation = $ConversationManager.AddConversation();
    [void]$Conversation.AddParticipant($LyncClient.Self.Contact)
    [Void]$Conversation.Modalities['InstantMessage'].
      BeginSendMessage($Greet,$null,$null);
}
Send-SelfIM -Greet "Hi, I am parameterized!"
```

Client-side object model – SharePoint Online

What is CSOM? What can it do for SharePoint developers and IT professionals? Most of the SharePoint developers use CSOM in the code and all are familiar with .NET. So, in this topic we would like to share CSOM and its importance. CSOM includes **JavaScript object model (JSOM)**. Developers think a lot before consuming REST, CSOM, and web services for either developing or helping IT Professionals in automation tasks. Each has its own pros and cons. It depends on when and how we use it. So, let us ignore REST and web service for now, and focus on CSOM, because this works based on the .NET Client-side object model of the SharePoint platform.

- CSOM is an acronym for Client-side object model
- CSOM provides a subset of the Server Object Model
- CSOM supports remote execution via JavaScript and .NET
- CSOM allows **Collaborative Application Markup Language** (**CAML**) query to query SharePoint lists
- CSOM has three distinct API, these are:
    1. .NET managed client object.

       This has more subsets of functionalities which allow developers and IT professionals to make use of it
    2. ECMAScript.
    3. Silverlight client object model.

Following are the download links:

- SharePoint 2010 CSOM can be downloaded from `http://www.microsoft.com/en-us/download/details.aspx?id=21786`

- SharePoint 2013 CSOM can be downloaded from `http://www.microsoft.com/en-us/download/details.aspx?id=35585`

- SharePoint Online CSOM can be downloaded from `http://www.microsoft.com/en-us/download/details.aspx?id=42038`

- Refer to the following CodePlex link and make use of it—please do read the documentation before you commit changes in the SharePoint environment: `http://sharepointpowershell.codeplex.com/`

The installation is similar to LYNC SDK—just download the required version and proceed with installation.

How does CSOM Work?

The basic usage of Windows PowerShell is by declaring a variable, we load the context, execute the query, and get the result from the variable. To know more about request batching using CAML, LINQ, and so on, refer to the following link:

`https://msdn.microsoft.com/en-us/library/ff798388.aspx?f=255&MSPPError=-2147217396`

In this exercise we will do different tasks on the SharePoint Online site using CSOM and PowerShell.

We have some basic information about the CSOM; this greatly integrates SharePoint IT professionals and developers.

 If you are looking for PowerShell tools for your Visual Studio, refer to the following link:

`https://visualstudiogallery.msdn.microsoft.com/c9eb3ba8-0c59-4944-9a62-6eee37294597`

One most common scenario in SharePoint is to audit a user profile; most of the organizations need it either to audit, or to ensure users align with corporate standards by updating their profile information. Most of the fields are mapped with active directory with a few exceptions for fields like date of birth, skills, interests, or any custom property we created in SharePoint user profile application.

In this topic we will cover a demo of below tasks using CSOM:

- Exporting user profiles
- Creating and deleting Lists
- Manipulating web settings

Using PowerShell and CSOM we can easily query the user profile information and export to CSV. Execute the following code:

```
#Import the required DLL
Import-Module 'C:\Program Files\Common Files\Microsoft Shared\
  Web Server Extensions\15\ISAPI\
  Microsoft.SharePoint.Client.UserProfiles.dll'
#Mysite URL
$site = 'https://Domain-my.sharepoint.com/'
#Admin User Principal Name
$admin = 'Admin@Domain.OnMicrosoft.Com'
#Get Password as secure String
$password = Read-Host 'Enter Password' -AsSecureString
#Get the Client Context and Bind the Site Collection
$context = New-Object Microsoft.SharePoint.Client.ClientContext(
  $site)
#Authenticate
$credentials = New-Object Microsoft.SharePoint.Client.
  SharePointOnlineCredentials($admin , $password)
$context.Credentials = $credentials
#Fetch the users in Site Collection
$users = $context.Web.SiteUsers
$context.Load($users)
$context.ExecuteQuery()
#Create an Object [People Manager] to retrieve profile information
$people = New-Object Microsoft.SharePoint.Client.UserProfiles.
  PeopleManager($context)
$collection = @()
Foreach($user in $users)
{
    $userprofile = $people.GetPropertiesFor($user.LoginName)
    $context.Load($userprofile)
    $context.ExecuteQuery()
```

```
    if($userprofile.Email -ne $null)
    {
        $upp = $userprofile.UserProfileProperties

        foreach($ups in $upp)
        {
            $profileData = "" | Select "FirstName" , "LastName" ,
              "WorkEmail" , "Title" , "Responsibility"

            $profileData.FirstName = $ups.FirstName

            $profileData.LastName = $ups.LastName

            $profileData.WorkEmail = $ups.WorkEmail

            $profileData.Responsibility = $ups.'SPS-Responsibility'

            $collection += $profileData

        }

    }

}
$collection | Export-Csv C:\Temp\SPO-UserInformation.csv
  -NoTypeInformation -Encoding UTF8
```

The output is illustrated in the following screenshot:

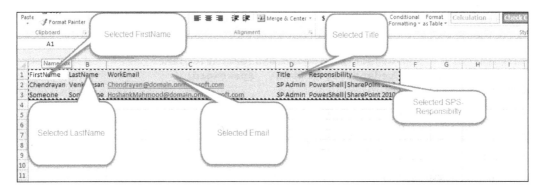

We can add the properties to get more information based on settings in your SharePoint farm.

Creating and deleting list

Using CSOM we can create lists and delete lists—below is the code for the same.

Following is the code for creating list:

```
#Import the required DLL

Import-Module 'C:\Temp\CSOM\Microsoft.SharePoint.Client.dll'

Import-Module 'C:\Temp\CSOM\Microsoft.SharePoint.Client.Runtime.dll'

$site = 'https://Chensoffice365.sharepoint.com/'

$admin = 'Chendrayan@Chensoffice365.OnMicrosoft.Com'

$password = Read-Host 'Enter Password' -AsSecureString

$context = New-Object Microsoft.SharePoint.Client.ClientContext(
  $site)

$credentials = New-Object Microsoft.SharePoint.Client.
  SharePointOnlineCredentials($admin , $password)

$context.Credentials = $credentials

$site = $context.Web

$context.Load($site)

$context.ExecuteQuery()

#Create List

$listinfo =New-Object Microsoft.SharePoint.Client.
  ListCreationInformation

$listinfo.Title = 'CSOM List'

$listinfo.TemplateType = [Microsoft.SharePoint.Client.
  ListTemplateType] 'GenericList'

$list = $Site.Lists.Add($listinfo)

$context.ExecuteQuery()

Write-Host "Successfully Created List $($listinfo.Title)"
```

After the successful execution of this code we can see the list in our site as shown in the following image:

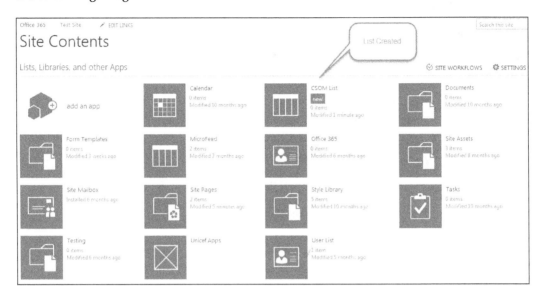

The following code simply deletes the list. Please ensure to check the names and ID:

```
Import-Module 'C:\Program Files\Common Files\Microsoft Shared\Web Server
Extensions\15\ISAPI\Microsoft.SharePoint.Client.Runtime.dll'
#OR
Add-Type -Path 'C:\Program Files\Common Files\Microsoft Shared\Web Server
Extensions\15\ISAPI\Microsoft.SharePoint.Client.dll'
#Site URL
$site = 'https://Domain.sharepoint.com/'
#Admin User Principal Name
$admin = 'Admin@Chensoffice365.OnMicrosoft.Com'
#Get Password as secure String
$password = Read-Host 'Enter Password' -AsSecureString
#Get the Client Context and Bind the Site Collection
$context = New-Object Microsoft.SharePoint.Client.ClientContext($site)
#Authenticate
$credentials = New-Object Microsoft.SharePoint.Client.SharePointOnlineCre
dentials($admin , $password)
$context.Credentials = $credentials
#Delete List
```

```
$list = $context.Web.Lists.GetByTitle('PowerShell CSOM')
$context.Load($list)
$list.DeleteObject()
$list.Update()
```

Making PowerShell modules with SDKs

So far we have seen three different technologies, namely Exchange Online, Lync and SharePoint along with creating smaller tasks using the API with DLL and web services. In the next exercise we will build another binary module which combines all the above sample code and delivers nice PowerShell cmdlets to do the tasks. This is just a sample code you can start building on your own for your environment.

The following code is a binary module built using C# which has three cmdlets:

- `Add-LyncPersonalNote`: Adds/updates your LYNC personal note status
- `Get-OSInformation`: Retrieves OS information—just .NET way
- `Get-PhotoStatus`: Retrieves LYNC photo status

The code is as follows:

```
using System;
using System.Collections.Generic;
using System.Linq;
using System.Text;
using System.Threading.Tasks;
using System.Management.Automation;
using Microsoft.Lync.Model;
using System.Collections.ObjectModel;
namespace OfficeServers
{
    [Cmdlet(VerbsCommon.Get,"PhotoStatus")]
    public class PhotoStatus : PSCmdlet
    {
        protected override void ProcessRecord()
        {
            //base.ProcessRecord();
            Console.WriteLine("Lync Group Name Information....");
            var cl = LyncClient.GetClient();
```

```
        bool photo = cl.Self.PhotoDisplayed;
        if(photo == true)
        {
            Console.WriteLine("Photo will be visible to
              others!");
        }
        else
        {
            Console.WriteLine("Photo is hidden!");
        }
    }
}
[Cmdlet(VerbsCommon.Get,"OSInformation")]
public class OSInformation : PSCmdlet
{
    protected override void ProcessRecord()
    {
        //base.ProcessRecord();
        Console.WriteLine("OS Version is {0}",
          (Environment.OSVersion).ToString());
    }
}
[Cmdlet(VerbsCommon.Add, "LyncPersonalNote")]
public class LyncPersonalNote : PSCmdlet
{
    [Parameter(Mandatory = true)]
    public string notetext{get;set;}
    protected override void ProcessRecord()
    {
        //base.ProcessRecord();
        var cl = LyncClient.GetClient();
        var self = cl.Self;
        var noteinfo = new System.Collections.Generic.
          Dictionary<Microsoft.Lync.Model.
          PublishableContactInformationType, Object>();
```

```
noteinfo.Add(Microsoft.Lync.Model.
   PublishableContactInformationType.PersonalNote,
   notetext);

self.BeginPublishContactInformation(noteinfo,null,null);

//self.EndPublishContactInformation(noteinfo);

      }

   }

}
```

After building the solution, the DLL will be located in the project folder. So, we need to import the module and test the output. Following are the steps:

1. Following is the command to import cmdlets:

   ```
   Import-Module C:\Temp\OfficeServers\OfficeServers\bin\
      Debug\OfficeServers.dll -Verbose
   ```

   This code will import the cmdlets as illustrated in the following figure:

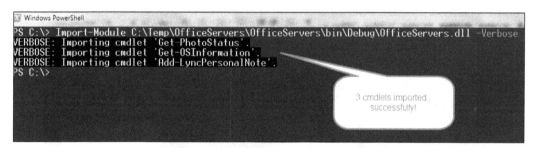

2. Following command lists all cmdlets in the OfficeServers module:

   ```
   Get-Command -Module OfficeServers
   ```

   Following figure illustrates the output of this command:

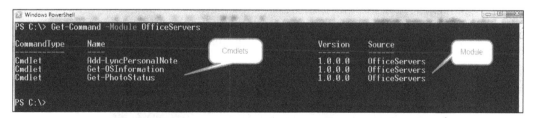

3. Let's test the following command:

```
Add-LyncPersonalNote -notetext "This is Automated!"
```

Following figure illustrates the output of this command:

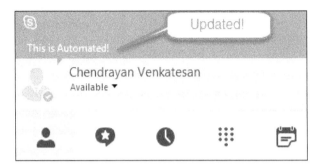

Execute the following command:

```
Get-OSInformation
```

Following figure illustrates the output of this command:

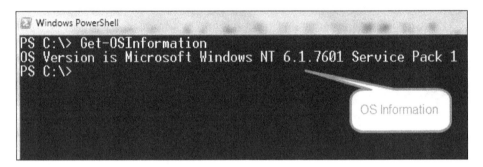

Execute the following command:

```
Get-PhotoStatus
```

Following figure illustrates the output of this command:

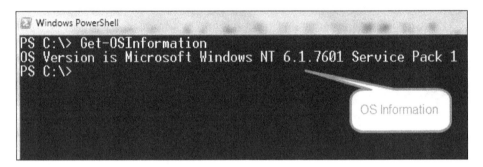

Summary

In this chapter we have covered the key benefits of API and using it in Windows PowerShell. It has made IT professional's and developer's lives a lot easier than before. We know how to use API in C# and PowerShell, and making custom modules for PowerShell using C#. With reference to this you can explore more and plan for a real case scenario in your environment as well as automate tasks. So, Windows PowerShell and DSC is considered to be a one stop shop for IT pros and developers looking for swift automation, chaos free deployments, remote troubleshooting, and so on.

We have covered Exchange Web Services, LYNC client side API and SharePoint client-side object model with a walkthrough demo, creating a PowerShell module in C# for office servers.

Index

Symbols

.NET Framework
about 4
types, extending 124-128
URL, for download 180
.NET objects
creating 121, 122
exploring 120, 121
extending, for Administrations and
Development tasks 122-124

A

advanced functions
versus compiled cmdlets 80
advanced modules
building 128-141
advanced scripts
building 128-141
aliases
using 36-41
**Application Lifecycle
Management (ALM) 255**
**Application Programming
Interface (API)**
about 261
Exchange Web Services (EWS) API, for
managing Exchange Online 269
exploring, PowerShell used 266-268
items, deleting from mailbox folder 277
items, purging in mailbox folder 274, 275
Source code API 261
types 261
Web Services API 261

**Authoring phase, Desired State
Configuration 147**
Automation
exploring 108-119
Azure Resource Manager (ARM) 255

B

binary modules 166-171
breakpoints
command breakpoint 175
line breakpoint 174
managing 174
variable breakpoint 175

C

certification authority (CA) 205
CIM
about 89, 197
basics 97-101
cmdlets, benefits 101
commands, exploring 206-209
methods, exploring 209-211
used, for querying remote machines 212
client-side object model (CSOM)
about 262, 289, 290
list, creating 293, 294
list, deleting 293, 294
PowerShell modules,
creating with SDKs 295-298
working 290-292
cmdlet definition XML (CDXML) 102
cmdlets
about 2, 29
commands 29

H

help
  obtaining 32-35
here-string 124

I

imperative programming
  versus declarative programming 185-188
interactive shell
  aliases, using 36-41
  cmdlets, using 29-32
  filtering 56-65
  formatting 56-65
  help, obtaining 32-35
  objects 47-50
  pipelines 51-53
  regular expressions (regex) 41-47
  snippets, exploring in PowerShell ISE 66-68
  using 28

J

JavaScript object model (JSOM) 289
JavaScript Object Notation (JSON)
  exploring 256-258

L

line breakpoint 174
line-of-business (LOB) 277
Local Configuration
  Manager (LCM) 148, 192
Lync 2013
  about 277
  client settings, exploring 281-285
  IM, with contacts 287-289
  test calls, automating 285
Lync Extensibility API
  URL 277
Lync Model API
  URL 277
LYNC SDK
  installing 277-280
  URL 277

M

Managed Object Format (MOF)
  about 195, 196
  file 92
  tasks, performing 195
  URL 195
  used, for creating configurations 213-215
Management OData Schema Designer
  URL 240
Management OData Web Service
  URL 240
manifest modules 171, 172
Measure-Command cmdlet 87
Microsoft Connect
  URL 2
Microsoft Online Services Module for
    Windows PowerShell
  URL, for downloading 107
Microsoft Online Services Sign-In Assistant
  URL, for downloading 107
modules
  about 164
  binary modules 166-171
  dynamic module 173
  manifest modules 171, 172
  script modules 165, 166
MSDN
  URL 269

N

New-Variable cmdlet 71

O

objects
  using 47-50
OCSPowerShell
  URL 203
Open Data Protocol (OData)
  about 237
  IIS Extensions, managing 237, 239
  Management OData web service,
    creating 240

U

Uniform Resource Identifier (URI) 240
Universal Description, Discovery, and
    Integration (UDDI) 246
Updatable Help feature 171
Update-Help cmdlet 34
use case of classes, WMF 5.0
  about 148-152
  constructors 153, 154

V

variable breakpoint 175
variables
  using 69, 70
Visual Studio
  URL 290

W

web requests
  exploring 240-242
  files, downloading from Internet 243
  files, reading from Internet 244, 245
web services
  building 250-252
  exploring 246
  URL 246
  using 246-249
Web Services API 261
Web Services Description Language
    (WSDL) 246
Web Services Management (WS-Man)
  abilities 197, 198
  cmdlets, exploring 198-203
  cmdlets, URL 198
Where-Object cmdlet 57
Windows API
  URL 262
Windows Data Protection API 107
Windows Management Framework 5.0
  installing 4-8
Windows Management Instrumentation
    (WMI)
  about 206
  basics 90-97
  references 90

Windows PowerShell
  about 3
  URL 3
Windows PowerShell 5.0
  about 89, 142
  basics, of Desired State
    Configuration 143-146
  highlights 142
  Package Management, exploring 158-162
  PowerShellGet, exploring 162, 163
  reference link 2
  reference link, for benefits 142
Windows PowerShell console host
  about 9-11
  setting up, GUI used 11-16
  setting up, PowerShell used 16-20
Windows PowerShell ISE host
  about 9
  benefits 25
  exploring, GUI used 21-25
  Script Browser 26, 27
Windows Remote Management (WinRM)
  about 197, 206
  HTTP/HTTPS Listener 203-205
WMF 4.0
  URL, for download 180
WMF 5.0
  use case of classes 148-152
WMF 5.0 April 2015 preview
  installing 182-185
  URL 182, 216
WMIClass type accelerators
  [WMI] 91
  [WMIClass] 91
  [WMISearcher] 91
WMI Query Language (WQL) 92
WSMan
  about 100
  object 97
WS-Management (WS-Man) 206

X

xHotfix resource 182
XML
  about 89
  working with 102-108

Thank you for buying
Windows PowerShell for .NET Developers
Second Edition

About Packt Publishing

Packt, pronounced 'packed', published its first book, *Mastering phpMyAdmin for Effective MySQL Management*, in April 2004, and subsequently continued to specialize in publishing highly focused books on specific technologies and solutions.

Our books and publications share the experiences of your fellow IT professionals in adapting and customizing today's systems, applications, and frameworks. Our solution-based books give you the knowledge and power to customize the software and technologies you're using to get the job done. Packt books are more specific and less general than the IT books you have seen in the past. Our unique business model allows us to bring you more focused information, giving you more of what you need to know, and less of what you don't.

Packt is a modern yet unique publishing company that focuses on producing quality, cutting-edge books for communities of developers, administrators, and newbies alike. For more information, please visit our website at www.packtpub.com.

About Packt Enterprise

In 2010, Packt launched two new brands, Packt Enterprise and Packt Open Source, in order to continue its focus on specialization. This book is part of the Packt Enterprise brand, home to books published on enterprise software – software created by major vendors, including (but not limited to) IBM, Microsoft, and Oracle, often for use in other corporations. Its titles will offer information relevant to a range of users of this software, including administrators, developers, architects, and end users.

Writing for Packt

We welcome all inquiries from people who are interested in authoring. Book proposals should be sent to author@packtpub.com. If your book idea is still at an early stage and you would like to discuss it first before writing a formal book proposal, then please contact us; one of our commissioning editors will get in touch with you.

We're not just looking for published authors; if you have strong technical skills but no writing experience, our experienced editors can help you develop a writing career, or simply get some additional reward for your expertise.

Mastering Windows PowerShell Scripting

ISBN: 978-1-78217-355-7   Paperback: 282 pages

Master the art of automating and managing your Windows environment using PowerShell

1. Construct scripts by following proven best practices to automate redundant tasks.

2. Delve into real-world examples to understand how to simplify the management of your Windows environment.

3. Get to grips with PowerShell's advanced functions and effectively administer your system.

Microsoft SharePoint 2010 and Windows PowerShell 2.0: Expert Cookbook

ISBN: 978-1-84968-410-1   Paperback: 310 pages

50 advanced recipes for administrators and IT Pros to master Microsoft SharePoint 2010 and Microsoft PowerShell 2.0 automation

1. Dive straight into expert recipes for SharePoint and PowerShell administration without dwelling on the basics.

2. Master how to administer BCS in SharePoint, automate the configuration of records management features, create custom PowerShell cmdlets, and much more in this book and e-book.

Please check **www.PacktPub.com** for information on our titles

Windows PowerShell 3.0 Windows
Management Instrumentation Starter

Explore new abilities of Powershell 3.0 to interact with Windows
Management Instrumentation (WMI) through the use of the new
CIM cmdlets and realistic management scenarios

Brenton J.W. Blawat   [PACKT]

Instant Windows Powershell 3.0 Windows Management Instrumentation Starter

ISBN: 978-1-84968-962-5   Paperback: 66 pages

Explore new abilities of Powershell 3.0 to interact with Windows Management Instrumentation (WMI) through the use of the new CIM cmdlets and realistic management scenarios

1. Learn something new in an Instant!
   A short, fast, focused guide delivering immediate results.

2. Create CIM sessions to local and remote systems.

3. Execute WMI queries using Windows Remote Management.

Windows PowerShell

Manage and automate your Windows Server Environment efficiently
using PowerShell

Vinith Menon   [PACKT]

Instant Windows PowerShell

ISBN: 978-1-84968-874-1   Paperback: 54 pages

Manage and automate your Windows Server Environment efficiently using PowerShell

1. Learn something new in an Instant!
   A short, fast, focused guide delivering immediate results.

2. Learn to use PowerShell web access to secure Windows management anywhere, any time, on any device.

3. Understand to secure and sign the scripts you write using the script signing feature in PowerShell.

Please check **www.PacktPub.com** for information on our titles

www.ingramcontent.com/pod-product-compliance
Lightning Source LLC
Chambersburg PA
CBHW062103050326

40690CB00016B/3184